MW00718276

Distributed Systems Management

Distributed Systems Management

Alwyn Langsford

United Kingdom Atomic Energy Authority

Jonathan D. Moffett

Department of Computer Science, University of York

ADDISON-WESLEY
PUBLISHING
COMPANY

Wokingham, England · Reading, Massachusetts · Menlo Park, California · New York
Don Mills, Ontario · Amsterdam · Bonn · Sydney · Singapore
Tokyo · Madrid · San Juan · Milan · Paris · Mexico City · Seoul · Taipei

© 1993 Addison-Wesley Publishers Ltd.
© 1993 Addison-Wesley Publishing Company Inc.

All rights reserved. No part of this publication may be reproduced, stored in a retrieval system, or transmitted in any form of by any means, electronic, mechanical, photocopying, recording or otherwise, without prior written permission of the publisher.

The programs in this book have been included for their instructional value. They have been tested with care but are not guaranteed for any particular purpose. The publisher does not offer any warranties or representations nor does it accept any liabilities with respect to the programs.

Many of the designations used by manufacturers and sellers to distinguish their products are claimed as trademarks. Addison-Wesley has made every attempt to supply trademark information about manufacturers and their products mentioned in this book. A list of the trademark designations and their owners appears on page x.

Cover designed by Chris Eley
and printed by The Riverside Printing Co. (Reading) Ltd.
Typeset by Colset Private Ltd, Singapore.
Printed and bound in Great Britain by T.J. Press (Padstow) Ltd, Cornwall.

First printed 1992

ISBN 0-201-63176-8

British Library Cataloguing in Publication Data
A catalogue record for this book is available from the British Library.

Library of Congress Cataloging in Publication Data is available

Preface

This book has its origins in the activities of the Special Interest Group in Distributed Systems Management (SIGDSM). The Special Interest Group is a gathering of individuals, in the United Kingdom, who have a particular interest in the topics of distributed processing and the management of the distributed processing environment. The members of the group first came together in 1986 to share experience and discuss their problems. Its members represent users, computing consultants, computer and communication equipment suppliers, research laboratories and academia. The group had amassed over one hundred working documents and organized three specialist workshops in the course of its work. The group considered that this material could, with additional specialist contributions, provide the material for a book on distributed systems management.

The aim of this book is to provide a guide to good practice in the management of distributed systems. Advances in computing, communication and workstation technologies are showing that networked systems, where the processing is distributed over the system elements, are being preferred for their robustness and adaptability. They also meet the management style of today's organizations, which require that responsibility and day-to-day control be devolved to the component parts of an enterprise. Such devolution is readily applicable to distributed systems, which can therefore support the organization of business and add to its efficient operation.

Experience has shown that while managers of computing and communication equipment are familiar with the hardware and software technology of these systems, they have less familiarity with the associated management requirements. Often the systems have grown by the accretion of smaller systems and this process has brought with it recognized management problems but few solutions. Even where manufacturers supply management products, these are essentially targeted at their own hardware and software environments.

This book is, above all, a guide for the practitioner. It aims to identify the factors which those who wish to make the case for managed distributed systems should put before their senior managers. It provides guidance to those managers on the issues they should expect to be addressed when such cases are presented to them. It discusses factors which affect the design, organization, operation and maintenance of distributed systems. It explores the impact of the ISO and CCITT standards for management which are now emerging. This book is therefore appropriate to the whole range of an organization's staff from the corporate director for information processing systems, through operations managers, to their technical support staff and the consultants who advise them.

The authors have made extensive reference to the particular specialisms and experience of the members of SIGDSM and wish to acknowledge that contribution here. In this way, the book represents the combined experience of many specialists. Particular acknowledgement is due to:

- Stephen Baker for his contribution to Chapter 3 on the business aspects of the case for distributed systems management;
- John Davies for his research on business requirements in Chapter 2;
- David Holden for his many contributions to Chapter 6 on user support services;
- Simon Jones for his help in compiling a list of terms and their definitions;
- Tony Law for his help on user requirements and training needs;
- Phil Phillips for his contributions on security and risk;
- Robin Sherman for his contributions on security and risk and his overall contributions on management issues as they affect business and commerce;
- Morris Sloman for his contributions to Chapter 4 (on management functions and services) and Chapter 8 (on distributed systems management's technical concepts);
- Norman Spink for his contributions on documentation and help facilities;
- Barry Varley for his contribution on accounting;
- David Vinograd and John Winterbotham for their general contributions to discussion, helpful comments and suggestions.

All members of SIGDSM acknowledge the support of our sponsoring organizations for allowing us the opportunity to take part in the work of this Special Interest Group.

Naturally, with the diversity of SIGDSM's background material, there has had to be considerable rewriting before a book could be produced. So, while acknowledging the stimulus and help provided by our colleagues, the authors have to take the responsibility for the finished product. We thank our colleagues for any virtues which the book may possess, and hope that they will forgive any faults that we may have introduced.

Above all, we wish to thank our wives, Margaret and Jennifer, for their encouragement and forbearance while the book was being written and, in acknowledgement of that support, we dedicate this book to them.

Alwyn Langsford, Jonathan Moffett
July 1992

Contents

1 Rationale for distributed systems management   1

   1.1 Trends in corporate information processing   2

   1.2 The need for management   3

   1.3 Distributed systems   5

   1.4 What is distributed systems management?   7

   1.5 Strategy for distributed systems management   14

   1.6 Management services for distributed processing   17

   1.7 Models for distributed systems management   19

   1.8 Organization of the chapters   25

2 Uses and users of distributed systems   29

   2.1 Introduction   30

   2.2 Characteristics of organizations   31

   2.3 Business sectors   32

   2.4 Business cultures   38

   2.5 People in distributed system management   41

   2.6 Management implications   46

3 Business aspects of distributed systems management   53

   3.1 Informing corporate management   54

   3.2 Categories of information technology management   56

   3.3 Establishing the requirement   57

   3.4 Risk assessment and management   59

   3.5 Financial considerations   60

   3.6 Managing the implementation   61

   3.7 Business recommendations   62

4   Management functions and management services   **65**

4.1   Introduction   66

4.2   Management activities and functions   67

4.3   Monitoring   70

4.4   Services supporting monitoring   71

4.5   Fault handling   74

4.6   Performance management   84

4.7   Configuration management   93

4.8   Accounting   97

4.9   Name management   103

4.10   Interrelationship of functions and services   107

5   Security and distributed systems   **111**

5.1   Introduction   112

5.2   Special factors of security in distributed systems   112

5.3   Security framework   115

5.4   Security mechanisms   118

5.5   Security policies   124

5.6   Risk assessment and management   133

5.7   Managing security   134

5.8   Security standards   135

6   Supporting services   **141**

6.1   Support service characteristics   142

6.2   Business risk management   143

6.3   Auditing and accountability   145

6.4   Help services   148

6.5   Directories and related information services   153

6.6   User-related management tools   156

6.7   Support environments   160

6.8   The automation of support services   164

7   **Installation, operation and maintenance**   **167**

   7.1   Introduction   168

   7.2   Installation   168

   7.3   System integration and testing   172

   7.4   Operations and user support   178

   7.5   Documentation needs   180

   7.6   Maintenance   183

8   **Distributed systems management concepts**   **189**

   8.1   Introduction   190

   8.2   Objects and object models   190

   8.3   Domains   194

   8.4   Management policies   206

   8.5   Policies and objects   210

   8.6   Authorization policies   215

   8.7   Management control concepts   221

   8.8   Delegation of authority using management role objects 223

   8.9   Responsibility   225

   8.10 Conclusions   226

9   **Standards for distributed systems management**   **231**

   9.1   Relevant standards activities   232

   9.2   Organization of OSI management standards   233

   9.3   Conformance to OSI management standards   247

   9.4   Alternative approaches to management protocols   250

   9.5   Other CCITT management standards   252

   9.6   Open issues in management standards   253

10 **Current practice and future directions**   **261**

   10.1 Distributed systems management products today   262

   10.2 The need for tool integration   265

   10.3 Future directions   268

10.4 Applying open standards to management products   271

10.5 The application of distributed systems management   273

10.6 Conclusions   278

Appendix A   Checklist for the distributed systems manager   283

Appendix B   Terms and abbreviations   295

Subject Index   305

Trademark Notice
Accumaster®, Accumaster Integrator® are trademarks of AT&T.
Concert®, Prestel™ are trademarks of British Telecom.
DECmcc™ is a trademark of Digital Equipment Corporation.
CM-APT™ is a trademark of Groupe Bull.
OpenView™, Postmaster™, Software Distribution Facilities™ are
trademarks of Hewlett-Packard; NetLS™ is a trademark of Hewlett-
Packard and Gradient Technologies.
Community Management™ is a trademark of ICL.
Data Engine™, NetView™ are trademarks of International Business
Machines Corporation.
LAN Manager™ is a trademark of Microsoft Corporation.
Netware™ is a trademark of Novell.
OSF™, Motif™ is a trademark of the Open Software Foundation.
HUGS™, objcall™, Object Despatcher™ are trademarks of Tivoli
Systems.
UNIX™ is a trademark of UNIX System Laboratories, Inc.
NeL™ is a trademark of Wang Corporation.

1

Rationale for distributed systems management

Objectives

- to explain the need for systems management
- to introduce distributed systems concepts
- to explain the main concerns of distributed systems management: complexity and integration
- to outline a strategy for distributed systems management
- to introduce distributed systems management services and functions
- to comment upon models of distributed systems management

1.1 Trends in corporate information processing

Networks, distributed processing and, in particular, their management are now on everyone's agenda. Advances in information technology, especially in telecommunications and workstation design, and the ready availability of low priced personal computers are changing the approach to computing. Organizations have always been aware that, because of their need for information, their data flows cover the whole of their enterprise and interact with those of other organizations. Whereas in the past, data has been processed manually, it can now be communicated and processed using the products of information technology. The consequence of this change results in a major rethink, away from reliance on the mainframe, where any interactive work is through dumb terminal access, to the computer network. The advances involve new technologies, both in the way data is transmitted and in the way communications are integrated with data processing capability. However, being technology-led, these advances have often paid most attention to transporting large volumes of data at high transmission speeds. Only recently has the focus shifted to consider the complementary need to organize and control the resulting computing and communications environment.

The European Community has recognized that the single European market will be an electronic market. Information flow has always been one of the dominant elements in trade. With technology now able to carry significantly more information between trading partners, banks and administrations, the underlying information systems will become determining factors in the success of the single market's operation.

As the technology of computing and communications has advanced to interconnect computer systems through communications networks, computer users have had to become aware of the distributed nature of their information processing environment. As a result, it has been the users who have had to organize, monitor and control their computer applications as best they may. In many instances this has become a barrier to progress and to more effective use of the distributed computing environment, because users' interests are primarily in their computing applications and not in the technology required to support them. More recently, some computer networks have begun to hide the consequences of distribution from their users and to offer true distributed computing. Freeing the users from the burden of organizing, monitoring and controlling the environment has resulted in a shift of this responsibility on to the distributed systems support and to the system's operators and managers.

As well as providing an information processing environment better matched to the information processing needs of business, distributed systems are able to offer other advantages. The newer networks and their computer systems offer the potential for **openness**. This reduces the necessity to be tied to the products of a particular manufacturer. Networking and the distribution of information processing offer added flexibility and resilience and better capability to handle evolving information processing needs. But, with openness and the dispersion of processing away from the mainframe and into the personal computer and workstation, comes added **complexity**. Even though the individual components may be relatively simple, combining them into a coherent and effective whole demands a significant level of management support. Thus, these benefits do not come at zero cost.

Writing in the European Commission's *XII Magazine*, the head of the Office and Business Systems Division has commented on the significance of openness and complexity. He identifies the following as significant factors influencing where resources are likely to be committed:

> A movement away from proprietary systems towards open systems and standards, and away from a reliance on single-vendor solutions towards open, multivendor, heterogenous systems.
>
> The increasing complexity facing user organisations as they find themselves having to build integrated systems from the non-homogeneous realities of the marketplace and of their own organisations. (Stajano, 1992)

These are among the factors which this book addresses in presenting the requirement for distributed systems management and the extent to which that requirement can be satisfied.

1.2 The need for management

All organizations plan the introduction of their technologies to a certain extent. However, there are few guidelines as to what constitutes good practice for managing distributed systems, and many networks are being developed in an *ad hoc* manner. Also, autonomous decision making in different parts of the organization may hinder coordinated planning. Distributed systems are often complex and they often evolve by implementing existing services on new equipment. All these factors make management more difficult.

Although there are many networking products, some of which provide some distributed processing capabilities, there are relatively few networking products that are well equipped with management functions. Management products have hitherto provided some monitoring and a little control, mainly of the communication components, with little attempt to manage the processing environment as a whole. They have been concerned to monitor and control individual components but not the system. This is beginning to change. Influenced by the development of open system standards for computing and communications, new products entering the market are beginning to respond to the need for equipment (both hardware and software) to manage the distributed system as a coherent entity.

The value and importance of good management discipline and good management tools within business enterprises is well recognized. As information technology begins to mature, management discipline applied to information technology systems, and especially to distributed systems, is becoming equally valued. To recognize the importance of good management tools, consider the case of a financial trading house. The organization's trading turnover will be of the order of £1 billion (10^9) per day. Such an organization will typically have an information processing system consisting of hundreds of user terminals served by a similar number of processors all linked through one of the newer networking products. A single failure which is not quickly detected, diagnosed and corrected can result in lost business, and the cost of a lost business opportunity may easily exceed the entire cost of that system. The value of tools that can prevent failures of this kind can therefore be appreciated. Experience shows that it is not appropriate to rely on the technical awareness of the system's users to help in problem diagnosis. Their expertise lies in understanding financial markets, not in trouble-shooting computer networks. The requirement is for appropriate systems management capability.

It is not only in financial dealing that the management of distributed processing is being recognized as necessary. The food retailing industry has linked its check-out terminals to its stock control systems to ensure 'just in time' provisioning of its stores. Similarly, videotape shops are becoming linked by networks to expedite their orders and distribution. A failure of the computing or communications systems can lead to the retail outlet running out of stock. If these failures happen frequently, they lead to customer dissatisfaction and loss of trade to competing retailers. A well publicized failure could put at risk the commercial viability of a company operating an ineffectively managed distributed system. There is therefore a significant element of corporate self-interest in ensuring that risks are fully assessed and that the distributed system is operated effectively. This must be planned. Evidence from analyses after the event have shown that the cost of recovery and the cost of time lost are always more significant than people imagine. Although these costs may not always be as large as those that could be incurred in the financial system described above, and may not even be large in terms of the organization's turnover, they can nevertheless be a substantial proportion of a company's operating margin, a factor that should carry significant weight with a company's accountants when making a case for distributed systems management. In short, whenever distributed systems are installed, their needs for management are determined by the operational needs of the organizations and not by their size or business sector.

It is against this background that this guide to the management of distributed information processing has been produced. The authors' objectives are to present the management issues that organizations encounter when they install and operate distributed processing systems. This is a fast moving technical field in which every distributed system has a different configuration, and the management objectives of owning enterprises differ one from another. Consequently it is impossible to offer a detailed prescription for management that is appropriate to everyone. Rather, this book aims to identify the principles of management as they apply to distributed systems, and the issues which must be recognized. By these means, it aims to help those who have to take technical and management decisions about the use, installation and operation of information processing equipment.

1.3 Distributed systems

The term **distributed systems** is variously applied to collections of computing, communication and data storage configurations. In this book a distributed system is considered to be one in which several autonomous processors, together with their data stores, cooperate to achieve an information processing goal. These information processing components are not expected to be placed at one location but are placed wherever it suits their purpose. This distribution of people and processing results in a need for a communication system to allow interaction between the components. As an illustration, consider the distributed system for a hypothetical organization (ABC Ltd.) shown schematically in Figure 1.1. Here the financial department has its own departmental network of clerical workstations with back-up data storage and report printing facilities. This is linked to the production units, some of which may be on remote sites, which have specialist production control processing to perform. There are stores systems to maintain inventories, sales departments which generate invoices and so on. All these separate parts of the organization need to be in communication with the corporate centre. Their information contributes to corporate planning and their actions respond to corporate policy. It is an illustration of a system which performs a vital part in both the operation and the management of a modern business. It therefore needs to be managed.

    This book also makes frequent reference to the term **distributed processing** as a general description of the information processing activities performed by the distributed system. The **distributed processing environment** is that aspect of the distributed system which provides the hardware and software for the distributed system's data processing, storage, peripherals and communications. It excludes those aspects which concern its operators and managers and their interaction with the system.

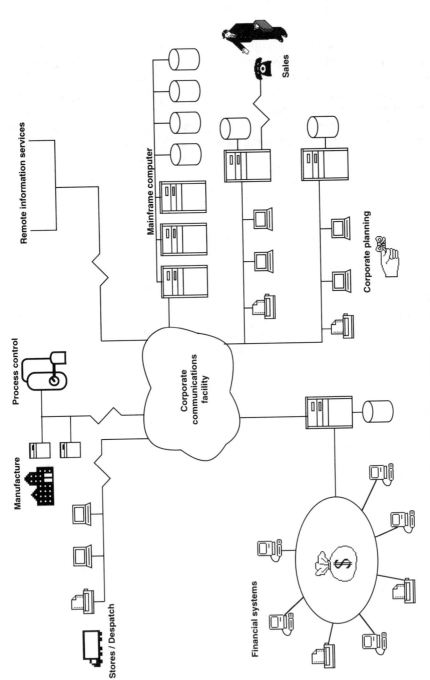

Figure 1.1   Corporate distributed processing systems.

1.4 What is distributed systems management?

Management of any resource – and therefore of any computer system, large or small, localized or distributed – involves five activities: planning, organizing, supervising the resource, controlling the resource, and accounting for its use. Therefore, in the context of the distributed systems and the communications which support distributed processing, management comprises all those actions and responses needed to:

- permit and influence the processing and storage of data,

- ensure the availability and integrity of the data,

- control and monitor the flow of data, with the aim of ensuring that resources are used efficiently and effectively.

Even the data manipulations needed to meet the objectives of the enterprise are included in the scope of distributed systems management because these too must be capable of being managed. Only the details of the specific application code and its data can be said to lie outside the scope of management.

Two aspects of the management of distributed systems ought to be distinguished. Firstly, there is the organizational aspect. This is about how to manage any significant component which contributes to the overall effectiveness of an enterprise. The distributed system is but one of these components. This aspect is concerned with preparing a business justification and with planning, operation and maintenance of the component. This aspect of management is always complex and its operation always needs to be planned, formally monitored and controlled to ensure effective performance from the networked components, both individually and as a whole. Secondly, there is the technical aspect. This concerns the information technology tools and methods that can be provided to automate or otherwise support distributed systems to ensure that they are manageable. This aspect is concerned with systems architecture, software engineering and open distributed processing standards.

The organizational aspect of distributed systems management will ensure that the resources of staff and equipment are available to meet identified requirements. It will be concerned to identify trends and, by performing analyses of likely future operations scenarios, plan for the management of change. It will ensure not only that equipment is adequate to meet the anticipated demands but also that staff receive appropriate training. To meet operational needs, it will estimate the costs of adopting a given method of operation, the likely benefits and the risks associated with a given operational strategy.

The technical aspect is concerned with the management functions and services required to facilitate the operational management requirements. It concerns mechanisms for determining and resolving fault conditions (which can occur anywhere within the geographically dispersed environment); reconfiguring the location and connectivity of network components to recover from faults, meet user needs and performance objectives, or support the evolution of the system over time; accounting for resource utilization; and ensuring the secure operation of resources.

1.4.1 Distributed systems management and complexity

Distributed systems management is particularly complex for the following reasons:

- A distributed processing application may span the computer systems belonging to a number of different organizations. There is no central authority in such systems and the management of the application as well as the underlying communication and processing resources will have to operate across organizational and, possibly, legislative boundaries.

- The systems being managed can have components that use different technologies and range in size from simple microcomputers to large, multi-user mainframes. These components may be providing very diverse facilities, from simply providing time and date to providing sophisticated distributed database services. All these facilities can interact and have to be managed.

- Components and services may be provided by different vendors with diverse and potentially incompatible management interfaces. These can make it difficult to apply a consistent integrated approach to management. Modern distributed systems incorporate multiple interconnected local and wide area networks, with the latter often under the control of one or more independent telecommunications authorities.

- The components and services being managed are physically distributed with genuine parallelism between components. This makes it difficult to obtain consistent global state information on which to base management decisions, or to synchronize management actions on different components.

- The size and complexity of large distributed systems introduce problems of scale due to the number of components that have to be managed. As businesses become ever more international and choose to interact more and more using the products of information technology, these distributed systems can become very large. This makes it impossible to treat each component or user as an independent entity for management purposes. Some rationale is needed to group components and users of the system into units which it is realistic to manage.

Response to this complexity underlies three particular themes in this book. They are: (i) the need to provide an integrated view of the various tasks of management; (ii) the need to provide managers with as much automated support as possible; and (iii) the challenge of providing management facilities which give an integrated and unified view to the manager of a distributed and heterogeneous environment.

1.4.2 The need to integrate

No true view of a distributed system will be uniform, because the system itself is not uniform. Moreover, there are two completely different reasons for the view being heterogeneous. One is that the components are themselves heterogeneous, and the manager must be able to see this fact. The other is that the tools that are used to view and manage the system are themselves also heterogeneous, and so present different views of similar things. Part of the system is based on one manufacturer's products, and part on another's, and the management tools that these manufacturers provide can be quite different. This second kind of reason for heterogeneous views has few, if any merits, but the reason it occurs is simple; the system has grown up incrementally, and incorporates diverse separate systems. Even on those rare occasions that a distributed system has initially been installed using the products of a single supplier, the three factors of system evolution, devolution of management and the use of open technologies will, together, inevitably lead to heterogeneity.

Figures 1.2 and 1.3 illustrate the system shown in Figure 1.1 from two other points of view. Figure 1.2 shows the network managers and their views of what they manage. It shows several different network management centres, arising from the networks that existed before the systems were integrated. They cover most, but not all, of the communications links, and they overlap in places. Figure 1.3 shows the system managers and the computing facilities which they cover. They are closely related to the network picture, but not identical, and they cover almost all the computers, except that a few enterprising users have brought in some unregistered personal computers, which they find they can quite satisfactorily attach to the network. The full complexity of the situation can be appreciated by superimposing the pictures to reveal the possible complexities in organization. To this can be added the physical complexity of handling different manufacturers' products with their different 'in-house' standards. It is clear that the managers' jobs are made more difficult by the complexity of the situation, and that managers are rendered less effective by the overlap in some areas of responsibility and by their incomplete coverage of other areas.

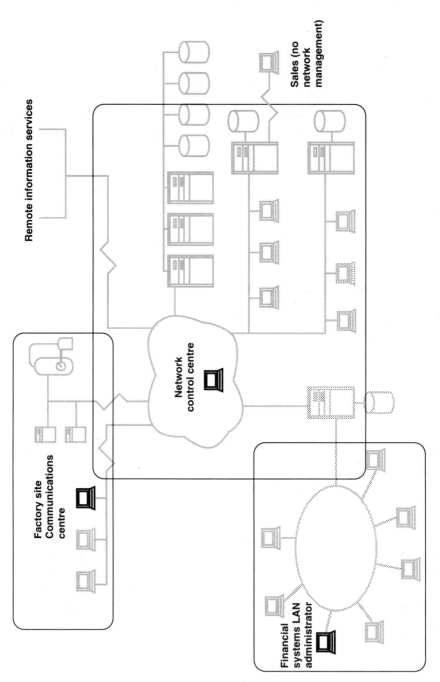

Figure 1.2   Network management centres.

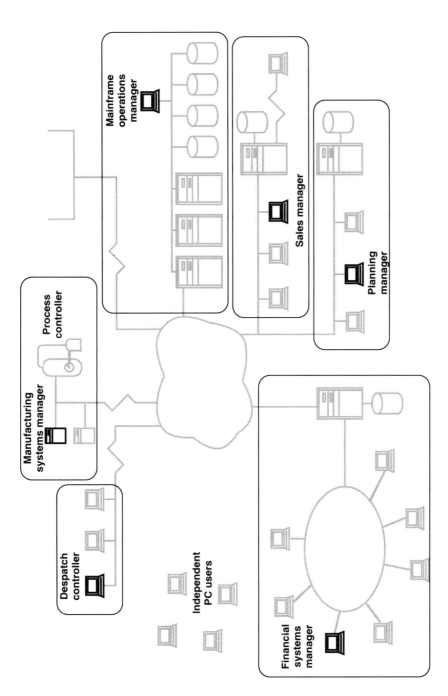

Figure 1.3 Systems management.

The solution of 10 years ago was to impose uniformity centrally. It is no longer an option that the users will tolerate. Today's solution has to recognize and accept diversity, turning it to the users' advantage while presenting an integrated and complete picture to managers. This book points the way towards a solution, and identifies what is being done to achieve that solution and what has still to be achieved.

1.4.3 Why manage distributed systems?

The reason for managing distributed systems ought to be self-evident to its users. However, experience of looking at distributed systems and their supporting products has convinced the authors that the question has to be properly addressed and the need for management justified. To some extent the lack of management in distributed systems has resulted from a lack of distributed systems management products. It is also a consequence of the way distributed systems have come into being. They frequently originate as relatively small, independent departmental computing activities organized through either an isolated local area network or a small to medium sized computer with a terminal network. For a small, stand-alone system, an informal management organization may be considered adequate. As the individual components become interconnected and the scale of the distributed system increases, the informal ways in which the components were managed in isolation from each other cease to be appropriate. These are explanations but they should not be excuses for how systems are to be managed in future. Even if goodwill and technical interest are currently sustaining distributed system operation, there is a risk of complacency, which could prove fatal to a system if it were permitted to continue indefinitely. Many aspects of management concern the way the responsibilities of a system are organized. Because this does not depend upon the availability of hardware or software, the lack of products is not, by itself, a justification for not providing an adequate degree of management.

What are the justifications for committing resources to managing the distributed processing environment and what are the benefits? The example of the trading house shows how the cost of a system fault which takes time to fix can be greater than the cost of the information processing system, let alone its management. The obvious benefits to be gained from distributed processing (in-built evolutionary potential, resilience and flexibility) cannot be achieved efficiently without the monitoring and controlling functions of management. Without management, planning for future development, if it takes place at all, must be haphazard. Management of the distributed processing environment enables an organization to get the best out of its investment and to be seen to be getting the best from it. Finally, it is important that corporate managers can be reassured that the information technology aspects of corporate activity are in safe hands; they may then 'sleep more soundly' and conserve their energies for other corporate problems.

Management of any component of a distributed information process-ing system helps to ensure that the component can be controlled so that it can meet its requirements to provide a service in support of the enterprise. Distributed systems management helps to ensure that the system as a whole can be controlled to meet those requirements. This is the most direct benefit of management, but others include:

- evolutionary potential, through incremental build-up and keeping pace with technical and business change,
- robust design with fall-back and partial, constrained system degrada-tion in the event of failure,
- minimized information flow bottlenecks.

Distributed systems can be large and complex and their life span is many years, even decades. During this time they do not remain static. Rather, they evolve in response to changing demands and in recognition of the benefits of new technologies, which are introduced to give better value for an organiza-tion's investment. For example, changing business requirements may make it worth while to invest in systems to support technical functions (for example, graphics workstations for product design) and these may be linked into a net-work which had previously only carried administrative traffic. This evolution in use leads to an evolution of technology and demonstrates the need to plan ahead. The new applications will lead to additional processing requirements and generate additional communications traffic. Typically, demands for net-work bandwidth grow at a rate of between 15% and 25% per annum, so the installation of network capacity that meets only current applications' needs can be short-sighted. It may be better to install high capacity data networks (possibly using fibre optics) some time ahead of actual need rather than rely upon cheaper, lower bandwidth cabling which might soon prove unable to meet expanding needs. Whatever technology is chosen, its performance needs to be continually monitored to ensure that any performance constraints can be identified before they begin to affect business performance and growth potential.

Evolution, both of requirements and of technology, leads to changes of distributed system configuration, which take place over relatively long time-scales, perhaps taking several years. Configurations can also change over a much shorter time span. Networking and distribution have the flexibility which allows the ready incorporation of information processing resources from other distributed systems should the need arise. It is possible to take advantage of this intrinsic potential of distributed systems to provide alternative sources of processing capacity. An example is the ability to handle peak loads detected in some parts of the distributed system by off-loading them to other parts that are less busy. Redistribution of processing activity can also arise when providing back-up if a part of the system becomes unavailable as a result of component failure. As well as illustrating the problems of short-term planning for distributed systems, these examples illustrate some of their advantages over centralized systems.

Applying management offers the benefits of:

- planned and economical expansion to meet user needs, minimizing both waste through early upgrade and degraded service through delaying it too long,
- efficient fault rectification,
- security and accountability for provision and use of the services,
- audit for both efficiency and integrity.

These are pointers to the value of management in respect of distributed processing. They are developed and elaborated in the following chapters. But sufficient should have been said so far to convince even the sceptic of the importance of management in this new area which has been opened up by the advance of technology.

1.5 Strategy for distributed system management

For distributed system management to be effective and to achieve the above benefits, it must have clear strategic goals. The overall objectives and management policy needed to achieve effective management for the distributed system must be clearly specified. Six environmental factors influence distributed system management strategy and hence affect those things which management seeks to achieve. The factors are:

- the business objectives of the enterprise,
- legal framework,
- organizational and administrative structure,
- inter-organizational trust,
- technology,
- the incremental nature of distributed systems.

The first of these factors, the business objectives, determines what the distributed system is used for, how it is used and the management policies that influence that use. Policy affects the importance given to system security and availability and this, in turn, determines the requirement for and constraints upon handling system faults, monitoring system performance and the scope for secure interaction between organizations. The objectives depend on the type of enterprise. Examples in the next chapter will show that a financial enterprise typically rates availability as of prime importance and integrity a close second. Efficient utilization of resources is less important. On the other hand, a computing system in an academic institution, where resources may be comparatively scarce and security relatively unimportant, puts significant management effort into obtaining high resource utilization. Therefore, the first requirement of any strategy for managing distributed systems is for its managers to identify the enterprise goals and constraints. The managers must determine how they influence the policies for the use of the enterprise's distributed processing resources.

Whatever the aspirations of an enterprise, its management has to work within the framework of national and international laws and regulations. Managers of information systems have to comply with the terms of their national data protection laws. There can be requirements for regular audit of the data generated and manipulated by computing applications. The laws and regulations define what managers are obliged to do and act as constraints on what they are permitted to do. They must be taken into account in the design and operation of distributed systems. For transnational systems the legal framework includes international agreements and laws which may explicitly regulate cross-border data flows.

The organizational and administrative structure of an enterprise influences the requirements for and style of distributed systems management. Some aspects of management may be based on individual departments whereas other aspects may be centralized for a site or at an enterprise's head-quarters. Large distributed systems, even within a single organization, will increasingly cross management boundaries, requiring interaction between semi-autonomous administrative units. In these cases, it can be more effective to work as if the units operated as independent partners, rather than to invoke a sufficiently senior level of management in an attempt to unify the information processing requirements and procedures of the units. Senior managers will set an overall framework and leave consensus formation to the units so that they can still meet their individual objectives. However, such independence must be exercised with flexibility. Although it must respect the autonomy of units, it must nevertheless permit some (possibly very limited) management of resources in other units where corporate policy requires it. This may call for units to negotiate management relationships where none currently exist. The technical response to this requirement is to identify **domains** of management whose component resources and activities are circumscribed by management policy. (This topic is discussed in detail in Chapter 8.) Hence, the management strategy is strongly influenced by policies which influence management style and the degree to which authority is delegated within an organization.

The degree of inter-organizational trust which can be established between independent organizations is a major factor in determining the interaction between distributed systems management components. Activities in independent distributed systems can only safely be interconnected to the extent that the organizations trust each other. Interconnection and subsequent intercommunication are strongly influenced by the security policies of the organizations concerned and the way in which the distributed system meets the security requirements. For example, an organization's security policy may specify that very limited access is permitted to its resources by cooperating organizations if they are not fully trusted. Thus, if sales persons are visiting customer sites and wish to make use of an inter-organization distributed processing facility, they would not normally be permitted to access their organization's resources as freely as they would when operating from within their own organization, even though they might be able to validate themselves as bona fide employees of the organization. One of the advantages of physical distribution of processing and data storage within organizations is that very sensitive material can be segregated, so reducing the risk of inadvertent disclosure to external enquiry. Managers of system components have the power to control how resources are made available. Hence, one potential application to which remote access could be allowed is that of system management itself. However, the degree of trust to allow remote management must be significantly higher and subject to even more stringent safeguards than for normal information processing and data handling transactions. If management action were to be incorrectly or maliciously applied, the result could compromise the integrity of the distributed system and even paralyse its operation completely.

Technology also has a major influence on the management strategy. Clearly, the degree to which computing resources can be managed depends on what management functions they support. Resources which have only rudimentary management facilities will constrain the effectiveness of management policies which demand extensive monitoring and control. A distributed system is made up of a large number of different types of computing resources, such as communications devices and their interconnecting data links, processors, file servers, terminals, printers, operating systems and various applications. Some of the devices supporting the communications environment already provide quite sophisticated management capability. These can provide prolific amounts of data relating to throughput and other performance factors. The devices providing these data are often technology-specific and, although they allow a measure of control for that technology, there are few examples on the market of management systems which integrate control across technologies. Facilities for monitoring and controlling processing systems are even more vendor-specific. Even where there are management capabilities, each component which processes management data tends to provide its management capabilities in its own fashion. Providing a coherent management capability in a heterogeneous, multi-vendor environment is only practicable where there are management tools conforming to suitable standards. These standards need to apply to the ways in which people manage information systems, in the same way as standards apply to the technology for data exchange and the languages in which program code and data are specified. That is, they provide common ways of referencing policy objectives, just as protocol standards provide common ways of specifying communications preferences.

Large distributed systems typically span multiple network segments. These will probably include a mixture of local area (that is, within a building or within a campus) networks and wide area (that is, inter-site or inter-organizational) networks. Whereas the former usually belong to one enterprise, the latter are often managed by a third party (a telecommunications carrier) on behalf of one or more enterprises. These large networks frequently support a number of different internal communication mechanisms (dictated by the different technological constraints imposed by the network suppliers), and there is a need to coordinate the heterogeneous management practices of third-party communications suppliers with the practices of the organizations which they interconnect.

Distributed systems are, by nature, incremental, growing and interconnecting in response to demand. Few organizations can expect to be blessed with a 'green field' within which to install a complete and new distributed system with its supporting management. They are more likely to move to distributed processing by interconnecting existing systems and applying management resources to make interworking possible. A viable management strategy is one which anticipates that a system and its management capability will exhibit incremental growth. The management system must incorporate management tools. These will be modified as the system evolves and as improved tools become available, so adding to the investment in hardware and software.

It will be obvious from the discussion of these factors that one of the key requirements for management is to be flexible enough to respond to the diversity and continual change expected of distributed systems and the distributed processing environment. In summary, the management strategy needs to provide for:

- a range of different management objectives and policies,
- a variety of hierarchical and federated organizational structures,
- the ability to manage a very disparate collection of entities supplied by multiple vendors and interconnected by many different networks.

Above all, management must expect that computing facilities will be installed incrementally into a distributed system.

1.6 Management services for distributed processing

Following work in the early 1980s by the International Organization for Standardization (ISO) committee developing standards for the management of the communications environment (ISO/IEC 7498-4), it has been common to discuss management in terms of five functional areas. These areas are:

- Accounting management
- Configuration management
- Fault management
- Performance management
- Security management

This partitioning is useful in helping to structure and dimension the problem of management, although it is not ideal for a technical consideration of management requirements and it fails to recognize that some aspects of management functionality apply to more than one area. Ultimately the quality of management is judged by the quality of the service it is able to deliver. The phrase 'quality of service' is easy to use but difficult to define concisely. Like all issues of quality, it is concerned with fitness for purpose and it is only achieved through good management organization. In the management of distributed processing there are four key services.

First, distributed systems management should provide the service of gathering, processing and maintaining the statistical data that is vital to effective policy making in an organization. It may extend to providing summaries and reports of system operation, performance and cost. This service provides the basis on which accounting, fault management and performance management applications can be constructed. For example, it includes the ability to search through historic records looking for parallels that can help with fault diagnosis. It may offer intelligent analyses based upon that data, which help to ensure *and demonstrate* that the distributed processing environment is operated effectively (performance management). It may also provide support for security management applications, in the form of an audit trail.

Second, distributed systems management should provide the capability to grant or deny access to resources and to control the mechanisms by which such access rules are maintained. The services to do this and to provide warnings and historical records when such rules are transgressed may be gathered under the umbrella of security management.

Third, distributed systems management should provide the service to control the installation, operation and maintenance of systems. It should provide services to put resources into service and to take them out again. It should control the initiation and termination of resource activities. These services fall within the scope of configuration management.

Fourth, planning services allow managers and operators to ask 'what if' questions about particular management scenarios. The results of such option analyses can lead to proposals for modification of the organization of system resources, for the introduction of new resources or the removal of obsolete ones.

1.7 Models for distributed systems management

Because of distribution and complexity, it is not possible to take a single view of the task of distributed systems management which covers all of its features. Several different perspectives are required in order to formulate an adequate technical approach. Various authors have sought ways in which to order the complexity. Some of the more recent approaches are identified below.

1.7.1 Open distributed processing (ODP)

Arising from a need to specify standards for open distributed processing (ODP), ISO has identified five viewpoints which it finds are able to assist in the analysis of distributed processing requirements (ISO/IEC 10746). These are the *enterprise, information, computational, engineering,* and *technology* viewpoints. Each contributes to the overall picture of distributed processing and its management.

The enterprise viewpoint considers the requirement from the perspective of general business objectives, and in terms of the management tasks which need to be approached from the different points of view that exist in any organization. Once it is appreciated that different management requirements and different cultures in an organization each require a particular approach, there emerges the possibility of establishing a methodology which can satisfy the goals of organizations.

The information viewpoint helps to establish what data is being handled and what data needs to be communicated between its various information handling components. It identifies some data as specific to individual resources, some data as applying to complete computer systems or to local sub-networks of computers and other data as relevant to the distributed system as a whole.

The computational viewpoint takes a more functional look at the distributed processing activity by asking what information transformations take place. Again, some transformations apply to an individual parameter in a single component, others affect a computer system while some interactions (for example, the update to system-wide data following reconfiguration) need to be coordinated across the entire distributed system.

The engineering and technical viewpoints take explicit account of the way in which a system is distributed, considering how both its construction and operation are affected by its technology. Technologies which enable rapid dissemination of data over a geographically very large network may take radically different approaches to the way in which reconfiguration updates are handled, compared with technologies which offer only slow, point to point communication through a message store and forward network.

A complementary perspective, which focuses upon the management problem itself, has been provided by one of the studies carried out in the ANSA project (ANSA, 1989). This project investigated the characteristics of an advanced network systems architecture (ANSA) which would support distributed processing. It has already led to the successful realization of distributed systems. Its management model proposes a four-layer hierarchy (see Figure 1.4) at the apex of which is the expression of management policy. This is supported by administrative services which put the policy into effect. At a lower level are the distributed management activities which provide local realizations of the policies by selecting appropriate management algorithms to monitor the behaviour of a system and control its operation. It is at the lowest, operation, level that this control is directly exercised and the basic monitoring operations are performed. There is a progressive decrease in generality as one descends through the layers.

Even with these viewpoints, the size and complexity of distributed systems and the very nature of distribution may make it impossible for individuals to hold in their minds the complete design and operating regime of a system. Indeed, to attempt to do so would be counter to one of the assumptions of this book – that a distributed system consists of multiple autonomous organizations which need to cooperate with, but may not necessarily be directly managed by, each other. These considerations lead to the adoption of specific concepts for distributed systems and their management, which are discussed in Chapter 8. There are two crucial concepts. The first is an object based approach which enables organizations to separate the

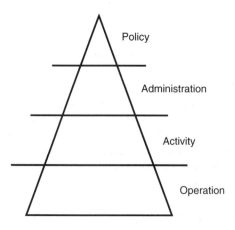

Figure 1.4   The ANSA layered model for management.

concerns relating to the external view of components from their internal operation. The second is the structuring of objects into domains to enable the management of groups of objects to be considered on a larger scale than is possible in a model which consists of individual objects.

1.7.2 The NETMAN cube model

Helpful as the ANSA model is, it suffers from being one-dimensional. Management is more complex than that. On the other hand, the multi-dimensional ODP viewpoint approach gives little guidance on how the features appearing in each of the viewpoints might be related. The European NETMAN project (Wells, 1991), which is part of the European Commission sponsored RACE programme, has proposed a three-dimensional perspective of the management problem, albeit applied only to the management of the infrastructure for the Telecommunications Management Network of integrated broadband communications which could be used to support a distributed system. Although the scope of the NETMAN project is not as wide as that of distributed systems management in general, modern communications systems have their own distributed processing activities. Consequently, there is much in the NETMAN approach that provides a viable perspective for distributed systems management. The NETMAN model, because of its three-dimensional characteristic, is described as the **cube** model (see Figure 1.5).

The model shows the orthogonality of three aspects of management, the *organization* dimension, the *functional* dimension and the *control* dimension. The organization dimension has much in common with the ANSA model and, although the terms employed by the two models are different because NETMAN is conceived specifically in terms of a communications network, there is a close similarity in the functions and control which the four hierarchical levels perform.

The functional dimension has more aspects than the five that were identified for the purpose of standardization of management. It considers not only those on-line management functions but also the design and planning functions which are vital for the development of a coherent, managed distributed system and also the functions needed to support the user of the system.

The control dimension is a recognition of the way information must flow for management functions to relate to each other and to the organizational requirements. The need for management action and control depends upon awareness that some situation is occurring which is not in accordance with policy objectives. As a result of gathering suitable data, a decision or set of decisions is made and implemented (through the choice of appropriate functions) to effect management control. By using the elements of the cube model, common terminology is available to describe management scenarios. For example, a policy requirement for giving a certain level of service

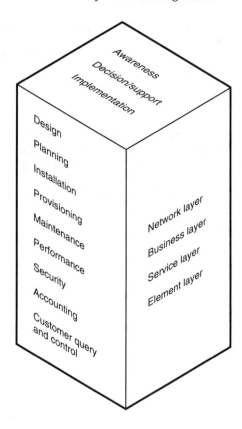

Figure 1.5   The NETMAN cube model.

availability will result not only in the design and provision of certain resources but also in a series of management activities to perform regular performance monitoring. On recognizing that performance is falling below that required by the policy, an analysis of system behaviour could lead to a decision to exercise the maintenance functions and so reconfigure the available resources.

1.7.3 Hierarchical approaches

One important modelling requirement is to provide a description in which both the technology of providing distributed systems management and the human activities of management can be combined. Management comes from the interplay of manager entities and the resources and activities for which they have responsibility. Management activity is concerned with the formulation of policies in respect of the resources being managed, in the planning of how to attain management goals subject to physical and (possibly) legal constraints, and in the exercise of supervision and control over the resources. Both policy making and formulating the plans needed to realize the policy influence the activity of managing the resources. Planning takes account of the policy requirements and relies for its success both on the manager's experience and on the availability of a reservoir of knowledge in dealing with analogous situations. In outline, the task of managing the resources first requires that the operational parameters, which govern resource behaviour and initiate that behaviour, have their values set. This is followed by a supervisory phase in which the manager assesses the behaviour to determine whether it meets policy objectives. If it does not, corrective action can be taken. This can take the form of further control commands being issued to the resources or, where this would be ineffective, reassessment of the policy and the reformulation of plans.

The strength of this model (shown in Figure 1.6) lies in the clear identification of feedback in the policy making, planning and control activities

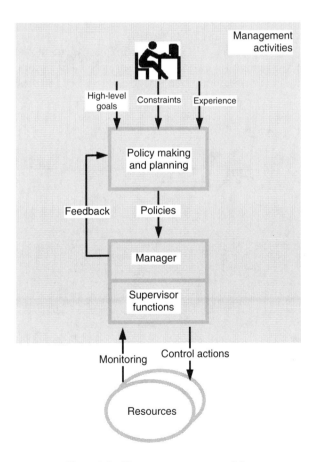

Figure 1.6   Human management activity.

of the manager. There is nothing intrinsic to the model which constrains the manager to being either a person or a computer program except perhaps a recognition that higher-order policy making is generally a human activity. The model can be elaborated by noting that the manager may delegate some of the supervisory functions to other entities (and even the policy making and planning activities). This is a natural way in which business managers delegate authority for a subset of management activities to more junior managers. Information technology systems facilitate the option to delegate well-defined subsets of management activity to computers.

Models that exhibit these characteristics include those developed in the Domino (Sloman and Moffett, 1989) and DOMAINS (Fink, 1991) research programmes and by Digital Equipment Corporation in their Enterprise Management Architecture (Strutt and Shurtleff, 1989). Figure 1.7 illustrates the approach, showing a hierarchical interaction between a human manager and an automated management activity to which certain responsibilities have been delegated. It assigns the policy making function to the human manager while the simple decision making functions are delegated to the automated manager. In the current state of the art the latter are functions where, as a result of analysis carried out when formulating management plans, the consequences of management operation can be foreseen. The automated management component is here represented by the supervisory function with control and monitoring interfaces to the resources. These are the subject of delegated

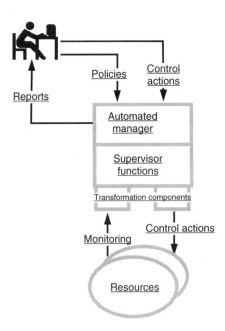

Figure 1.7 Automated management activity.

management, which is provided through any necessary data transformation components. Finally, there is a presentation component through which the automated manager communicates to the human to provide reports of delegated activity. It is through this interaction that the human may monitor, and hence supervise, the success of the activity. The reader will no doubt have recognized the similarity to the ANSA model. Delegation of responsibility to resources with a more limited management capability can continue down the management hierarchy to the component which exercises direct control operations over unintelligent processing components. The consequences of this model for automated management are discussed further in Chapter 8.

The models discussed in this section are all helpful in giving structure to the management problem. None is perfect and the authors consider that it is unlikely that any single model can ever be applicable to every type of managed distributed system, unless the model were to exhibit the very complexity which is an intrinsic part of management. Nevertheless, the reader is encouraged to remain aware of them while reading the remaining chapters.

1.8 Organization of the chapters

This chapter has served to set the scene by providing a general introduction, explaining the need for distributed system management and the general factors that affect it. It has identified the benefits, issues and possible approaches that can be taken. The two following chapters are concerned with the business and organizational aspects of management. They place particular emphasis upon the special factors introduced because the information processing is distributed. Chapter 2 discusses some requirements for distributed systems, their management in a particular organization and some related human factors. Chapter 3 identifies the factors to be taken into account when making a case for investing in distributed system management products, including the benefits, the risks and the costs.

The remaining chapters are more technically orientated. Chapter 4 covers the basic management services and functions that are needed, in addition to security, which is covered separately in Chapter 5. Chapter 6 identifies the additional supporting services needed and Chapter 7 covers installation and maintenance. These chapters constitute the core of the technical material. Chapter 8 then covers distributed system management from a more conceptual and theoretical point of view.

Chapter 9 discusses the important role of open systems standards in distributed systems management and identifies which standards exist and which have yet to be developed to support open distributed management. Finally, Chapter 10 explores distributed systems management in terms of current practice and current research to show what is available, what is under development and what has still to be provided.

The book contains two appendices. Appendix A summarizes significant points as a checklist for those whose task is to provide the management systems for their organization's distributed system. It also provides a guide to the risk analysis factors that managers should consider when installing or augmenting a distributed system. As terms are introduced and defined throughout this book they are shown in **bold**. *Italic* is used for emphasis and to highlight terms that are defined elsewhere. Appendix B provides a summary of many of the important definitions whose technical meaning specializes the normal use of the term. It also lists the abbreviations used in this book. In compiling the book, it became obvious that different authors give different meanings to the same terms and sometimes use different terms to convey the same meaning. Appendix B provides these different meanings to expose the overloaded use of technical terms and indicates the authors' preferences.

Summing up

- The need for system management grows as enterprises become more dependent upon information processing systems to help them meet their corporate objectives.

- Distributed systems are systems in which autonomous computers cooperate through communications networks to achieve common goals.

- Distributed systems are almost always complex: they typically evolve through the federation of heterogeneous independent systems and it is this which determines the need for integration.

- A strategy for distributed systems management must take into account environmental factors, business objectives, the external business environment and technology.

- A 'quality of service' agreement between the users and system managers is met by the application of the appropriate management functions and services (accounting, configuration, fault, performance, security and monitoring).

- Of the several models of distributed systems management, no model is complete and all simplify the complexity of the subject.

References

ANSA (1989). *ANSA: An Engineer's Introduction to the Architecture*. APM Ltd., Poseidon House, Castle Park, Cambridge CB3 0RD, UK

Fink B. (1991). DOMAINS basic concepts for management of distributed systems. In *Proc. 5th RACE TMN Conf.*, 1991

ISO/IEC 7498-4: 1989. *Information Technology – Open Systems Interconnection – Part 4: Management Framework*

ISO/IEC 10746. *Information technology – Open Distributed Processing* (in development)

Sloman M.S. and Moffett J.D. (1989). Domain management for distributed systems. In *Proc. IFIP Sym. on Integrated Network Management*, Boston, MA, May 1989 (Meandzija B. and Westcott J., eds.), pp. 505-16. Amsterdam: North-Holland

Stajano A. (1992). ESPRIT business systems. *XII Magazine*, March (5), 20-1

Strutt C. and Shurtleff D. (1989). Architecture for an integrated, extensible enterprise management director. In *Proc. IFIP Sym. on Integrated Network Management*, Boston, MA, May 1989 (Meandzija B. and Westcott J., eds.), pp. 61-72. Amsterdam: North-Holland

Wells A. (1991). Functional description of network management. *British Telecom Technology J.*, **9**(3), 9-17

2

Uses and users of distributed systems

Objectives

- to identify user and business requirements
- to consider typical business cultures
- to note how distributed systems influence and are influenced by human factors
- to consider training for distributed systems managers and operators

2.1 Introduction

Information technology systems and the communication of information (both in its processed form and as raw data) are tools that facilitate the activities of industry and commerce on a day by day basis. Yet, with the exception of the computing and communications industries themselves, these tools are a secondary part of their businesses and exist only to serve them. If distributed systems and their management are to prove effective, it is vital that they are based upon the real needs of the business activities they support. In the past, the evidence has often appeared to be that computing and communication have been led by the technology rather than driven by the needs of their users. Before moving on to more technical aspects of distributed systems, their organization and their operational management, it is important to consider some typical uses for the technology and some of the factors that motivate its users and its managers.

This chapter focuses upon the business environment and those who work in it. Its themes are the requirements for distributed systems within business enterprises and for the management of those systems. It considers their effect upon people, especially those who operate and manage the distributed system. Users of computing facilities and their organizations measure their business success in terms of their goals and objectives. In consequence, much of the discussion in this chapter is in terms of the perceptions by users of the distributed processing environment and of the organizations that provide the service. It is based upon current practice and recognizes that distributed systems are now in use and serving genuine applications. Organizations differ and, to obtain a rounded picture of their requirements, it is important to consider them from a number of viewpoints. This provides a starting point for considering how business requirements relate to distributed processing and how the availability of distributed processing reacts back on business.

Distributed processing is influenced by the distributed nature of organizations and their interactions as much as by the specific applications of information technology. For that reason, the investigation of requirements is not constrained to a particular technology of distributed processing nor to any specific hardware or software architecture. Similarly it does not distinguish between organizations in the public and private sectors except where these have truly sector-specific characteristics. Thus, for the purpose of this chapter, the words 'organization', 'business' and 'corporation' may be regarded as interchangeable. Given the diversity of business applications, the authors can make no claim to provide a complete coverage of all possible aspects of all businesses. Rather, the aim is to cover at least some major areas and sectors that are reasonably representative.

The discussion begins by identifying concepts that characterize the structure of organizations. These are used to identify particular characteristics of organizations in a number of business sectors. Although industries may differ in their products and their specific use of information technology, many features of business life are similar and common cultures, with common roles, pervade the business environment. Some representative cultures are also explored. In its investigation of the impact of distributed system technologies on people, the chapter briefly explores some human factors issues and the implications for training. The chapter ends by summarizing the general objectives of management and the implications of a unified approach to distributed systems management.

2.2 Characteristics of organizations

People within business regard themselves as operating primarily in a business environment. Even when the environment is highly technical, they relate only to the technically defined environment where they see business advantage. This is true of all technologies, including information technology. At one end of the range of user perception, users may see information technology as offering a rich field for complex interactions which materially assist their work. At the other extreme, they may see the impact of technology as being hostile to their preferred way of working, although this antipathy to the use of information technology is often the result of lack of familiarity, the novelty of concepts, the rapid pace of technical change and, above all, its threat to displace people who perform routine tasks.

Some structural aspects of organizations whose characteristics span a number of functions and sectors of application are common to all of them. Although people may see themselves as having the authority to act in a relatively unconstrained or in an autonomous manner for some aspects of their business activities, there are always interaction constraints. There are distinct differences in interaction style and content depending upon whether the interactions are between the component parts of an organization, or the interactions are with other organizations; and whether these interactions are between peers who are collaborating in some activity of the organization, or hierarchical, when one person takes responsibility for and exercises authority over people.

Peer interactions between individuals occur at many levels within an organization. They relate to performing the operational tasks of an organization (like production or administration) but not to its management. Management interactions within an organization are essentially hierarchical though managers frequently receive peer support to assist in their tasks. This is the usual way in which businesses choose to manage their internal operations. Particularly significant, for their influence upon managing distributed systems, are peer interactions between organizations or between departments within organizations. In the conventional sense, hierarchical interactions between organizations cannot occur because they are obliged to treat one another as equals. However, when independent organizations need to collaborate to achieve a mutually desirable goal, they often invoke a superior authority for the purpose, by agreeing to contracts that are backed by the force of law. In addition there are hierarchical relationships which stem from regulations where, in respect of some particular aspect of business activity, the responsibilities of an organization are prescribed by an external body. These may be established by national governments or by international authority.

These interactions are further affected by the distribution of the interacting entities. There is the physical aspect of distribution which leads to a recognition that interactions within a single geographical site are simpler than those between different sites, even when the sites belong to the same organization. Sometimes this is because communication is physically easier, but often it is because communication and interaction are *culturally* easier. Members of the workforce identify with both their place of work and their colleagues in adjoining offices and workshops rather than with those in distant locations or in other departments. In multinational businesses, these relationships can add political and legal dimensions to distribution. Organizations can find their activities constrained by the different regulations which apply to businesses operating within the country where they are registered and to those where they are trading internationally. This is particularly true where there are differences in the freedom with which people may have access to certain data or where there are differences in the way data of a personal nature must be secured.

2.3 Business sectors

Five major business sectors have been chosen to illustrate the analysis because they provide a broad spread across the spectrum of information technology applications. The sectors are: financial, retail, petrochemical, government, and academic organizations.

2.3.1 Financial enterprises

Financial organizations operate within a well defined legal framework and are characterized by the extent of their inter-organizational dealings and their goals for growth. They see growth arising from increasing world trade and prosperity, the acquisition of smaller, less successful financial information service organizations or by mergers and partnerships with other enterprises offering complementary financial services. However, this is not a universal development paradigm. There are examples of demerger, with alliances being unmade where they have not shown themselves cost-effective.

Financial information systems are prime users of information technology. They rely on the timely provision of information, often from worldwide sources. Telecommunication and the processing power and data storage capabilities of computers have led to financial organizations becoming big users of distributed processing. They have two main components:

- front office, where trading takes place
- back office, where deals are resolved

These are distinctions of function. It is the back office which has been the long established user of information technology. This used to be primarily a batch operation. Now back office services contribute to the general pool of financial information, of which some is provided by third-party sources. There are still examples where the back office obtains its information from the front office by batch transfer, often in the form of re-keyed paper forms. However, networked and distributed processing technologies which have been applied to the front office are becoming generally adopted. In the front office, sophisticated ways of presenting the information from internal and third-party sources upon which deals are based have spread widely. Typically, they employ local area networks, long-haul data links and video. One consequence is that this application area is necessarily heterogeneous even within the same building or site.

Users of financial systems are impatient with technical difficulties and unconcerned about its issues. They demand not only business-orientated help desk services but 'instant' response by technical staff to any fault or problem. The back office is characterized by a demand for security and integrity: the former to ensure that financial data and the funds they often represent are passed only to those authorized to receive them; the latter to ensure that funds are neither inadvertently lost nor spuriously created. These two requirements are also necessary in the front office. Here they are supplemented by the requirement for information availability. In trading, considerable stakes can rest upon the timely availability of financial and business data.

2.3.2 Retail enterprises

The modern retail business is highly competitive and the introduction of information technology, initially seen as offering a competitive edge, is now an essential part of the business. The business itself is highly distributed, taking its supplies from a number of national (and international) wholesale distribution points. Its customers are dispersed and may choose to use cashless means to pay for purchases. As a result, there is a growing interaction between retail and banking businesses (see Figure 2.1).

The retailer with multiple outlets typically has computing and communication requirements for the following functions: evaluation and transfer of price and sales information to and from shops; delivery schedules to

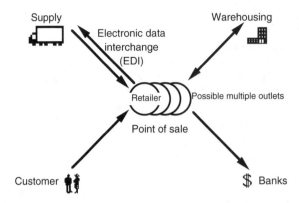

Figure 2.1 Interactions between business and the retail sector.

and from distribution depots; banking and financial services; on-line order entry at display terminals; and point-of-sale (POS) systems. Requirements for data processing are often conventional (that is, through batch processing services) accounts and payroll processing. The retail sector is a pioneer user of electronic data interchange (EDI) for transfer of trading data and therefore has peer relationships (usually via third-party supported networks) with companies acting as suppliers.

In shops, end users of information technology, whether at the cash desk or behind the scenes in storage areas, are almost without exception non-technical. Nevertheless, they must place total reliance on information technology and POS systems. As a result, there is a systems requirement for high reliability, fast fault location, and (in some cases) fall-back capability.

2.3.3 The petrochemical industry

The petrochemical industry is a prime example of a major production industry transforming raw materials into finished products. Like other chemical and manufacturing industries, its sources of materials, its operations and its markets are world-wide. The petrochemical industry can essentially be divided into three major areas of activity:

- upstream: exploration and extraction of crude oil
- refining: where a range of chemical products are generated from the crude oil
- downstream: marketing and distribution of refined products

Their interaction, and the data flows between the components of the business are illustrated in Figure 2.2.

Upstream

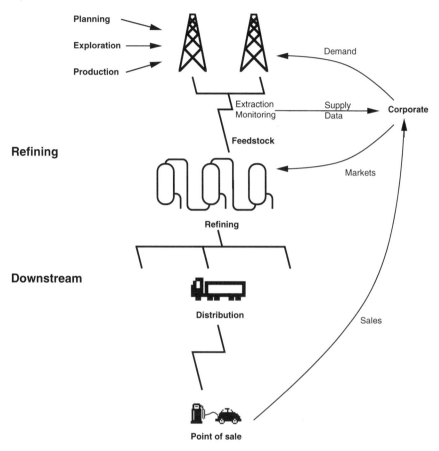

Figure 2.2 Petrochemical activities and data flows.

The division is again by function and also, within each functional area, by product and its market. The international nature of its business has significant implications for its computing and computational needs. Within each functional area and each type of business there is a desire to achieve common standards to ease information interchange. These requirements must also be tempered by the overall need for a corporate view of the state of the business as a whole. Upstream activities have significant requirements for computationally intensive processing of oil well production data and for exploration data analysis. There is a significant security requirement since the results of analysis are closely-guarded commercial secrets. Central to refining are conventional process control computing requirements, with a strong emphasis on safety. Downstream activities have the more conventional commercial trading requirements for computing, whether wholesale or retail. Their security requirements are to avoid the risk of fraud, which can be a source of loss at the point of sale or delivery, and to maintain system availability.

Within the three areas, the users have many different requirements for information technology. The industry employs staff with a range of backgrounds and a diversity of practical, technological and scientific skills, so users have varying levels of information technology expertise. Like the computing and communication systems users in the finance industry, the majority of those in the petrochemical industry are also intolerant of any of its technical difficulties. They see themselves as 'oil people' rather than as 'computer people'.

2.3.4 Governments and administrations as enterprises

Governments and administrations, both national and local, exhibit typical enterprise requirements. In common with other corporate entities, they divide administrative functions into personnel, finance, stock control, management, etc. However, government is very much engaged in the business of national and local administration and these corporate activities are often matched by an operational division which performs those administrative functions on behalf of the public. For example national governments are not only concerned with the management of their own staff (division by function), they are also concerned with handling national employment (division by product). The outlets to the public who are the customers for administrative products are widely distributed, usually through local offices. At the same time there is a strong requirement for data to be centrally coordinated. This results in a heavy demand for office automation, communication and conventional data processing. The interactions are not just within an area concerned with a typical administrative product, like finance or employment. They are between both functions and products, for example in the need to have common internal personnel policies, irrespective of the specific public service which is being provided.

Government, with its supporting judiciary, is instrumental in setting a legal framework not just for the activities of its citizens but also for those of business enterprises. As already observed in Section 2.1, legal frameworks impose hierarchical authority over business in the sense that national laws constrain the policies which business can adopt. Yet because governments do business with industry and commerce, there are also close peer linkages. With significant data flows between the public and the business sectors, there are advantages to governments and their administrations in having efficient connections between their computing and communication facilities and the corresponding distributed systems of industry and commerce.

Although there are many similarities between governments and business enterprises, governments differ in two key respects. The above examples of financial, retail and petrochemical enterprises have all shown the need for some measure of security concerning personnel and commercial information. This is largely a response to normal commercial pressures. However, the government sector is responsible for national security and for law and public order. These place additional demands upon the requirements for security, which are at a significantly higher level of protection than those normally encountered in business.

The second difference concerns the desirability of growth. Whereas it is typical that a commercial or industrial enterprise will seek to grow, this goal is absent from governmental policy. Indeed some governments have aimed, as one of their policies, to reduce the national and local administrative burden they inevitably must impose. Yet in spite of such policies, there appears to be a tendency for administrative bureaucracy to increase. This seems to be a natural consequence of the increasing complexity of public affairs and the increasing interactions between government departments. Both result from improved communication and increased general mobility, both of which have generated increased business and political interactions. The net effect on computation and communication is that growth of distributed processing and changes to the distributed systems are features of this sector even when they are not explicitly sought after.

2.3.5 Academic enterprises

Institutions such as universities and polytechnics are traditionally independent bodies, the spirit of independence often being found within the departments they contain. Thus, significant characteristics of the academic enterprise are the peer interactions between departments and the considerably weaker hierarchical dependencies upon a corporate centre than are found in business or government. Yet in spite of this desire for independence and academic freedom, funding arrangements for both teaching and research are often organized centrally and across institutions. Much of this funding is public, which brings with it a requirement for academia to adhere to goals that are broadly set by its national paymasters.

Each academic institution has a defined geographical base. Yet, because they are usually large enterprises, their property is frequently spread throughout a town or city and, in some countries, can cover a significant part of a state. This distribution raises its own communication requirements. Even where the division is in terms of functions (that is, by academic discipline), the requirements for interdisciplinary interactions add to the communication requirement.

In terms of their computing needs, academic staff show a wide diversity of requirements and expertise. This can range from the highly demanding technical specialist who is well informed about the potential of the technology to the more routine data processing requirements of payroll and record keeping. Users of these computing and communication systems vary not only in their technical capability but also in their responsibility and attitude (first year undergraduates to full-time administrators).

There is a similar variety in the degree of autonomy of academic staff. This can range from individual users wholly dependent on a central service to departments and even to individual research projects with their own computing and communication systems (often with considerable processing power) supported by their own administrative and technical staff. Hence, there is no simple management hierarchy and the overall situation is analogous to that of a number of loosely associated companies in the private sector. Only in the central services supporting all aspects of the institution is there likely to be a hierarchical management discipline.

2.4 Business cultures

Cultures are the expression of the social aspects of the individuals and groups within organizations. A common thread which joins the requirements of those fulfilling similar roles within different organizations is their culture. This contrasts with the more formal structures and roles of corporate bodies. The following set of cultures is typical of many within business sectors. The interest here derives from the impact of information technology and the requirements that these cultures place upon that technology, its distribution and its management. The list is by no means exhaustive but serves to illustrate principal requirements:

- Business strategists
- Administration
- Secretarial and the office environment
- Information technologists

2.4.1 The business strategist culture

Business planners are becoming aware that distributed systems and the networks which support them are particularly important in the support of business. Traditionally, the business strategist has not been involved with distributed or even centralized information technology systems directly. The studies of the Advanced Network Systems Architecture (ANSA, 1989) project, while committed to establishing requirements for distributed processing, explicitly excluded them from the scope of its analysis of distributed systems requirements. However, their needs cannot be ignored. As a group they are demanding better deterministic business models and more realistic business data to support strategic planning activities. These requirements generate demands from planning departments who need access to powerful systems for business modelling and to corporate data upon which to base their models.

Business strategists are concerned about the risk to which a business is exposed. This includes both the risk which arises from normal business transactions and also the risk which is inherent in placing considerable reliance on distributed systems (see Chapters 5 and 6). They are also concerned about the costs of resource utilization and hence about the charging strategies that should be applied for use of the distributed processing infrastructure. For example, should distributed processing be treated as a general service and charged as an overhead on all enterprise activities; or should it be charged on the basis of usage? There is clear evidence that, in the formative stages of distributed processing activity, the former strategy is the correct one to adopt. During the initial transition to the distributed system, there will be few users. If these few are burdened with the full economic cost of the distributed system, the charging rate will be far higher than when the use of the distributed system has matured. Levying high charges will tend to diminish usage and so increase the fraction of total cost that must be born by those users who remain. As the cost to these remaining users increases further, they too will be discouraged. Only when distributed processing is well established and there is keen competition for resources are accounting strategies which charge by usage likely to have their desired effect: that is, to ration the availability of limited resources by price.

2.4.2 Administrative cultures

Administrative cultures provide the supporting infrastructure of business, handling day-to-day planning and monitoring of business activity. It is within the administrative culture that automated management mechanisms meet the largely manual mechanisms of higher management. Administrators have used computer systems for some time, often for financial reporting, invoicing and maintaining business statistics. The culture has adapted well. As administrative information processing becomes further distributed, this culture finds it needs to evolve yet further to meet the challenges of business interactions between many sites and between many businesses. Because this culture is not trained in the technology of the distributed processing environment, distribution of functionality must be transparent to it. That is, the distributed nature of the processing environment must be suitably hidden from its users.

2.4.3 The office and secretarial culture

Office and secretarial services provide support for management at many levels. This is a service culture, of professionals and their supporting staff, who have not generally been provided with basic information technology training. They are increasingly being given the responsibility for the day-to-day administration and control of small departmental systems and networks, for example, office automation systems. They are, in effect, users who have become small-scale system managers. Their numbers are increasing rather than diminishing with the increasing complexity of office requirements. Those who belong to this culture are highly dependent upon the successful application of information technology yet, in some cases, their jobs are often threatened by it because they are often ill-trained in understanding the potential it offers them. The result of this lack of training is that neither their work nor their use of information technology tools is as efficient and as cost-effective as it could be.

A further feature associated with this culture is that it is only those parts of the staff's task which can easily be programmed and automated which receive computer assistance. The result is a need to change back and forth between manual and computerized methods. Users and industry have frequently failed to integrate the benefits of information technology with the everyday operations of the office. This results in unnecessary work as typed documents are sent by conventional mail services to be manually amended and then returned for editing or retyping. Not surprisingly, there is frustration with the only partially implemented and imperfectly integrated distributed systems.

2.4.4 The information technologist culture

The information technologist culture covers central services management, data communication and the maintenance of information technology resources. It is a management and operations culture with its focus of attention upon the technology and its efficient use. To the extent that members of the culture are concerned to provide a resilient service because they recognize the strategic role of information technology within the enterprise, the culture is concerned with the availability and cost-effectiveness of the technology.

One of the complaints levied against this culture is that its specialists too often regard the technology as an end in itself rather than as just one of the important mechanisms for attaining an enterprise's goals. In this, those exhibiting the information technology culture are at variance with others in the enterprise who, as has been shown above, identify with the enterprise rather than with particular aspects of its information technology systems. It is therefore important that the leaders within this culture encourage its practitioners to hide as much as possible of the unnecessary details of computing and communication from its users. This means that they have to plan for system imperfections and develop culture-related strategies which encourage robust system design, able to provide continuity of service even in the event of failure.

Within this culture is a maintenance sub-culture whose mode of operation has hitherto been largely reactive. To some extent, this reactive mentality has arisen through a lack of appropriate tools, whose use would enable incipient problems to be identified and diagnosed before they become serious. In some situations, the monitoring capabilities of existing systems are so inadequate that operators respond to maintenance calls as a result of requests from system users. In extreme cases, maintenance staff have been known to seek faults in financial information systems by 'floor walking'. Clearly, there is a need for better management discipline in this area. However, in its defence it must be noted that not all failure modes can be anticipated. Therefore an enterprise must be prepared to invest in resources which will enable its information technologists to resolve problems speedily. It must also invest in the appropriate level of training for this culture and recognize that skilled operators are scarce and valuable resources.

2.5 People in distributed system management

2.5.1 User cultures

Although not listed as one of the four cultures, it is important to take users into account, even to examine the extent to which there can be said to be a user culture. This has been separated out, not because users are the least important – indeed they are the reason that the technology is provided – but because users constitute an ill-defined group. Consequently, they have the least coherent of the cultures. Users' experiences range from a academic scientist on an open, toll-free, network to the home-based user of public electronic mail and the office clerical assistant. A common factor is the universal desire for human-to-computer interfaces of high quality which match the user's application and skill. This requires a capability for interfaces to be customized for the particular activity users are undertaking. Ideally, it requires the system to offer differentiated levels of help services. These should range from help that is suitable for the occasional or novice user right through to help appropriate to the expert.

Because so many enterprises now rely upon the support of information technology, the cultures of its information technology users deserve particular attention. Enterprise managers need to commit specific resources to making the users conversant with both the strengths and the weaknesses of the systems which have been installed. In this way it may become possible to bridge the cultural gap that frequently exists between the technology specialist and the majority of the technology's users. Only in this way will it be possible for users, operating from their remote workstations, to assist the technical specialists, who are themselves distributed throughout the system, to resolve problems and respond to system failures when no automatic recovery is possible.

2.5.2 Interfacing people to the distributed system

Within a distributed system service, individual functions may be carried out in different ways. Some require analysis and insight, and so fall into the human domain, while others are routine and can be delegated to automatic (or semi-automatic) processing. System management functions and services may therefore be shared between computers and the people who interact with them. Whereas it is possible to throw the onus for taking management decisions or performing refined analyses upon the person when the system is simple, there are several reasons for seeking to automate whenever possible:

- The speed with which modern information processing and communication systems operate means that people cannot be expected to respond fast enough to critical situations which might develop (say through security breach, component failure or operational overload).
- The complexity of the distributed processing environment means that raw data needs to be processed before a comprehensible digest is presented to managers and operational staff.
- Human resources trained in distributed systems management are a scarce and expensive commodity. Distributed systems may need to be operated continuously and the cost of automated management is essentially independent of the duration of their operation. Furthermore, whereas computers do not tire, people do.

Management imposes its effects over a range of time-scales. Each management activity, whether performed by humans or delegated to systems, has associated with it a longer term supervisory function in which the operation of the system being managed is monitored against the policy which guides that activity. Typical management time-scales are summarized in Table 2.1. They range from fractions of seconds to years. Generally the break point between management activities that are left to people and those that are delegated to computer systems occurs at about the 1-minute level. As the speed of computation and communication continues to increase, this means

Table 2.1   Typical systems management time-scales.

Activity	Time-scale
Computing and communication processes	Seconds or less
System operations	Seconds/minutes
Operations reporting	Hours
Change control	Days/months
Planning	Weeks
Budgeting	Months
Technology and business evolution	Years/decades

that more and more significant aspects of distributed systems management must be delegated to machines.

For all these reasons distributed systems management activity is typically exercised through a combination of human and computer processing. For the interface between computer processing and the human operator to be effective and contribute to the quality of the management service itself, its design and implementation requirements deserve as much attention as do the other aspects of distributed processing and its management. Managers should be prepared to invest in good human–computer interface technology in order to capitalize upon its investment in both.

In managing and operating a distributed processing environment, one is, in effect, monitoring and controlling a large real-time process control environment. This requires the capability to observe many things at any one time and to partition them into different spheres of operational interest. Technology is already providing excellent tools in the shape of computer workstations with large screens and windowing software, which permit several concurrent activities to be updated and displayed simultaneously. However, there are limits to how many items it is sensible to display at any one time. Partly this is conditioned by the space available on workstation screens for representing a large network and its many attachments. Because management frequently requires access to different types of data at the same time, there is competition between them for space. Even where windowing techniques are used to enable the user to scroll through the representations, the space limitation remains.

But an even more significant constraining factor is the amount of information that should be presented to the operator. Studies show that the effectiveness of a person to comprehend a situation and to respond diminishes when presented with too much information at any one time (Miller, 1975). These studies show that there is considerably more to the human–computer interface than the ability to display concurrent activities and different features of the distributed processing environment on a windowing workstation. The type of management information should determine the way in which the display is realized. Alarms need to be highlighted to capture the operator's attention and may be supplemented with audible warnings. Reports demand tabular or textual rendering. Topological relationships are best handled graphically through mimic diagrams. Trends may require both numerical data and graphical representation as histograms or other form of charting. As well as being displayed, these representations of management data may also need to be generated in the form of a printed report. A report format which is suitable for window display usually needs to be considerably modified in order to communicate its message effectively when it appears as a print-out.

The modes of input can be equally diverse. There are two types of input: those which manipulate the presentation of data and those which control the distributed processing environment. Both can lead to direct interaction with the display using any one of a number of input styles (keyboard, mouse, touch-sensitive screen). The consequences of the data manipulation operations will not affect the operational system, only the way in which data is rendered. On the other hand, those operations which influence system behaviour must be subject to both access control and other control checks. Access control ensures that operator identities have been authenticated and operators have the authority to institute changes. But additional control checks are needed; it could be disastrous to remove from service an active system which is providing the only instance of a particular corporate database.

Integration is an important concept for the human–computer interface. The human operators should have a uniform style of access to all the resources under their control. The most basic form of integration is at the technology level. Separate workstations for separate subsystems should be unnecessary. Yet, at present, it is all too common to find that different groups of resources are handled independently by different management systems. For example, each component local area network has its own management workstation; so too do the interconnecting wide area networks. The connected terminal access, data storage and processing subsystems again have their independent workstations for subsystem monitoring and control. There is no technical reason why the management data pertaining to these subsystems should not be consolidated and made available at a single workstation.

This requirement for integration and uniform access should not be taken as implying that all distributed systems management has to be carried out through a single workstation, only that it should be possible given a powerful enough workstation. However, the ensuing management task for a large-scale distributed system would be beyond the capabilities of a single person. A single operator could neither appreciate all aspects of the system in sufficient detail nor respond to the multiplicity of situations which would arise within the system. It is at this stage that management policy and the logistics of managing a large and diverse distributed processing environment take effect by distributing the task of its operation and control among several people. This may require several workstations.

Given that a large distributed system has several operators and several workstations, there needs to be a more sophisticated level of integration. This concerns the style of interaction. Whatever the means for input and output, it is essential that equivalent operations, carried out upon diverse resources, should convey the same 'look and feel' irrespective of location, vendor or resource class. Failure to do so makes an already complicated management environment even more difficult to manage. A common look and feel will make it possible for operators to move within the business environment without the need to retrain them for each specific user interface.

The present generation of network and distributed systems management products are not usually integrated at either level. Suppliers are aware of the need for more integration and some have, within a narrow product range, satisfied this requirement in part. However, many management systems still remain unintegrated even at the technology level. Organizations proposing to purchase management systems need to make allowance for the multiplicity of management support systems which may be required. Analysis has shown that over 80% of *The Times* Top 600 companies use three or more communication protocols in their systems and almost 60% use two or more different types of wiring schemes (Benchmark Research, 1991).

2.5.3 Skills, staffing and training

One feature which underlies many of the practical difficulties faced by managers of distributed systems is the need to staff the system with people who have the right type of management skills. These people need to:

- understand the management policy and its implications for the system,
- appreciate the technology,
- have experience in knowing how to deal with the 'unexpected' problems which can always occur in a real-time system.

The manager, trying to build a team of suitable people, is faced with the issues of skill and staffing which apply to all computer systems, whether centralized or distributed. Scarcity of specialist skills and the drive to reduce costs by cutting down on staff numbers are particularly significant. Two additional factors arise from distribution:

- the need to manage at a distance, since it is not practical to put a specialist everywhere,
- the extra demands placed on staff by the complexity of the system as a whole, even if the individual components are simpler than a centralized system.

These all have implications for staff development. No job stays constant. Continual retraining is needed simply to keep abreast of changing requirements and changing technology. Yesterday's computer operator is today's first-line support. If scarce staff are to be retained, it is necessary to ensure that they can see their careers developing satisfactorily.

Help services, backed up by good documentation, are considered to be essential to the satisfactory operation and management of distributed systems. The characteristics of help services and the ways in which they contribute to user and operator training are discussed in Chapter 6. Documentation and the way it adds to training support is considered in Chapter 7.

A prerequisite for a successfully managed system is that attention is given to manager and operator training. Whenever a new product is introduced, its users need to spend time on learning its characteristics and how to use it most efficiently. For some simple products and talented users, learning by use is effective. For many products, though, time and money spent on formal training sessions is more cost-effective. The hidden costs of learning slowly and making mistakes on the job usually outweigh the visible costs of training sessions. In a distributed system, an operator error could affect hundreds of people who might be far away from the scene of the error. A training programme is required for each staff member, identifying the skills required and planning how they will be acquired.

Training has to be backed up by good documentation. This must include: documentation for the resources and activities being managed; the procedures for their management; and the rationale for decisions taken. Without documentation, the management of the system will not survive the departure of key staff. The danger of relying upon the detailed personal knowledge of a few information technology staff and communication specialists is particularly acute. Both classes of staff are in high demand and there is a high rate of staff turnover. The pressure on them to solve urgent day-to-day problems often takes precedence over the need to commit their knowledge to a form where it can be used by others. Managers must resist this pressure. Although experts' knowledge could be put on paper, it is also important to have their knowledge consolidated into an on-line knowledge base. This makes it available through the same distributed processing environment that the operator is seeking to monitor and control. As a knowledge base, it can be accessed through an expert system. Having the expertise of the specialist readily accessible to operational staff in this way complements and reinforces their training.

The need for technical training, which gives familiarity with the distributed system, is obvious, but the need for management training, especially for distributed systems, is as great. The operator and the manager have to be given awareness of equipment which they may never actually see yet whose behaviour is vital to some part of the system for which they are responsible. Its malfunction could vitally affect overall performance. Management training should ensure three things. One is to ensure that staff are fully aware of the requirements for and disciplines of resource management. The second is that the corporate objectives of their employing organization are explained to them. The third is that they learn to recognize the relationship of their technology skills to the objectives of their parent organization and so relate the system management need to the corporate need.

2.6 Management implications

Management is about the establishment of policies to meet enterprise goals, turning those policies into plans and supervising the activities of resources to ensure that their operations meet the policy requirements of the enterprise. Policies are characterized by motivation and authority; managers need to have both the motivation and authority to perform the tasks required of them (see Section 8.4).

In whatever way managers operate within a business and interact with distributed systems they are primarily concerned with the delivery of products and services on behalf of their organization. Management, of whatever type of enterprise, has some objectives which are common. These include:

- Minimization of cost – or, more realistically, the control and pre-dictability of costs.

- Minimization of complexity – management of large systems is a complex matter and simplification into manageable subsystems is an important element of strategy for systems managers and users.

- Delivered performance – the balance between pure performance and the broader issue of cost/benefit will vary mainly according to sector (contrast the financial and retail sectors). As with costs, the general objective for providers of information technology services to corporate users is predictability of performance.

- Integrity – particularly the consistency of information in both space and time so that all users and managers of distributed systems have as near identical views of it as possible. Much effort has been expended towards attempting to achieve high degrees of integrity in applications (for example, in airline reservation applications), in systems (distributed transaction processing systems) and in standards (for example, through commitment and concurrency protocols).

- Resilience – system distribution offers the potential for resilience. Independent of degrees of distribution, resilience has an importance which is highly application-specific and time-dependent. For example, process control and retail POS systems have resilience requirements which exhibit both high degrees of distribution and low tolerance of even short-term failures.

- Security – distribution of highly secure systems raises a security risk by exposing data in transit. In highly sensitive computing applications, this perceived vulnerability may inhibit the acceptance of distribution as a technique.

- Commercial interest – the specific objectives of end user organizations are not usually met in any direct way by distribution in itself but by the capabilities which distribution delivers, such as resilience and performance.

For all except the smallest organization, its staff and resources and their interactions with other organizations have an element of distribution. With size and distribution comes the need to delegate. Therefore, the essence of a distributed system's architecture is the delegation of responsibility to a number of discrete entities. While distributed systems management need not necessarily be distributed to the same extent as the systems managed, some degree of distribution of management is probably inevitable. Modern management styles have tended towards the distribution of authority. Where an information technology infrastructure is essential to the business then delegation must extend, to some degree, to the corresponding distributed systems. This means that the various layers of management need to consider carefully which elements are delegated to lower layers and how peer interaction occurs. It has often been observed that where clear policies on system intercommunication and compatibility are absent, enterprises are adversely affected.

The rationale for applying information technology within organizations is to provide the technology where it is needed. In a distributed system, it is natural for the management task to be distributed to a number of individuals who are given responsibility for different parts of the total system. This partitioning of management may be on regional or functional grounds. It is vital that the areas of authority are properly delineated. Partition by region is the easiest to visualize and consequently it is the easiest to implement. Where partition is by function, it will cover operational, security and data management. Because security and data are less overt aspects of systems, the requirement for coherent management policies can be overlooked when the systems in which they occur are distributed. The importance of security in individual systems is already recognized by businesses. However, the security of communication is often handled by the communication specialist, not the security specialist. For that reason, the organization must appoint a security administrator to have a coordinating role across all systems to which security is applicable. Although distribution of corporate data within computer systems is a relatively novel concept, similar attention needs to be given to analogous procedures for managing data.

Roles in both distributed human management and distributed systems have an impact upon, and generate requirements for, distributed systems management. In the same way that human management roles mirror corporate structure, distributed systems management roles should be influenced by the elements of corporate structure. That said, information technology systems are influencing corporate structure either directly (through the use of advanced communication and corporate information systems) or indirectly (by their influence on general business activity). The interaction between human roles and structures and the corresponding distributed system structures is already complex and must be expected to become more so. As a result, technologies may both subvert the formal structure and threaten cultures in a wide variety of environments. One of the more obvious examples of this has been the almost anarchic effect caused in some industries by the introduction and uncontrolled proliferation of personal computer systems.

Regulatory authorities and regulators have a special position in respect of management activities. They exercise some of the elements of hierarchical authority by virtue of the general authority which governments exercise over companies. At the same time, they must maintain peer group interactions since, at the working level, the staff of regulatory bodies make their effect largely by consultation and consensus. Although regulatory authorities are an essential aspect of the complete picture of management, the mixed formal and informal character of their role makes them difficult to accommodate into any standard scheme. Fortunately, this difficulty is not a stumbling block to an understanding of distributed systems and their management. The interests of regulators are quite narrowly confined by the legislative framework which they exist to enforce. The detail of their regulatory requirements and their impact upon the distributed system can usually be contained in a relatively simple manner compared with the requirements of the corporate hierarchy under regulation.

To achieve organizational effectiveness in the use of distributed systems, there are advantages in developing both the distributed system structure and the corresponding management structure in parallel to take full advantage of the technology. Departmental and technical managers must anticipate user needs as systems are pushed out further into areas where users cannot or will not generate their own management systems. System designers and operators must recognize that these users' needs will be different from the needs of users who are readily serviced by a local computer centre. As the discussion on enterprises and on cultures has shown, fault management at both the tactical and strategic levels needs to move towards a situation where faults can be detected and put under control well before they impact users. If this type of defence fails, management activities must ensure that faults are contained before vital functions are compromised.

There is always a danger that over-zealous management can lead to control instability as managers in each area within the distributed processing environment seek to optimize their local operations. In a move to avoid this, there is an inevitable temptation to move the point of control upwards in the management hierarchy. But moving the locus of control away from the immediate area which it affects introduces another danger, one that is familiar to control engineers. The delays which long feedback paths introduce into the controlling system can themselves introduce instabilities. Also, senior managers, often associated with the centralization of control, cannot fully anticipate the future and hence cannot know all the control requirements of the devolved parts of the system. Some measure of control must always be delegated to operate at the local level. The consequence is that managers must perform a dynamic 'balancing act' so that the efficiencies gained from the distribution of application functionality are not negated by being subject to over-constraining central control.

Distributed systems have already allowed informal structures to arise within organizations. This has been particularly noticeable where distribution of functionality into personal computers and workstations has not been accompanied by the application of formal management to the process. This lack of control makes distributed processing difficult to account for and risks giving such systems a bad name. Partly, this is because the investment in the local communication network infrastructure is not readily perceived as a corporate asset with a defined cost and value. When the management activity fails to deliver important characteristics which should be provided in an effective distributed system, then drastic measures inevitably become necessary. Consider the situation in which the system fails to provide security. A piecemeal approach may develop, with critical applications kept off the network because of perceived inadequacies in security. This negates the advantages of distribution and can deny it to a class of users within an organization. Investigations by business consultants frequently find, in a wide variety of organizations, that critical capabilities have become dependent upon under-managed personal computer systems. A disaster striking them (for example through virus contamination or loss of data which has not been backed up) risks a corporate catastrophe. More subtly, there can be a significant waste of resources if unskilled staff attempt to solve problems, especially where these problems arise from the interaction of several computer systems. A management policy to distribute computing also needs a policy of providing trained managers to deal with system organization and trained personnel to deal with problems. These factors need to come to the attention of senior managers if the unmanaged introduction of distribution is not to prejudice organizational effectiveness. What managers cannot clearly see they cannot effectively control.

Summing up

- Distributed systems' users identify with their organizations and businesses and not with distributed system technologies.

- Distributed systems' managers must respond to corporate management needs and style, because all organizations have a mixture of hierarchical and peer-to-peer interactions.

- The user culture is strongly influenced by the quality of the human-computer interface.

- Technology is needed to support operational staff and to help them cope with distributed system speed and complexity.

- Even where authority and responsibility are devolved, a coherent management overview of the distributed system must be maintained. Management roles and distributed systems interact with each other in increasingly complex ways and organizations must develop to take this into account.

References

ANSA (1989). *ANSA: An Engineer's Introduction to the Architecture*. APM Ltd., Poseidon House, Castle Park, Cambridge CB3 0RD, UK

Benchmark Research (1991). *The Complexity Crisis – A report commissioned by 3 Com UK*. Benchmark Research, pub. 3 Com UK

Miller G.A. (1975). *The Psychology of Communication* 2nd edn. New York: Basic Books

3

Business aspects of distributed systems management

Objectives

- to discuss how to make the business case for distributed systems management
- to consider the different classes of manager who are involved in the business case
- to identify financial factors and risk factors that affect the requirement

3.1 Informing corporate management

Persuading someone to put money into a product, whether it be a consumer item or a concept, is fundamental to the successful outcome of every business activity. In the context of distributed systems management the product is a strategy for adopting a managed distributed processing environment and the payment is a commitment of funds for the purchase and operation of a system. With today's profit-driven business objectives it is even more important that the underlying reasons for introducing management products and skills should be quantified in terms of monetary and other benefits to the business. This assertion is as true of the introduction of networking and distributed processing to an organization as it is of introducing a new stock control scheme or product line.

This chapter looks at the information that managers need if they are to make sound decisions about installing distributed systems and, above all, ensuring that those systems are manageable. The perspective taken is of the requirements which the manager must address in preparing a sound business case. By implication this identifies the points that senior managers expect to find when a proposal for a managed distributed system is presented to them.

An investment in a managed, distributed processing environment arises from the interplay of three categories of management activity within an organization. To put the discussion into context, a notional business structure is used, as illustrated in Figure 3.1, in which three kinds of managers play roles. First, there are senior managers who set and respond to the corporate strategies, and monitor and control other managers. Second, there are business managers who are responsible for a defined part of the organization's mainstream activities. They produce the products upon which the organization primarily depends, according to their own business strategy plan. Third, there are support managers, among whom are the information technology (IT) managers. They provide services and support for the business

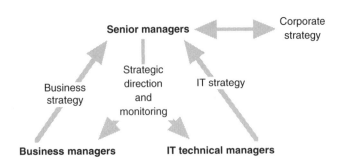

Figure 3.1 Management interactions.

managers, in accordance with the organization's information technology strategy.

All three categories of manager, and also the system users, have an impact on the investment decision about a distributed system, as illustrated in Figure 3.2. Firstly, the business managers and their staff (potential system users) identify the requirement and the benefit to their work. They also inform the IT managers of their required information technology services. Secondly, the IT managers have the task of identifying the technical solutions that can meet the requirement. They include the managers who will be responsible for supporting and managing the equipment when it has been installed. It is they who can, and must, establish the feasibility and cost of the technical aspects of any proposed solution. The business managers make their case to senior managers, who perceive the advantages to be gained by integrating the information handling activities of their staff and equipment resources into an information processing capability which can support their business objectives. They expect to decide their case on business grounds and they are not specifically concerned with the technicalities of the systems which will result, except that their staff will be its users. They also have to take into account any corporate business constraints, as they must ensure that any proposal is robust in terms of the investment risk they are being asked to undertake and that the proposals are in line with corporate objectives.

Whereas the business manager's staff (identifying the need) and the IT manager (identifying the system to meet the need) could readily be distinguished from each other when the technical solution proposed was to provide a mainframe computer, the 'downsizing' introduced by distributed processing is drawing these two categories into the same type of person. In an ideal management world, one would wish to distinguish the role of generating the requirement from the role of proposing the system which meets the requirement. However, one must be pragmatic and recognize that in the real world where systems evolve, the computer-literate users of today can, and often do, fulfil both roles.

Business and IT managers have the responsibility for ensuring that senior managers understand the need for and the value of managing the

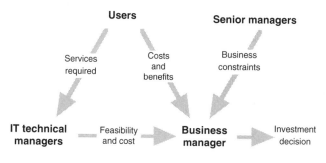

Figure 3.2 Management activities and the IT investment decisions.

distributed system. This value must be expressed not in technical jargon but in terms of satisfying the objectives of the business. In the technical disciplines of computing, ongoing management costs associated with the operational life cycle have not always been quantified when making the case for an information processing system. The cost of subsequent system evolution, operation and maintenance, all areas which place significant demands upon management, can be as much as two or even three times the initial system cost. Because of the complexity of distributed systems and their potential for continual evolution, this need to quantify operational and management cost is even more essential. The method by which a distributed system is to be operated, maintained and allowed to evolve with business needs must be addressed by the IT managers and budgeted for by the business manager from the outset. Senior managers have a responsibility to ensure that these issues are addressed before assenting to provision of the information processing system.

Although there will be cases when a distributed system is introduced at a 'green field' location, most distributed systems come into being through evolution from existing, often centralized, systems. The evolution is generally piecemeal. It is the usual way that distributed systems come into existence, continuing to grow by a process of accretion. There are several factors which tend towards the growth being uncontrolled: first, introduction of a distributed solution is often seen by users as a way of escaping the restrictions of a centralized solution; second, it may be a means of integrating information currently available at several independent sites, and may require *ad hoc* methods for integration; and third, diverse users may adopt several of the diverse solutions that are on offer in the market-place.

In the face of such pressures towards divergent solutions, the only long-term remedy is a strategy for convergence of distributed systems. This is one of the primary reasons why management needs to maintain a firm control upon their growth. Without that control, there is every likelihood of the system's developing in an unplanned and uncoordinated manner. Managers and computer specialists are all too familiar with computer programs which develop in this way. They carry the twin dangers of uncontrolled time-scale to completion and uncontrolled expenditure. There are obvious parallels if the corporate information processing system itself develops in an uncoordinated way.

3.2 Categories of information technology management

There are three categories of IT management that need to be considered:

- management of hardware and software, including system software and applications software

- management of system support services, such as naming, addressing, controlling system access, accounting, security and audit
- management of user support services, such as those for trouble-shooting and training

Each category has its own objectives and procedures. Collectively, they provide the umbrella under which the applications are delivered to the end user. It is important that IT managers identify what is required and why; and that business managers demand to know how much it will cost and identify what benefits it will bring to the organization. This latter point is the key to the whole exercise. In any business plan, there is no value in advocating a policy where the costs exceed the perceived benefits. Furthermore, managers should identify the mechanisms by which both costs and benefits can be judged. They need to do this both for the distributed system itself and for the way it will be managed in practice.

3.3 Establishing the requirement

The value of improved facilities for handling corporate information may well be recognized by both senior and business managers. However, the translation of that rationale into a set of technical requirements for a managed distributed processing environment is likely to be refined and developed through the technical push of their information technology specialists and advisors. It is all too common for such technical staff to express these requirements and the justifications for their proposals in purely technical terms. The danger is that they show how the system will operate rather than what it will deliver. Proposals based purely upon technology are not acceptable to senior managers, however technically literate they may be; the focus of concern at corporate level is upon the strategic value of an investment, not upon its technical merit.

Business managers, irrespective of their own information technology background or expertise, will be looking to the 'bottom line' of cost versus benefit. They will be less interested in the technology itself. In this context, managers think in terms of four business objectives:

- Cost savings
- Productivity increases
- Image to the customer
- Increased market share

The opportunities for information technology lie in the ability of IT managers to deliver and support applications in a way that addresses these four business objectives. To do that, they must be clear about the value of the applications to their users. These can be classified as:

- Strategic to the business activity
- Supportive of the business activity

The way in which the spectrum of information processing applications divides into these two classes is often highly company specific. But, as illustrations, the following are strategic:

- Dealing room systems
- Electronic funds transfer
- Business-integrated electronic data interchange
- Computer integrated manufacturing

and the following are supportive:

- Payroll
- Stock control
- Billing and invoicing

Therefore, the technical proposals should reflect the business objectives, emphasizing the business value for each objective and showing attendant risks. To advocate it effectively, the concept and value of distributed systems management needs to be promoted both as a pro-active and as a reactive investment. It is pro-active in the sense that effective management can, with confidence, increase opportunities. It is reactive when it shows how risks can be minimized or costs saved.

There are further important reasons for considering the technical management requirement in corporate terms. Experience has shown that the successful distributed systems are those whose management styles match the corporate style. Senior managers who favour the devolution of responsibilities will respond well to proposals where the responsibility for operating and managing the corporate processing environment is distributed. Conversely, those managers who prefer a centralized mode of management control will wish to see this style reflected in the management of the corporate network. Even if the processing capability is distributed, the management need not be.

Styles of management evolve just as much as do network requirements and network technologies. The astute technical advisor will recognize that styles of corporate management are as subject to fashion as are many other human activities. There is evidence that management style alternates over several years between being devolved and being centralized. A managed, distributed processing environment designed to operate over a long period of corporate evolution must be capable of responding to changing fashion. This introduces a very important factor into the organization of the underlying systems management technology. The intrinsic distributed systems management approach must be one of distribution of responsibility, for while it is a relatively simple matter to arrange that a distributed system is controlled centrally, it is impossible to operate a purely centralized system in a distributed fashion.

The requirement is to devise an approach which, having identified the technical and corporate management objectives, expresses them according to the needs of the target audience. From a technology point of view this can be achieved in a fairly structured way either through personal experience and skill or through the use of some form of check-list, such as provided by Appendix A.

Finally, the need for distributed systems management to prevent loss of control has already been mentioned, but the positive benefits of distributed systems management should also be described. They have already been introduced, in Chapter 1, but it is important to bring them to the forefront when discussing investment in information technology. The benefits of both distributed systems in general, and management, need to be made explicit.

3.4 Risk assessment and management

The term 'risk' is frequently used in relation to information systems. Both the significance of risk, and the relevance of risk management, need to be clarified for distributed systems. Two quite different forms of risk need to be distinguished: **security risk** and **business risk**. Security risk is concerned with future occurrences which can lead only to loss: from fraud or equipment failure, for example. Business risk can result in either loss or gain. It arises as a result of the normal management decisions of a business. The use of distributed systems carries business risk in the same way as, for example, the decision to develop and launch a new product.

Information systems represent value to the business not only in the tangible assets (computer hardware, networks, software) but even more in the value of the data which they store and process. The analysis of risk must extend to these, and to the organizational infrastructure which surrounds them. A major defect in an important distributed system could have a significant impact on a wide area of a business. The likelihood and potential consequences of failure have to be assessed and understood in order to define the need for preventive measures and back-up facilities and to identify the resources to be allocated to them. Inadequate risk management practices also carry their own, very real, risks.

There is now a growing corpus of security risk management and safeguard selection techniques, to identify and implement appropriate and effective controls against both accidental and deliberate attacks. Analysis of risk presupposes that all losses can be quantified, although some losses are more easily quantifiable than others. Human loss (accident or death) could be treated separately but, as even this can be given an actuarial cost, it does not contradict the assumption of risk analysis. Most methods of risk analysis begin from the identification and valuation of assets, from where they carry out loss calculations to establish a cost-effective risk management programme. This is most effective when carried out during the specification and design phases of a development, where the riskier features of design decisions can be identified alongside the security requirements and their consequences can be established. Identifying potential weaknesses before committing significant resources itself minimizes risk.

Where distributed systems may come into existence by the joining of existing isolated systems, the ideal policy just outlined is seldom practical. None the less, risk analysis can identify and help to remedy points of vulnerability, whether previously unidentified or introduced by joining systems. This then provides a baseline for future analyses as the system evolves. The two forms of risk are discussed in more detail later in the book. Security risk is analysed in Chapter 5, which is concerned with security matters in general. The analysis of business risk is considered in Chapter 6 along with other services which support distributed systems management.

3.5 Financial considerations

Senior managers in industry are increasingly using 'value for money' assessments to judge the merits of technology-based investment proposals. They are taking a keen interest not only in being convinced that technology is required but also that it is cost-effective in its implementation. Managers in government departments are also taking a very businesslike approach in their procurement policies and operations. Although distributed systems are a long-term investment, senior managers will tend to discount the distant future and look for a short pay-back period.

Because the costs of providing distribution and of managing risk are important factors by which the proposal will be judged, it is important that the financial case is presented in the best format to ensure approval. As well as the usual presentation techniques, two additional means of representation are often used to aid the financial case. These are life cycle costing and marginal costing.

It should not be forgotten that maintaining the availability of applications and ensuring that they continue to meet users' needs both have life-time costs associated with them. Some of these costs may arise because the separate activities of business development and business operations are controlled by separate interests within a company. When presenting a financial case for the infrastructure to support applications, the significance of applications maintenance is an important factor in helping to justify the cost of management. Good management can reduce the cost of applications maintenance. Of course, it has to be recognized that the cost of developing some applications looks attractive only until the ongoing operations and maintenance costs are added. In the past, life cycle costing has been little practised by technical managers. However, it is the only means by which senior managers can assess the true cost of the service. If the development of the application would not be approved if maintenance costs were included, then it is better to expose the fact at the outset rather than seek expensive remedies later.

Technical advisers might also take into consideration any benefits of marginal costing which result from the way business overheads are costed. Although some companies deprecate such an approach and argue that each activity must bear the costs associated with it, others recognize that there is some merit in advocating that a proportion of activity costs may be allocated to related activities which derive benefit. Computing is a prime example of an activity which provides basic and effective infrastructure support. In the 'battle of the budgets', it is always worth while identifying and attributing the true cost and beneficiaries of shared resources, and one of the benefits of distributed processing capability and resources is their ability to be shared. Although the shared resources will probably be placed under the responsibility of one manager for sound operational reasons, the beneficiaries can be expected to pay towards their cost. This may be done either directly or as an overhead if senior managers decide that they constitute a common good to the organization.

3.6 Managing the implementation

Having overcome the first major hurdle of convincing senior managers of a need and that there is a sound business case, technical managers have still to convince them that the desired goals are achievable. A detailed plan must be produced which shows how the project will be implemented and operated over its lifetime. Those developing these plans need to recognize that management commitment can be lost through failing to maintain good relationships with users and their managers. No installation process occurs instantaneously, and requirements can evolve and change even during installation. Failure to keep in touch means that evolutionary changes can sometimes appear to happen with surprising rapidity. Senior managers have an interest in assuring that money continues to be spent wisely, and managers of activities affected by the installation will continue to be concerned that any support they gave to the project is still deserved. Thus, in the human management of the distributed processing activity, especially where the implementation process can take the form of a long-term, evolutionary upgrade of system capabilities, it is essential that technical managers and their staff work continuously to carry the support, not only of senior managers but also of their peers; that is, the business managers and the system users. Those advocating the provision of the managed, distributed processing environment need to promote widespread appreciation of the less tangible benefits of a managed system as being a matter of self-interest to the users of the system and hence to the organization as a whole.

In a project which by its nature is evolutionary, the post-project review is difficult to handle. Since there is no definitive final completion for such a system, the review may go by default. Senior managers will not wish that to occur. There is still a need to be assured of the effectiveness of the investment and to check that the promised benefits accrue. An effective way to handle this situation is, having established a long-term policy goal, to consider both the initial installation and the subsequent evolutionary developments as mini-projects, each of which is subject to review. The cost and the immediate benefit of each step will then be known as it is completed. Even so, it may be some time before a true picture can be gained because the longer term benefits can only be apparent after months or even years of operation. The gains from one step in the evolutionary process are frequently influenced by earlier steps and further modified by later developments. Senior managers need to be aware of this evolutionary characteristic of distributed systems when the initial system goals are being agreed. As with all long-term planning, a degree of faith in the future is required and the merits of investment in management need reassessing as the requirements (and the system to service them) evolve. For these reasons, and recognizing the requirement for sensible short-term pay-back, planning needs to be robust so that earlier investment is not totally written off as a result of change.

The information technologist should note that the benefits of having a managed distributed system may, in the final analysis, be better appreciated by the distributed system's users rather than by its IT managers. The users will see more cost-effective services whereas the technical support team may have some of their controlling involvement taken over by the management services of the system itself. These factors need to be taken into consideration by all who are part of the project proposal and review process, at whatever level in the organization's management hierarchy and at all stages of the project. The mechanism for project review can become complex, but some of this complexity is avoidable where development is incremental through mini-projects. But a word of caution; the use of mini-projects runs the danger of fragmenting the management process, because decisions that are correct in the context of one small project may be incorrect when the system is viewed as a coherent whole.

3.7 Business recommendations

There is still much to discuss about the technical aspects of distributed systems management and of managing a distributed system. This discussion forms the theme of the remaining chapters. But from the perspective of business managers it is already possible to summarize the arguments and to draw firm conclusions.

Distributed systems need to be managed. Management is vital to handle the complexity exhibited by the distributed processing environment and to contain its diversity. There is an ever-present danger that a system which grows by evolution and through accretion of its component parts, often as a response to some perceived technical or production need, will ignore the management requirement. An ill-managed system invites inefficiency and risks disaster.

The goals of the management system are derived from the goals of the organization which owns it. Therefore the style of management of the distributed system should reflect the management style and objectives of the organization. Even when the management style is centralized, it is a more robust strategy to construct the distributed system recognizing that management is itself a distributed processing activity, rather than to centralize the management of the information technology system. Management styles evolve just as much as do an organization's requirements. Therefore the organization of the management of a distributed system will also evolve, though on a longer time-scale than is typical for its components.

There is more to the management of a distributed processing environment than just the technical products and communication infrastructure that supports it. The investment in management should include the training of the operations and system management staff, not only in the art of distributed systems management, but also in the ethos of their employing organization. The investment will also include documentation not only of the static aspects of the system (that is, its configuration) but also its case histories and analyses of alternative scenarios.

How much should an organization invest in the management of its distributed processing environment? For a well-organized and smoothly operating system the temptation must be to believe that too much has been spent on providing that management. But the majority of today's industrial and commercial organizations are heavily dependent on timely and accurate processing of their corporate information. The cost of failure can easily outstrip the investment in the management tools which could have contained, if not circumvented, that failure. As indicated in Chapter 1, it can even exceed the investment in the processing system itself. Therefore an organization should value investment in managing its corporate distributed system as highly as it does its corporate management. That is to say, the investment in managing the processing environment as a fraction of the investment in information processing technology should be comparable with the fraction of the organization's resources that it commits to managing its corporate activity.

There is, unfortunately, no panacea for management. There is only a framework within which the individual and the individual's organization must decide which route is best for a particular system and supported enterprise. Even so, guidelines have been identified above and they are elaborated in later chapters. The guidelines can assist managers to be properly informed when investing in distributed systems projects. Much of the early mystique surrounding information systems and telecommunication systems is disappearing. Given time and experience with managed systems, the greater mystique which seems to surround the management of distributed systems should also disappear. Computing specialists recognize that information technology is not an end in itself but merely a means to an end. Eventually management will be recognized as a necessary support activity for the information processing technology.

If there is one overriding message that comes from business experience, it concerns the methods that technical managers use to express application requirements. To satisfy the needs of the senior managers, these requirements must not only be expressed in terms of technology and functionality but also provide an interpretation of that technology and functionality in terms of the financial and strategic objectives of the organization for which it will provide support. Financial commitment should only come, and will only be forthcoming, when senior managers are convinced that proposals are justified in the corporate context.

Summing up

- Distributed systems need to be managed in line with the management goals of their owning businesses.

- The case for computational support comes from the business manager, the rationale for the distributed system comes from the technical manager, the requirement that the distributed system is efficiently and effectively managed comes from senior management.

- Whereas it is a relatively simple matter to arrange that a distributed system is controlled centrally, it is impossible to operate a purely centralized system in a distributed fashion.

- The essence of the business case is non-technical but technical factors affect its realization.

- Planning for managed distributed systems is strongly influenced by risk analysis.

- System evolution adds to the difficulties of post-installation review.

- Each organization must decide the details of its own approach to managing its distributed processing environment.

4

Management functions and management services

Objectives

- to provide a detailed treatment of management services and functions
- to show that monitoring is the basic management service
- to illustrate the importance of services which support monitoring
- to describe fault detection, diagnosis and resolution
- to describe performance measurement and planning
- to describe configuration management
- to discuss accounting services
- to describe name management

4.1 Introduction

Chapter 2 has shown that distributed processing applications may span the computer systems not only of different parts of an organization but also those of a number of different organizations. In these latter cases there is no central authority and both the management of the application and the underlying communication and processing resources have to operate across organizational and legislative boundaries. Even where the cooperating computer systems are within the same organization, the activities and availability of the resources still need management over and above that which is required to run programs within single computers. This management entails the long term activity of planning in order to monitor and control the resources which support an enterprise's distributed processing applications. It also entails the supervisory services by which managers obtain feedback on the way in which enterprise objectives are being satisfied and take appropriate corrective actions when service deficiencies are encountered.

This chapter provides a detailed treatment of the management functions that are required, and the classes of management information that flow between distributed system components in order to provide management services. The emphasis is upon the functions that are required for operational management activities although the way in which they are used depends upon the organizational activities of policy making and planning. The operational functions are responsible for supervision and control. They ensure that a system can be maintained in an operational state. It is through them that performance can be monitored to demonstrate that the system continues to meet the quality of service it has been specified to deliver. They point the way for a system to evolve by incorporating changes in its functionality and resources. Through the exercise of other management functions, the organizational aspects of management receive feedback on the extent to which the operational system is meeting its organizational goals.

From this brief introduction, it might seem that management functions and services are independent of whether the system is centralized or distributed. Indeed, at a gross enough scale, this is largely true. Hence, for completeness, this chapter summarizes the general nature of management's operational requirements for functions and services and how these may be provided. But this is done primarily to serve as a background from which to highlight those distinguishing features that are introduced into management functions as a consequence of distributing processing, data storage and user access.

It is important to be reminded at the outset of the way in which resources provide management services and support its functionality. Every entity within an information processing environment has a normal functionality which expresses the particular service it provides. Thus, a file store provides functions for writing data to and reading data from files; a communication switch provides functions to route traffic from incoming to outgoing communication lines. If that entity is then to be a managed entity, it also provides a management functionality. This permits its normal activity to be monitored and possibly modified. The management functionality is provided directly by the entity or through the collaboration of several managed entities. For the file store it entails, for example, backing-up named files to archival media. For a data switch, it includes monitoring the performance of the routing algorithm and exercising control to maximize throughput. In some cases, deciding what is management and what is part of normal functionality may be rather more difficult. One criterion is that management should not be critical to an entity's normal operation. For example, an OSI Transport Layer entity's normal functionality is to set up and clear connections, send and receive messages. On the other hand, its management activity might be to monitor the entity's performance and optimize it by, for example, adjusting the number of buffers used for sending and receiving such messages. Similarly, the use of encryption is a normal security service whereas the distribution of keys used for encryption is a security management function.

4.2 Management activities and functions

Figure 4.1 provides a reminder of the basic management supervisory cycle modelled in Chapter 1. It illustrates the three kinds of activity carried out as part of operational management:

- monitoring the managed system to obtain information,
- making management decisions on the basis of that information and of management policy,
- performing management actions in order to control the managed system.

Chapter 1 also introduced the five functional areas of management for communications systems, identified in the development of the OSI Management Framework, namely: configuration, fault, performance, accounting and security management. Depending upon the planned response to management policy, these functional areas can be of differing significance. It is obvious that accounting management has more relevance if there is a policy of accounting for the use of resources. Where security is not an issue, management will not set as high a priority upon security management functions. For these reasons, it is worth dividing management functions into two principal categories: primary (or core) management functions and secondary functions. Primary functions are those that are necessary to enable management to carry out its primary task of maintaining the operational state of a system.

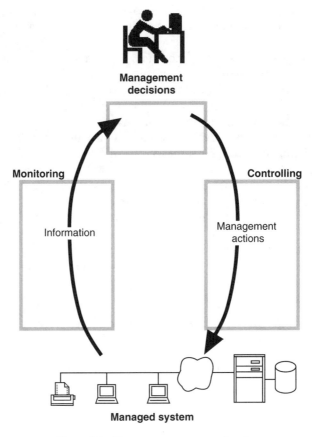

Figure 4.1   The management control cycle.

This is to ensure that the system performs correctly and efficiently so that it provides its users with the service for which they are paying. That is, management is the means by which the owners of the system ensure that their distributed information technology investment meets an essentially universal policy requirement; that the services are provided in a cost-effective manner. Primary management is concerned with maintaining the quality of service (QoS) of the information technology service and controlling the configuration needed to provide that service.

A user of a service requires, and will contract with the system supplier for, some specified quality of service. This can be in terms of responsiveness, processing performance (throughput), undetected error rate, etc. and could include security level. As in all 'quality' related matters, there are no absolutes. Quality is determined by the service's 'fitness for purpose'. It is related to the contract price which the user is prepare to pay the supplier for the cost of the service. Thus, managing the QoS requires a means of specifying the required QoS, maintaining required QoS and of notifying changes to

QoS if the specified quality cannot be maintained. It includes negotiating a different quality if the required one cannot be provided, and negotiating an alternative price. Because maintaining QoS includes determining both performance and fault behaviour, it is a generalization covering both the fault and the performance management functional areas.

Consider the following example of a company whose offices are spread throughout a country. Senior managers have decided that document distribution (which is by store and forward electronic mail services) shall not be subjected to a delay which is greater than five minutes. This is because it is a requirement that all executives and section leaders shall receive, with a measure of synchronized availability, regular finance and planning updates. This policy leads to an agreement being negotiated with the providers of the company's information technology services for an appropriate level of communications and message handling support for a service of the required quality. To perform their task, the operational staff of the distributed system need to ensure at all times within the working day that end system devices are operational. They need to ensure that these are properly connected to the corporate communications infrastructure. These are examples of management monitoring. If any attached device or communications line is defective, alternatives have to be made available and the executive or section leader informed of the operational change. This is an example of management control and also of reporting through the management hierarchy. Control and monitoring do not end there. The transit time of all messages has to be measured and their statistical distribution analysed to ensure that the total traffic load is not so high that delays greater than five minutes could occur. If communication message stores, switches or traffic routes show signs of overload, pre-emptive action has to be taken, for example, by pre-allocation of special, lightly used routes for critical traffic. This is one form of reconfiguration needed to maintain QoS.

When considering the behaviour of a system, it is natural to focus attention upon the activities which it performs most of the time. For management this focus is upon the normal state of system operations. Yet it must be recognized that, at some time, all systems and components have to be started into operation. It is a feature of distributed systems that they evolve and systems change to incorporate new functionality or new technology. It therefore follows that the initialization of systems is part of normal operation and a primary management activity. To start up a computer system so that it is connected to others through a communications network requires that an initial configuration of the hardware and software components of that system be specified. Other aspects of configuration management include specifying what classes of components are required, the component instances needed, the interconnection or binding of interfaces and the allocation of software to hardware. This, like the QoS example above, helps to draw attention to the fact that functions providing management services are closely interrelated.

The secondary management functions provide management features that are not intrinsic to the primary goal of maintaining the operational state of the distributed processing environment. Security management functions are provided to ensure that users' requirements for safeguarding their data are carried out and are seen to be carried out. That is, security management functions are concerned with facilitating the provision of a secure environment necessary for given applications. One way in which they contribute is by demonstrating, for example, through audit trails, that the security needs of the users have been upheld.

Accounting enables users to obtain information on usage of resources. It is needed to allow suppliers of services to charge for the use of those services. It is also needed for fair allocation of resources to prevent a user from monopolizing available resources within a service. Thus, accounting management provides the functions needed by an organization to ensure that information technology resources are used cost-effectively. Name management provides the mechanisms for generating names of entities together with the support services for locating entities by their names. Although checking for faults and determining performance have been identified as primary functions, some aspects of system testing and performance analysis can also be regarded as of a secondary nature since they serve to provide added value to the primary functions. Each of these functions and the services they help to provide are now considered in greater detail.

4.3 Monitoring

Monitoring is arguably the most basic of the management activities. It underpins the primary functions of statistical data capture for performance measurement and is the means by which fault-related data is obtained. It is the means by which management entities obtain configuration data about the state of the systems they are managing in order to make informed decisions and perform control actions. For example, traffic monitoring is required for performance optimization; monitoring of status changes and of error reports is needed for identifying the existence of faults; monitoring of usage can be important for accounting purposes; monitoring of configuration changes, unusual events and related state changes is needed to create an audit trail for security and other purposes.

Monitoring may be implemented as a management service which collects and collates predefined information for other aspects of management or for users (Holden, 1989). Components being monitored may be passive or active. Passive components must be polled by a monitoring process to read parameters values. Components may be capable of signalling the values which require to be monitored, chosen according to a management policy. One approach to monitoring is to provide a local monitoring agent in each computer within the distributed system. This collects data, time-stamps it and sends it to one or more servers, where it is filtered, logged, analysed and presented to administrators in a suitable format. If it is monitoring a passive component, it reads data and checks state periodically. An active component monitors its own state, and sends the resulting data to its monitoring agent. Data may be sent periodically or generated as a result of an internal event such as a state change or a counter value reaching a pre-set threshold.

It is desirable that monitored data be time-stamped at source. Doing so allows a consistent view of system events to be maintained, provided that time can be synchronized across all the components of the distributed system. Monitored data can also be time-stamped by the recipient but, due to communication delays within the distributed systems, this may introduce inconsistencies in the perception of causally related happenings. In some distributed systems raw data is collected at a central site for subsequent analysis. Whereas this is convenient in small distributed systems, it is an approach that scales badly when extended to large distributed systems. Resources which provide significant data processing capability should be responsible for their own monitoring so as to facilitate fault handling, accounting and performance monitoring for the purposes of future planning. This can be organized on a regional basis where a group of resources is being operated, for example, for a department or specific business area of a company.

Not all monitoring is carried out in order to determine system behaviour. It can be of value to users to help them to determine the performance characteristics of particular applications. In this instance, a user of computing services may wish to monitor transactions performed on application software in order to check the quality of each of the services. Monitoring an application's behaviour can also be an aid to the user who has to handle fault situations. Servers may also provide users with accounting information derived as a result of monitored usage.

4.4 Services supporting monitoring

Effective monitoring needs additional support services which add value to the basic monitoring process. These services include:

- Filtering
- Logging
- Time synchronization
- Scheduling

Filtering (sometimes referred to as discrimination) is needed:

- to reduce overload in both processing and communication systems and their management functions,

- to present only relevant information to operators and administrators to assist their decision making,

- to place constraints upon access to data which may be commercially sensitive if released to unauthorized users.

These examples are indicators of how filtering can be used. Consider a particular example. Real systems, constructed from real components, cannot be guaranteed to operate perfectly at all times. Effects such as noise can cause systems to operate erroneously from time to time but, because the effects are random, a repetition of the operation is unlikely to be subjected to the same error. This situation is familiar to communications engineers who design their communication protocols to provide error correction mechanisms. For performance reasons, it may be useful to collect data that provides a value for the rate at which these errors occur. However, it may not be necessary to advise management of each individual occurrence. On the other hand, if the error rate were to rise above a given discrimination threshold, this may be revealing symptoms of something more significant, requiring management intervention.

If the consequence of this type of incident could be localized and contained, it would result in a single message to management. But in distributed systems, these occurrences are seldom without knock-on effects. The services provided by one system component are used by other system components. Hence, something which affects the behaviour of one component can lead to unexpected changes in the behaviour of other components. If each component were to signal its changed behaviour, there could be an outburst of management messages, all stemming from one incident. Sometimes, managers need to be informed about the incident and all of its consequences. At other times, they may wish to avoid the resulting communication and processing overload. Discrimination is then used to filter out the unwanted messages so that only the most critical messages are forwarded. This filtering needs to be carried out as near to the message source as possible if its effect is to be maximized. The decision concerning which messages are of significance and which are trivial is an expression of management policy and discriminators are devices for handling policy-related rules concerning the significance of and destinations for information flows.

So much for overload as a result of spontaneously occurring incidents. Filtering may also be selective when obtaining management data by polling. Suppose one requires to read management data from components that are operational but it is not important to obtain the same data from components that are either inactive or disabled. The problem in distributed systems is that it may not be possible to know at a given time which components are in which state. One option is therefore to read both the state and the other data from all components. This delivers the required data but has two undesirable consequences: it results in possibly irrelevant data being communicated (so using up valuable communication bandwidth) and it forces the recipient to process every response to filter out the required data. An alternative scenario might be to poll all components to determine their state and then to poll only those components that are operational. If a considerable amount of management data were to be retrieved, this could reduce the total volume of data transmitted. This would save bandwidth but would introduce the delay of making a double enquiry, first to obtain state information and then to retrieve the desired data. But this approach suffers from a more fundamental flaw. In a distributed processing environment it does not guarantee to deliver the correct result. Between the first polling to determine state and the subsequent data retrieval, some operational components could have become inactive and other inactive components could have become operational. The appropriate mechanism is to perform a conditional monitoring enquiry. This entails passing both the request for data and a predicate for carrying out the request (in this instance, the desired activity state of the component). Only those components which satisfy the predicate need to respond. This dynamic filtering mechanism reduces the communications load in the distributed system and also the load upon the managers and operators who do not have to perform discrimination themselves. Note, however, that it shifts the requirement for decision making (to reply or not to reply) to the component. It therefore requires that components (and/or their immediate supporting environments) be equipped with additional intelligence in order to perform the filtering process.

Providing access control can be a simple extension of such filtering mechanisms. In this case, the predicate is determined by comparing an access token to a set of acceptable token values maintained by the monitored component. If there is a match, the data may be forwarded. Security mechanisms must be used to define boundaries for controlling access to monitored information. Security principles and mechanisms are discussed in detail in Chapter 5.

Logs provide a mechanism for long-term memory within systems whenever the resources being managed do not have the intrinsic capability to maintain historic records of their own behaviour. Monitored data may be maintained in logs from which it can be extracted for analysis purposes; for example, to establish trends, to build up activity profiles or to maintain accounting data. Logs and filters are resources that have to be provided to assist management to perform its management activity. As resources, they too need to be monitored and controlled. That is, management functions and management services must make provision for their own management. Without it, the system designer is faced with a seemingly endless regression of management concern in seeking to answer the question 'who manages the managers?' The answer is that management must contain its own intrinsic management capability.

Time synchronization has already been mentioned with respect to providing monitored data with time stamps. Maintaining this synchronization within the distributed processing environment is not trivial. Except in direct point-to-point broadcast communications, the variation in transmission delays and the impossibility of ensuring that all system clocks run at exactly the same rate mean that a unique time is not always available. As a result, it can be difficult to obtain consistent state information from different locations. Even if system clocks are synchronized at some particular time, they can drift with respect to each other over time. Yet to relate a monitored item of data from one system to an item from another system may require knowledge of which event was the primary cause which led to the generation of that data. Only then can one indicate a possible causal relationship between separate events. Unless all devices are able to accept a directly 'broadcast' time signal which has a known and constant propagation delay for source to destination, elaborate protocols are needed to perform synchronization over non-deterministic communication networks. Hence, the concept of time, in a distributed system, should always be qualified with a parameter indicating the level of accuracy which is appropriate to time stamps.

A scheduler may be regarded as an extension of discrimination activity whose selection criteria are not defined in terms of data values but in terms of a list of times at which discrimination may occur. This reflects the requirement that certain items of management data take on additional significance if they arise at specific times. For example, during periods of normally quiet activity (such as weekends or at night) when traffic is expected to be low, a sudden burst of activity might be an indicator of an unusual pattern of behaviour requiring management investigation. Or it may be important, for performance or accounting purposes, that certain data items are recorded only at peak times. Schedules can be set for arbitrary time periods or they can be regular and repetitive on a daily, weekly or other calendar basis.

4.5 Fault handling

Fault handling is the name given to the management of abnormalities in system operation. A fault (either a total failure of function or an error causing malfunction) may occur in a hardware or software component. If no recovery action is taken, the fault may result in a systems failure or malfunction. The fault may be detected by the component itself, by other components in the system or by human users. It may lead to a failure in the service provided by the system. As indicated in the discussion on filtering, some failures and errors are permanent and repeatable; for example, where they are caused by a hardware component failure or software error. Other failures are intermittent and are generated either by noise or by chance interactions between components. A transmission error or the rare loss of data from a memory location are examples of faults that can be due to noise. Failures due to chance interactions often arise because of conceptual or design errors that are intrinsic to the system and are often deeply embedded in its design. They can arise because a component designer did not take account of interactions with remote activities proceeding in parallel. Such failures are not of themselves intermittent but reveal themselves intermittently, for example, by being dependent on the work profile, the processing load or the environment in which the system is operational. Faults due to noise are not repeatable (due to the randomness of noise). Strictly, conceptual and design errors are repeatable provided that the precise conditions which lead to their appearance can be regenerated, but this is usually impractical to organize in a distributed system, if only because of the impossibility of obtaining strict system synchrony.

When a fault is detected, the first action is to take any immediate recovery action which is possible, so that the system can continue to perform its intended function, though possibly with some reduction in performance or functionality. The location of the fault and its cause are then diagnosed through analysis of the relevant system information. Finally, after the fault has been diagnosed, corrective action may be taken to resolve the fault. This entire process of fault management is vital for ensuring that the system can provide a satisfactory level of service. The sequence of fault detection, recovery, diagnosis and resolution is illustrated in Figures 4.2, 4.3, 4.4 and 4.6.

The sequence of recovery followed by diagnosis is not immutable, although the normal management strategy will be to recover from the failure as quickly as possible, for example by switching to back-up facilities, before performing detailed diagnosis at leisure. The intent is to minimize the mean time to recovery. This keeps the system live, maintaining, whenever possible, the contracted QoS. However, if the failure occurs at a point where a single component failure causes system failure, it may be necessary to perform the diagnosis and resolve the fault in order to recover.

4.5.1 Fault detection

Faults, as noted above, may be self-detected, detected by other system components, by (dedicated) monitoring facilities or by human users. The events handled by any fault management system are those caused by faults rather than those resulting from performance overload. The latter are the concern of performance management. However, it is clear that there will be a need for these two management activities to cooperate closely.

Figure 4.2 shows the process of fault detection. Suppose the primary fault occurs in the data link connecting two computers. If these computers can detect the fault, it may be located at the component level. The same fault can manifest itself at the network level if the data link failure were to result in the loss of communication between network components. Fault detection software in the network may even be aware of the failure of communication

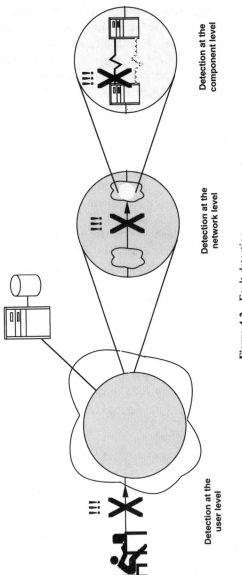

Detection at the
component level

Detection at the
network level

Detection at the
user level

Figure 4.2 Fault detection.

between several network subscribers and be able to correlate these failures so as to identify the failed data link. Finally, the fault can manifest itself at the user level by the user detecting a loss of service. Although noticing the loss, the user does not know where the fault has occurred or the nature of the fault and could suspect the problem to lie either at the local point of user interaction, in the remote service being accessed or in the intermediate communication environment (even assuming that the user was aware that the service was remote).

Detection needs to be carefully organized and the following techniques are available:

- active probing of services,
- regularly broadcast of service status,
- execution of diagnostic routines.

Detecting faults by monitoring according to a regular schedule is a highly data-intensive way of detecting faults. Wherever possible, it is preferable to employ components with sufficient intelligence to provide internal monitoring and announce the occurrence of a fault without continually having to be polled. Reporting facilities should provide the means for notifying problems to ordinary users and management agents, particularly those concerned with configuration management. Failure and error reports should also be logged so that histories can be analysed and possible trends detected. Fault reports may also be generated from fault management systems as a result of analysis and diagnosis (see below).

In many instances, it is possible to include a trivial function within each service that can be polled to check on the availability of the main service. This may be all that is required to provide the necessary fault detection intelligence. It can be cheap to implement and execute. However, it may not be capable of testing the complete service. This is particularly true of complicated components such as network gateways, relays and mail systems, where several processes have to collaborate to provide the complete service. In these latter instances it may be necessary to test the whole service by initiating an external interaction with the service. Yet even this may not exercise all the processes of the service component unless the interaction is elaborately constructed with a detailed knowledge of the internal functioning of the component.

Where fault reports are issued to a manager from composite or hierarchically structured services, there are advantages in coordinating these reports within a single entity. Coordination and consolidation, if performed close to the source of the fault, prevents a multiplicity of fault reports being sent by each sub-service to an end user. If the end user does not have detailed knowledge of the internal working of the service, fault reports that have not been consolidated by the service can appear to be inconsistent and conflicting. Reporting to users can be through user support services such as electronic mail systems and bulletin boards.

Not all detected errors are fatal and the distributed system, though downgraded, may have sufficient resilience to continue to perform. Sometimes a fault detected in one component is symptomatic of faulty behaviour elsewhere in the system. For example, the corruption of a message as a result of transmission noise is detected upon receipt, although there is no failure in the receiver. Figure 4.2 illustrates the possibility of detection at any of the levels. The error may be corrected by retransmission of the message, and more or less elaborate recovery schemes are usually specified as part of the transmission protocol. However, if the frequency of transmission errors is critically high, a service failure will have been deemed to have occurred since the quality of the message service will have fallen below a level of acceptability. At this level, the user becomes aware of the problems that low-level failures are causing. Thresholds on error rates can be used to warn of such conditions.

4.5.2 Fault recovery

When a severe fault condition, which results in a significant loss of service, has been identified it must be isolated and the service restored according to service level agreements. This could be performed through invocation of built-in redundancy or by operator intervention. Figure 4.3 shows fault recovery of the data link service by a process of reconfiguration in which alternative data link capacity is provided between the two components. This recovery may be automated if a stand-by (or secondary) data link is available and the components have the intelligence to synchronize the change in their intercommunication channel. Strictly speaking, either approach to fault recovery is an example of the use of reconfiguration services.

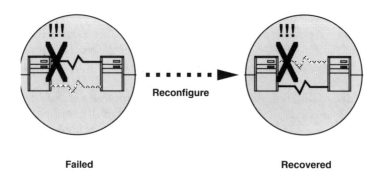

Failed   Recovered

Figure 4.3 Fault recovery.

4.5.3 Fault diagnosis

Having established the location of the fault and met the primary management objective by providing continuity of operation, the next step is to diagnose the nature of the fault and take permanent repair action. Referring to Figure 4.4, diagnosis at the system level will provide an indication of the fault's location and its type. In the example, it will show that the fault lies in the networking component. At the lower level, diagnostics will be able to establish the precise nature of the fault so that the appropriate repair action may be initiated. This may require the despatch of an engineer to change the faulty component or even to replace an entire unit.

The aims of fault diagnosis

Although not regarded as a primary function, fault diagnosis, leading to the determination of the exact cause and location of a fault, is a valuable aspect of fault handling. In distributed systems, diagnostics can be required for two types of reason:

* when a fault is announced but its cause is not specified,
* when a problem is suspected through observation of system behaviour but no fault is indicated.

To illustrate the first of these points, consider the situation in which a program is awaiting data from a remote filing system but is unable to proceed within the time allocated for the user to obtain a response because the remote system fails to deliver the file. There is a fault because the program has failed to meet its requirements. But the fault is not the program's, nor

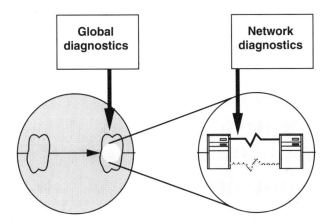

Figure 4.4 Fault diagnosis.

is it reasonable to expect the program to offer any further diagnostic other than

FILE NOT AVAILABLE

This message may be just about acceptable for the user but it does not assist in curing the fault. It is the task of the distributed system operator and the supporting management system to diagnose the real cause.

The second situation arises when, for example, some performance indicator reveals that a system throughput is not meeting expected performance criteria. In this case, the cause may not be the result of component failure, but a result of a system failure, say under-capacity elsewhere within the distributed environment, which is causing a knock-on effect.

Good diagnostic information can be used to shorten the mean time to effect a repair and increase confidence that the correct action has been taken when a component, believed to be faulty, is taken out of service for this purpose. Diagnostics can also be used in the absence of faults to give confidence that the system is operating according to specification. In the above examples, diagnostic services might again be brought into play to establish that repair, reconfiguration or provision of additional capacity had indeed rectified the problem. That is, diagnostics can be used in conjunction with performance measurement to demonstrate that systems are performing according to specification as much as they can be used to show that they are failing to do so.

The fault diagnosis process

Fault diagnosis may be achieved in three main ways:

- Execution of diagnostic tests
- Analysis of the symptoms (histories) associated with the event
- Analysis of normal event logs and performance reports

Diagnostic tests can be used to exercise a resource in order to reproduce errors, and supply more detailed information about the condition of the item under test. They must be able to initiate, suspend, resume and stop the running of tests, to trace their progress, and to load test software. Such test facilities (along with the detection methods described above) may also be used by management agents as confidence tests to detect fault conditions before they cause serious problems to users.

In the second and third cases, the analysis of the information needs to be centralized, although the gathering of the information on which to base the analysis must be distributed. This is an area where expert systems with knowledge bases may be used to aid fault diagnosis.

Whichever way diagnosis is obtained, the basic process is the same. It requires the ability to take the available data (a statement about the failure of communication or about the unavailability of the file) and follow some set of rules such as a fault tree analysis or series of diagnostic heuristics to establish the primary cause. In the above example of a failure associated with a file system, the first test could be to interrogate the filing system to establish whether the problem is operational or whether it is just a case of an inaccessible or non-existent file. Assuming the filing system is not operational, the operator or the management system would then seek to find out whether there is local diagnostic capability and, if so, seek to run it to subject the file system to software and hardware tests. This would continue until the fault is narrowed down to the extent that, either by operator command or by a visit from a service engineer, the fault can be rectified, although fault rectification is a follow-up activity and not a feature of fault diagnosis. Where the local diagnostics cannot be activated remotely, local operator action must be stimulated.

If the problem is one of overload, it is necessary to make a hypothesis as to the nature of the overload and then perform a diagnostic experiment to put the hypothesis to the test. Suppose the reason was a hardware problem and the sensitivity of the disc read head is marginal due to excessive noise. There would be a history of successive retries on that disc drive until, by luck, a block was retrieved satisfactorily. Diagnosis would need access to that history to confirm the hypothesis. But suppose that there was no history of failed reads and all reads were found to be successful the first time. It would be necessary to construct an alternative hypothesis. This could be to infer from the history that the rate of demands upon the filing system was the cause of the inadequate response. That is, there was no failure at the component level but a shortcoming at the system level. The solution would be to reconfigure to provide addition filing system capacity. This too is a follow-up action, one which is outside the scope of the diagnostic service.

These examples show the principal features of the diagnostic process. They first require that a test environment is established. Using a suitable search procedure (predefined and tree structured or context-dependent and heuristic) a starting situation is selected with others to follow. Each situation has an associated set of objective criteria and an expected pattern of behaviour against which it has to be tested. The results of the test are obtained and compared with the expected behaviour. This process is iterated according to the selected search procedure until the result and expectation match. That completes the diagnosis phase. When action has been taken, then the appropriate diagnostics can be repeated to show that the result of any changes leaves the distributed system still able to meet its objectives. This paradigm for diagnostic services is shown diagrammatically (as a flow chart) in Figure 4.5. This method of performing diagnostics to locate faults can be enhanced if the negative results of earlier tests are used to influence and thus modify the test sequence.

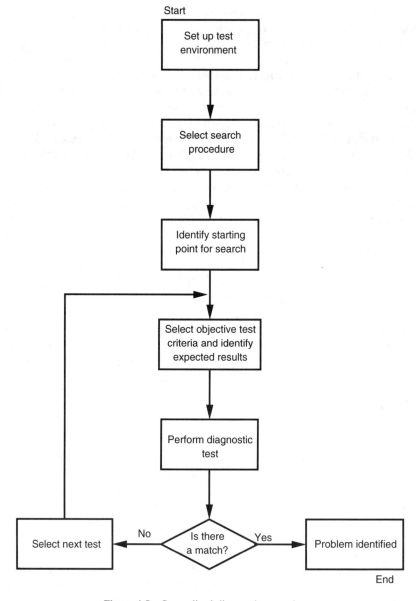

Figure 4.5   Generalized diagnostic procedure.

Fault diagnosis in distributed systems

Distribution exacerbates the difficulties of fault location since faults may be generated as a result of the interaction of processing elements in conjunction with communications elements. For example, the inability to obtain a response to a service request could be due to a communication failure or server failure. Also, the fault and the diagnostic equipment are often at different locations and require a reliable channel for diagnostic communication. Where a fault is suspected in the normal communication channel, an independent communication route may need to be set up for diagnostic purposes outside the normal communication band. In extreme cases, there may be no communication channel by which the diagnostic equipment can be connected.

Where the overall service is provided by a combination of sub-services under the control of different organizations, close cooperation between them is needed, with agreed common procedures and protocols for diagnosing faults. Ideally, there should be a single management entity responsible for coordinating overall fault diagnosis. As is sometimes the case for interconnected communication networks, with a local management entity responsible for each sub-service, the decision as to who or what acts as the coordinator may be determined by commercial or other policy constraints.

4.5.4 Fault resolution

Following fault detection, service recovery and fault diagnosis, management performs fault resolution. When the failure is in a hardware component, fault resolution usually takes the form of repair or replacement of the component, for which human intervention may be required. When the failure is found to be within system software, fault resolution may require re-initialization of system state to restore software to its proper state. This may have to be done by retrieving the software from local stable storage or by re-installing the component. The latter usually requires configuration management facilities.

Upon restoration of a repaired component, fault resolution reports may be issued to all affected users of that component to inform them that the fault has been cleared. The reports could add further information as to the nature of the fault and the recovery action that has been taken. In the example shown in Figure 4.2, fault resolution may result in the repaired link being reinstated as the primary link.

In the illustrated example, the left-hand diagram of Figure 4.6 shows the recovery situation in which a stand-by link has been introduced following failure detection. Following fault diagnosis and resolution, the repaired component (the data link) can be subjected to a series of confidence tests. At this point, it is possible to effect a further reconfiguration to return the stand-by link to its stand-by status, making the repaired link the primary once again. This would certainly be the case if the stand-by offered notably poorer performance than the primary link. But if both links were of comparable performance, it is likely that the repaired link would now be designated as the stand-by. This has the merit of retaining continuity of service and avoids the need for further network reconfiguration. It does, however, require that administrative records be updated to show the changeover in the status of the two data link components.

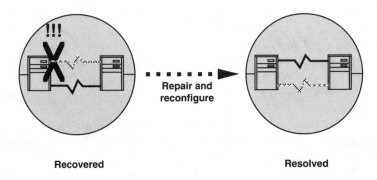

Figure 4.6 Fault resolution.

4.6 Performance management

There is no hard-and-fast distinction between performance objectives, reliability objectives and cost objectives. They are all aspects of the total QoS package offered to users. Performance management merely places the emphasis upon performance. Some aspects of performance are of direct interest to system users. They reflect the users' concerns to obtain effective performance from the distributed processing environment so that they might better meet the enterprise goals. Typical user performance objectives include:

- Overall response time
- System availability
- Error rates

and users and their representatives will negotiate these objectives with the system managers to ensure that their requirements can be satisfied.

Other performance objectives are of direct interest to system managers. They manifest themselves as sub-goals in meeting the overall objectives agreed with users. Examples include:

- Improving utilization of components (e.g. sharing load among printers)
- Minimizing delays on individual links (e.g. communications links)
- Maximizing throughput of services (e.g. network service)
- Reducing errors

Performance management is therefore concerned with:

- Setting performance targets and planning to bring the actual or predicted performance in line with the performance objectives
- Predicting future performance, by means of performance modelling
- Measuring actual performance against the objectives
- Performance optimization

Many of the features of performance management are independent of the distribution of users and their processing requirements. But once again, distribution and the scale of distributed systems add to the complexity of the management task and it is these factors which the following discussion aims to highlight. Performance targets and the ways in which they are set are specific to the enterprise and its management procedures. Some are concerned with the organizational aspects of management, others with its operational aspects. The following discussion can therefore give only illustrative examples. The approach adopted here is to consider firstly performance measurement, then the way in which performance can be modelled and, finally, performance optimization.

4.6.1 Performance measurement

The objectives of performance measurement are to enable managers to determine whether the present and planned performance objectives of the enterprise are being met and will continue to be met, and to identify whether cost savings can be made while meeting them. Two kinds of information are required. The first, the actual performance level of a system under a known load, tells managers whether a system is meeting its performance objectives. The second, the estimate of performance under a potential load, is required for sizing, detecting under-utilization and estimating the risks of offering a particular QoS or level of performance.

In order to carry out performance measurement, metrics have to be identified and defined. Relevant metrics must provide their data in a timely manner, provide the correct level of detail and, above all, be sufficiently accurate for their purpose. The level of detail and the accuracy required are, of course, dependent upon the particular performance measurement but, in general, measurements should be sufficiently precise that they are not invalidated by noise or operational errors. Performance metrics may not be amenable to simple measurement or directly available, but may have to be derived indirectly. Where there are random factors, for example in the utilization of a communication channel, it will be necessary to take several readings so as to derive an average value, thereby increasing the significance of the performance metric. And measurement of other performance metrics, for example total processing performance, can be obtained only by combining individual observations from all of the processing components.

Attempts to determine performance have to be realistic and practical.

Managers need to consider when, how, where, in what form and in what quantities data is needed, how data can be captured, and how it should be presented. Unless these questions can be answered, there is no value in making a commitment to measure performance. As with other supporting services, there may be security issues if, for example, managers need to obtain performance-related data from systems lying outside their immediate scope of responsibility and authority. It could be that sensitive information may be deduced from an analysis of performance-related data. For example, by discovering which parts of a system are vulnerable to overload it would be possible for an antagonist to inject spurious data and request operations to reduce system performance.

Performance measurement inevitably carries an overhead in computer and communications resources. This overhead will bias the results and may use vital storage space, processor time and channel bandwidth. These resources have an associated cost. It may cost more to derive some performance measurement than the benefit of its analysis could justify. This too is one of the practical factors which ought to influence an investment in performance measurement services. Performance management is often directed towards the minutiae of the system to determine parameter values such as the length of message queues, data flow rates across interfaces and processing times. This requires the corresponding computation and communication components to be provided with monitoring access (or to be self-monitoring) so that these values can be measured. While this can be invaluable for diagnostic purposes, it is essential that this type of detailed monitoring can be turned off so as to eliminate the measurement overhead. Often what is required is not microscopic detail but a macroscopic assessment of performance if the user or manager is trying to determine the overall performance of a file transfer or printing service. Hence, managers should continually ask two questions: 'Does the monitoring provide valuable knowledge?'; 'Just because performance data has proved to be of value in the past, is its continued gathering needed?' The feeling of comfort that managers might have merely because they can carry out performance measurements is quite misplaced if the data obtained no longer has significance.

There are some special factors which affect the application of performance measurement in a distributed system environment. They are:

- Inconsistency of measurement policies
- Inconsistency of metrics
- Inability to make measurement at all points in a system

These factors can lead to ambiguities and errors in performance measurements and can show unexpected fluctuations in measured values.

Inconsistencies and variations of a regular, permanent or more substantial nature can arise from deep-seated structural and organizational differences across the distributed processing system. They can be caused by differences in enterprise policies concerning what is legitimate to include in the measurement, what should be left out and what (for security reasons) cannot be made public. For example, different enterprises and even different departmental policies within an enterprise can give rise to conflicting needs for audit trails to retain and present evidence of performance measurements. It may not always be possible to derive a total picture or to correlate the requests from clients from one department with the services provided by another department. Variations in measured performance may also arise from variations in the nature or function of components of the system and the differences in measurement needs in different services and at different locations. These variations may lead to differences in the interpretation of the measurement's meaning.

Thus, measurements upon value added data services and their networks have shown variations in the measured performance of their end systems. The measured system performance for users who are making data requests has been observed to fall below its objectives. Yet performance of the transaction servers that are responding to those requests appears to meet the objectives set for those components. Each transaction is performed within its allotted time. What can be going wrong? In some instances the imbalance is due to the different management expectations of what constitutes good performance. Clients may have been led to expect a faster response to enquiries than the servers were capable of providing. In some cases that have been investigated, the server can respond to the demands of an individual client and meet the client's desired performance criteria but the distributed system has insufficient servers for the number of clients who are currently making requests. If the performance metrics ignore the lengths of server queues, there will continue to be a mismatch between expectations and reality. The experience from this example shows the value of being able to make measurements throughout the system and not just of specific components when this degree of diagnosis is required. But experience has shown that, with today's distributed systems, it is not always possible to establish a sufficient continuum of measurement points. In one case drawn to the authors' attention, the variation in measured performance probably arose from a bottle-neck in a part of the system which was inaccessible for performance measurement. It was likely that this was a result of queuing within an overloaded network which was administered by a third party. It serves as a reminder that where distributed systems are composed of independent systems supported through a carrier network there may be locations in between measurement points where performance data cannot be obtained. It is one of the factors leading user organizations to request access to certain management data from communications carrier services.

Because distributed systems have a tendency to evolve by adding components, some interactions may be unforeseen and it is these which can lead to unexpected fluctuations. The complexity of the distributed processing environment makes these fluctuations difficult to trace. Results may appear to be misleading. One cause is the difference in the ways in which performance-related data is obtained from subsystems, especially if these lie outside the direct responsibility of a given manager or there is inadequate synchronization between the performance parameters that are being compared. A more common cause of fluctuations arises from different loadings in other parts of the system. Although performance is often adequate, contention for resources can introduce temporary overloads in systems operating close to critical performance margins.

These effects can be minimized by:

- using agreed common standards of measurement,
- consistency in the tools and presentation facilities offered at different locations,
- awareness of the factors that can invalidate performance measurements.

But, in the final analysis, the only satisfactory way to judge performance is in terms of metrics which relate to the overall QoS which is delivered.

4.6.2 Performance planning and modelling

When faced with an obvious performance problem, the immediate reaction is to contemplate a system upgrade. While this might be considered as an acceptable strategy for a desktop computer system, it is not necessarily appropriate for a larger system and wholly inappropriate (as a first step) for a distributed processing system. The factors affecting distributed system performance are more complex, and a simple upgrade to a single system component may not have the intuitively expected effect. It may merely move the performance bottleneck to some other part of the system. It is in these situations that the ability to model projected system performance can be of critical importance.

The purposes of this modelling are threefold:

- to gain a clearer understanding of the way a system functions,
- to perform calculations of the likely behaviour of a system,
- to test hypotheses about the effect of alternative system designs.

The complexity of distributed systems results mainly from their capability for growth through accretion and from their interactions with other distributed systems in other enterprises. This makes it difficult to identify clear boundary conditions appropriate to the system whose performance is being investigated and means that large scale models may be needed. Nor should one forget that distributed systems are partially self-controlled systems with many feedback paths. Some of these paths introduce long delays and the paths may interact.

Different and potentially incompatible control algorithms or failure to gather relevant data during performance monitoring can modify the feedback, thereby giving the system different operational characteristics. These can be a serious problem for an approach, such as simulation, whose representation scales with the size of the system being modelled. Where there are multiple alternative routes available or multiple alternative processors, each capable of servicing a given requirement, there has to be a multi-dimensional model of comparable complexity.

The act of creating a performance model is one of producing a representation of those features that are thought to be relevant to the characteristics under investigation. The modelling must enable initial conditions to be established and then varied so as to establish sensitivity to various factors such as changes in behaviour, workload or reconfiguration. Two types of modelling methods are appropriate: parametric modelling and simulation. Parametric models are represented algebraically. They are speedy in operation but usually at the expense of gross oversimplification in the model. The simulation model's algorithm, or set of algorithms, provides an approximation which represents the resources together with the rules governing their behaviour. The model is then set running, fed by and interacting with stimuli. These are usually triggered using a pseudo-random event generator whose characteristics are chosen to match operational load conditions (Bratley *et al.*, 1983; Chu, 1969). While simulation models can resolve finer details of interactive behaviour than parametric models can, they do this at the expense of consuming more processing and storage resources. They suffer from lack of stability as the simulation becomes more detailed, experiencing deadlock problems if the simulation is overloaded. More seriously, they can miss system lock-up situations which would occur in the real system if operational conditions are poorly specified.

This highlights three issues which affect all types of performance model:

- Validation of the model
- Selecting the appropriate level of detail
- Understanding and interpreting the results

For distributed systems, model validation is particularly time-consuming. There are many independent, parallel activities, each of which has to be driven by a representative event stream. Care needs to be taken in the selection of a set of suitable algorithms for generating pseudo-random numbers which represent asynchronous events. It is important to ensure that the generators have very low repetition frequency and, more significantly, that there is no spurious coupling between event streams due to correlations between the pseudo-random numbers that are generated.

Techniques that can increase confidence in the model include:

- use of state table models, which are suited to problems with protocols, control algorithms, failure, lock-up and recovery, and transition paths;
- temporal logic models, which can help in the analysis of time-dependent problems.

However, for all but the simplest systems, model validation is likely to be subjective, that is, based on the experience and confidence of the model's designer and backed up by initial runs and statistical analysis.

Other factors that affect the simulation of distributed systems are:

- Distributed system size
- Diversity of components

and this influences the level of detail appropriate to model. If it is too coarse it fails to bring out essential features; if too fine, there are high costs in running the model with the added penalty of being swamped by detail.

The diversity of resources and of their behaviour can lead to very large simulation models with corresponding demands upon resources to create and maintain them. Getting past the initial settling period can take a lot of apparently unproductive use of computing time even for a non-distributed system simulation. Having to do it for a multi-subsystem model, where the cost can be an order of magnitude greater, may prove to be too expensive to be used on a regular basis, the cost of the simulation outweighing the anticipated benefit. Parametric models allow this diversity to be glossed over or represented by average characteristics.

Modelling distributed systems calls for considerable skills and, with only a limited number of distributed systems performance-modelling experts, these skills are not always readily available. For these reasons, a decision to construct and then manipulate a performance model should not be entered into lightly. A pragmatic approach to modelling a very large distributed processing environment is to adopt a mixture of models. Gross system characteristics are covered in one model and detailed analysis is performed only for relatively independent subsystems. The subsystem models, having relatively less complexity, can be probed in depth using simulation models. The system as a whole is modelled in a parametric representation to check that overall behaviour is reasonable and that attempts at local optimization have not compromised performance elsewhere. This approach allows the use of modelling to establish how certain controls affect local performance and it demonstrates the global characteristics of the system. This may be all that is required.

4.6.3 Performance optimization

Performance modelling provides some insight into the factors that can affect system behaviour and identifies suitable default values for parameters which affect system performance. However, model imperfections will mean that the results obtained do not guarantee that an enterprise is getting the most out of its investment. It could still be necessary to tune the operational system to optimize its performance.

Optimization is a complex matter. It requires more than the optimization of the use of each individual component at all times. Rather the objective should be to optimize the use of all resources and these include not only the distributed processing components but also the activities of its operators and users. The cost of people can be considerably higher than that of equipment and it may be that, in saving people cost, the enterprise obtains better overall performance in spite of the loss of component or distributed computing system efficiency. Part of the gain comes from recognizing that making continual adjustments, to ensure that all resources are appropriately loaded, is undesirable. The nuisance value of perpetually adjusting the operational environment may be sufficiently disruptive for its users that it reduces their effectiveness. The selection of optimization goals therefore depends upon the type of distributed system and the policy of its operating enterprise. Indeed, a broad optimization at subsystem level may be the best approach to adopt.

Performance optimization involves monitoring the system or subsystem, obtaining feedback on its usage, identifying weaknesses and exercising control to correct these weaknesses. Typical weaknesses include processing bottlenecks, communication delays and high error rates. Optimization is the responsibility of the service administrator, who must ensure that users obtain the best possible service from the system consistent with management policy. The main areas for overall performance optimization for a distributed system are:

- The communication subsystems
- The attached processing systems
- Overall system availability

The communication system is a critical part of any distributed system. The optimization objectives for it are usually to reduce delay and increase throughput. These can be achieved by adjusting parameters such as the number of buffers in individual nodes, retry time-outs and the routing algorithms, or changing the protocol used in a layer (Terplan, 1982). In situations where the optimum values for these parameters have already been set, any further performance enhancement can only be achieved by re-dimensioning the system, for example by adding new components or using new technology. Monitors observe traffic flow, packet size etc. Control can then be exercised and the network tuned, for example to maximize throughput. In local area sub-networks such as Ethernets, this can be achieved by a combination of selecting the optimum packet size and choosing the number of buffers to be provided in each network node.

Processing performance is affected by the allocation of software components to computers and is usually optimized through an equitable distribution of resources to software components. Memory usage, processing time, process priority, input/output overheads and communication delays are all factors to be taken into consideration when deciding upon software allocation. If the configuration is static, then this optimization must be performed at configuration time. For systems in which performance can be optimized dynamically by migrating software components, performance monitoring will identify those parts of the distributed environment that are lightly used and those that are more intensively used. Software components (including their current state) can then be redistributed between computing components. Note that care must be taken when reassigning software to lightly loaded computers with the objective of optimizing the performance of a dynamic system. If the processing duration of the software component is less than the time taken to effect the reassignment, then there is an obvious loss of performance. Less obviously, where there is insufficient control over migration policy (for example, different aspects of migration policy are independently carried out by two or more managing components) then instabilities in behaviour will be observed as software migrates to hitherto lightly loaded systems, only to overload them and so generate new processing bottlenecks elsewhere (Casavant and Kuhl, 1988; Eager *et al.*, 1986).

The availability of a system is a measure of its ability to work without a noticeable break in service for a given period of time. It can be improved either by increasing the reliability of individual system components or by fault tolerance, which requires the provision of additional resources, some of which can operate in a stand-by mode. The reliability of components can be improved by ensuring that environmental conditions (such as temperature and humidity) are properly adjusted and by replacing components that are prone to failure by more reliable ones. Fault tolerance can be improved by techniques which provide back-up resources, particularly through dynamic reconfiguration upon the detection of faults.

In summary, if the performance of the distributed processing environment as a whole is to be optimized, targets must be set and metrics adopted which provide objective, measurable quantities against which to judge the effect of optimization. The task requires:

- performance measurement tools to obtain information on which to make optimization decisions;
- modelling tools for decision making and planning that assess the effects of changes without having to affect the real system;

- control tools that allow parameters to be changed or the system to be reconfigured.

Performance optimization makes use of the configuration management service as discussed in the next section. Performance changes are reassessed after parameter or other configuration changes to see if these have resulted in overall performance improvement. Where improvement is detected, this gives an indication that a further and similar change could lead to greater improvement. However, this process of trial and error may, at best, lead only to sub-optimization. If it is to be employed as a serious method of performance optimization, it should be undertaken only in conjunction with an overall optimization plan, derived on the basis of a performance model.

4.7 Configuration management

Because the various management functions are so closely interrelated within the total management service, it has already been found necessary to make many passing references to configuration functions. Not only does configuration management assist in recovery after fault detection and provide support for performance optimization, it also supports initial configuration and subsequent evolutionary changes to the distributed processing environment. Kramer and colleagues (1990) have pointed to the advantages of a consistent approach to configuration management for both applications and support services.

Configuration management in a distributed system consists of the functions related to installing and interconnecting hardware and software components. Its functions are driven by statements specifying relationships between distributed systems components and the conditions (system states) under which those conditions shall apply. The use of modular programming techniques, with the emphasis on building both applications and support services from small reusable software components, is widely recognized (Wegner, 1984). Their use to aid reconfiguration is an example of 'programming in the large'. Reconfiguration functions must be executed when setting up a service instance and for system modifications to accommodate re-dimensioning. Control of the changes performed on a system, ensuring that they are performed in a consistent way, is referred to by some authors as **change management**. The term 'configuration management' is sometimes used to refer to managing the versions of software released during a service life cycle or the different versions required for a variety of hardware. The term **version control** is preferred for this activity.

The following list identifies some configuration management functions of services and of the systems which provide those services in a distributed processing environment:

- identification of hardware and software component classes to be used to provide a class of service;

- specification of the instances of components needed within a service. For example, there shall be five terminals each with its own terminal driver process;

- installation of hardware components for computers, peripherals, network interfaces and communication links. Although this requires manual intervention, it may be possible to change the state of a component under (remote) computer control, once a component is on-line. Typical state changes include active to passive, or normal to maintenance mode (Sloman, 1984);

- allocation of software components to hardware components. This may be performed automatically by means of a load-balancing resource manager or may be specified by the administrator responsible for configuring the service;

- allocation of resources such as code and data memory space to a software instance. These can either be pre-allocated for the lifetime of the instance, or allocation and release of resources can be performed dynamically on demand;

- binding imported interfaces to particular instances of exported interfaces;

- support for ability to stop, start, create, delete and query component instances.

A consideration of this list reveals three characteristics, which can be termed the **ABC** of configuration management functions:

- **A**dministrative functions
- **B**inding functions
- **C**ontrol functions

Administrative functions are those which identify components and assign services to them. They determine what hardware and software components are required for a system, and decide upon an optimum mapping of services onto components.

Binding functions establish, maintain and identify the interrelationships between components so that interfaces provided by components can be properly matched. For example a distributed database may make use of three particular file server instances, although there are many more file servers within the distributed system. Because most software components require a set of underlying support services, servers have to be bound to those specific servers which constitute their support environment. This is analogous to binding a program's I/O streams to particular I/O devices. Binding can also include checks that the interfaces are syntactically and semantically compatible. Language-based approaches to building distributed systems often perform type checking on interfaces (Birrell and Nelson, 1984). An information processing service may export a specification of its interface, thereby registering it with a directory or other information brokerage service. A client for a service finds the location of the server from the directory server and binds its imported interface to the exported one. Information obtained as a result of binding can take the form of topological maps which show the interconnectivity of components.

Control functions are responsible for establishing, monitoring and identifying the state and status of components by being able to create and delete services dynamically, suspend and resume the operation of services and, as with fault handling, use trivial functions within each service so that the state and status of each service can be polled, thereby determining the current state of the entire system or one of its subsystems. Taken in conjunction with binding functions, configuration management allows the bindings between interfaces to be changed so that one information processing service can make use of alternatives (this is analogous to being able to perform dynamic binding when making remote procedure calls (Birrell and Nelson, 1984)). It is like setting up a new connection to a different service access point within the communication system. Instances are usually created in a stopped state and must be started. Services may specify a particular start-up order for their components.

Binding functions can be combined with the administrative functions to provide a configuration management service to manage a software environment which supports distributed processing. Administrative functions will determine which software needs to be provided or updated, for example, to issue a new version of the protocol handlers to support improved routing of network traffic. These can be loaded using existing communications services. Binding functions will arrange that the interfaces of the newly loaded software are matched correctly to the environment in which they are loaded. Finally, control functions will arrange the changeover to the new software or effect recovery if there are software faults.

These configuration management functions can be performed in various ways. In some systems an initiator component starts up and performs all the actions required to install the service, by means of calls on the underlying support environment. In other systems, these functions are the responsibility of a third party. (In some **object oriented** systems (Goldberg and Robson, 1983), an object class manager provides a service for creating instances of the object class. Class managers are themselves software component instances.)

In small distributed systems configuration management can be static, that is, the service must be shut down and re-installed to make any changes. However, this is impractical for large-scale distributed system where dynamic (re-)configuration, at run-time, is the norm. There is a range of different types of dynamic configuration. Some systems dynamically create an instance of a service to handle each request, by creating a process to handle a transaction. Others allow new service classes to be dynamically installed in the system. Dynamic resource allocation can optimize the use of the resources (and hence reduce costs) but can also lead to resource starvation and, possibly, to deadlock. The code for a software component has to be loaded into the computer in which an instance is to be created, unless it has been loaded there already as a result of a previous instance invocation. As the size of the distributed environment increases and its components are required to remain operational at all possible times, there is a preference for configuration management techniques to be dynamic because they are 'scaleable', that is, they are essentially independent of the magnitude of the distributed system.

Configuration management may make use of commitment, concurrency and recovery controls to perform actions atomically. The controls are needed to maintain consistency when performing configuration operations over distributed sites should there be failures. As in the above example of software distribution or when installing a new version of the file service in a distributed database, it is advisable to change all instances which provide the service or to change none of them. This prevents any possibility of the service being left with incompatible versions of the service operating at its different sites. Commitment control is usually provided through a two-phase protocol. In the first phase all systems are primed to make the desired change but none does so. Each indicates its preparedness to make the change. Only if all systems acknowledge that the change can be made is the second phase entered, in which the change is committed. Even then, it may happen that a system fails to make the change. Provision is therefore made to recover to the original configuration if this is appropriate. However, the direct application of commitment, concurrency and recovery protocols, as used for example in transaction processing, may be inappropriate for managing the reconfiguration of distributed systems. If there has been an indication of a fault during the reconfiguration process, it may be quite inappropriate to recover to the original conditions. The way recovery takes place depends upon the nature of the fault and the recovery policy of the enterprise. Commitment control is also needed where there are multiple configuration managers within a system. In this case it is employed to prevent mutual interference between the managers. (See also Section 8.4.1.)

Configuration management requires a considerable amount of information about components, their state and their relationships. This includes the physical configuration of hardware components, the logical configuration of software components, information about service classes and their versions etc. Configuration management functions therefore benefit from the use of database or other information repository management services. Three types of information are needed. First, it is necessary to know the potential of the systems being managed; that is the classes of components that can be supported. Second, it is necessary to know the actual instances of the component classes that are being supported at any specific time. Third, the current state of each component needs to be known (is it operational, is it on stand-by, is it under repair, etc?) As the size of the distributed processing environment grows and, with it, the scale of the management need, the components of the database will become distributed both in the interests of resilience and for operational performance. The organization of the distributed processing activity associated with this database is itself distributed and requires management, just like any other distributed processing activity.

4.8 Accounting

Accounting management is a management service that collects and collates information about usage of services and resources; in other words, it is a specialized form of monitoring and reporting service. The two main objectives of accounting management are:

- to account for, and allocate a cost to, each instance of usage of a service or resource,
- to maintain and report accounting information covering many instances of service or resource usage.

To these can be added the supplementary service of controlling the availability of resources or access to services through an accounting quota, established through an accounting contract between a service provider and a subscriber to the service.

As with other monitoring services, accounting is enhanced by the additional support services described in Section 4.4, namely filtering, logging, time synchronization and scheduling. In fact, accounting management can be viewed as incomplete if logging is not available in the system because, without it, the second of the two main objectives cannot be met.

It is useful to maintain the distinction between service usage and resource usage. Resources, like disc storage space and communications bandwidth, are used in the provision of services, such as file storage or electronic mail. The important point for accounting is that services add value to the resources. Both users and service providers may require accounting services. Because users interact with a distributed system through the services it offers, they are interested only in service usage. On the other hand, service providers are interested in both service usage accounting and resource usage accounting, as the examples in this section will show.

Accounting for service usage requires the definition of what constitutes an instance of usage and how the quantity of service usage will be measured; both are determined by the service provider. One factor in the measurement of service usage is the resources used in providing the service. But the metric may also take into consideration factors such as the service provider's tariff policy, cross service subsidies and the costs of obtaining usage information. As a consequence, some service metrics are not directly related to all the resources used. One example is accounting for use of a print service by the number of pages printed while ignoring the amount of processing time it takes to print the pages. Some accounts are not directly proportional to the resources used as, for example, when accounting for the invocation of a service (such as a file transfer service) but not for the quantity of service used (the number of records transferred) in the invocation.

From these examples it is apparent that data on usage can be used for many purposes other than accounting, so what differentiates accounting management from other monitoring and logging services? Consider the provider of a service who decides that reading and writing to a database are two services on offer and that the service usage recorded is the quantity of data written or read each time the service is used. If the resulting audit trail were used so that users were held responsible for their actions, that would be an objective of security management. If the usage statistics were an aid to performance planning that would be a part of performance monitoring. Therefore, the definition of **accounting management** has to constrain the usage-determining function in a specific accounting sense; it is *a management service that collects, collates and logs usage information that is pertinent to the cost of using or providing a service*. As is shown below, the cost is not always directly expressed in cash terms.

It is not uncommon in distributed systems for one service, a **complex service**, to be provided through the use of other services. Where this is the case, the class of service can be classified in one of two ways:

- The users may not be aware that the provision of a particular service involves the use of another service or services. In this case, the complex service is referred to as a **compound service** and the underlying service(s) as the **component service**.

- The users may be aware that the provision of a particular service involves the use of other services. In this instance, the complex service is referred to as the **main service** and the other service(s) as the **enabling service**.

There may be services that are both compound services and main services. However, the reason for making these distinctions becomes clear when the cost of using a service is examined.

4.8.1 Resource usage accounting

Resource usage accounting is used:

- to determine the cost of a providing a service,
- to influence the efficiency of the system.

Although there are many factors influencing price, a service provider needs to determine the cost of providing a service, as a basis for deciding the price of the service to users. As with all monitoring activities, the level of detail is a matter of policy. The choice of the level of granularity of accounting information is always a balance between the benefits that can be derived from the information and the costs of obtaining and analysing the information. The cost of obtaining the information includes the cost of the distributed system's resources consumed in providing the accounting service and the cost of maintaining and improving it.

Resources can be divided into those that are reusable and those that are consumed. A reusable resource is 'borrowed' by a service for a period of time to be returned to the system once the service has finished with it. It is then available for use by another service. Disc storage space is an example of a reusable resource.

A consumable resource ceases to exist once it has been used by a service. There are two categories of consumable resources: durable resources and non-durable resources. Durable resource remain in existence until explicitly consumed by usage. Paper used for document printing is an example of a durable resource. A user who is given ten sheets of paper each working day but prints nothing for a week, can then print a document of fifty pages. When those pages have been printed the paper is no longer available for further use. A non-durable resource ceases to exist after a period of time, whether or not it is explicitly consumed. This is because the metric associated with the resource is intrinsically related to time in some way. An example is a unit of computation, measured, say, as a second of central processor time. If a central processing unit can handle a million instructions per second and is idle for one second, that resource is lost. The processor will not be able to handle two million instructions the next second. Non-durable resources have to be kept in constant use if the objective is to maximize usage. These two classes of consumable resource can be readily differentiated by considering the metrics used to account for their usage. Durable resources are expressed solely in terms of quantitative metrics (like the number of sheets of paper). Non-durable resources also have an associated temporal metric.

4.8.2 Service usage accounting

Service usage accounting is used:

- to bill subscribers,
- to determine the cost of using or providing a service,
- to influence and control user behaviour.

Billing subscribers

The provision of information with which to bill subscribers is a major motive for accounting management. A subscriber is an entity which enters into a contract with a service or resource provider so that users who are authorized by the subscriber may have access to the service (or use the resources). In many cases the subscriber and the user are the same entity but that need not always be so. A post, telecommunications and telephony (PTT) organization has a contract with a subscriber to provide communication services to an enterprise. Many of that enterprise's staff will be users of the service.

Many distributed utility services, such as telephone, electricity and gas, employ distributed monitoring of usage and centralized billing. These systems send usage information to a central site, where a bill is calculated to be delivered to the subscriber for payment. The tariff policy of a service provider determines the information that is collected for billing. For each instance of service usage the provider records the subscriber and, where possible, the user of the service. In most cases where there are instances of usage rather than continuous usage, the service provider also records a service instance identifier which is unique to the instance of service. However, there are some simple billing systems that record only usage on a subscriber's meter, which is read and reset periodically. To assist in providing a detailed bill and to handle a subscriber's queries, the provider may additionally record:

- The duration of usage
- The distance of the called server from the user (this is typical of communication services)
- The time and date
- The quantity of information manipulated or transferred
- The quality of service
- Other tariffed services used and not included in the basic service

Determining the cost of a service

Accounting for the cost of providing a compound complex service entails accounting for the cost of the component services it uses. If the component services and the compound service are all from the same service provider, then the tariff policy of the service provider may negate the need for detailed accounting of component service usage. In distributed systems, however, the services may be supplied by different organizations, and one instance of complex service usage may result in many instances of component service usage or enabling service usage, or both. The rationale for maintaining the distinction that has been made between compound/component service and main/enabling service is that there are two different ways of handling this.

In the first case (compound/component services) the subscriber views the service provider as the supplier of all the service. The subscriber is presented with a single consolidated bill which details the compound service usage and may or may not detail the component service usage. If component services are itemized they may or may not be directly related to the instances of compound service that used them. To relate them requires a usage instance identifier, which is passed from the compound service to the component service. While this improves the accountability of service usage, it is a significant accounting overhead and is therefore not commonly employed.

Because the compound service provider is accounting for all component services used, the compound service provider will be billed, in turn, by the component service providers. In commercial environments it is common for both parties to account for usage, so that when accounting information is exchanged it can be reconciled. Some subscribers also account for usage independently of the service provider, particularly where there is little trust placed in the accuracy of the service provider's accounting. Extreme cases exist where users inform the service provider of their service usage and the service provider does no accounting, but this requires a high level of trust. Both of these situations underline the need to evaluate the cost of accounting against the value of the accounting information.

The second case (main/enabling services) is where the subscribers and their associated users are aware that the service they wish to use is composed of more than one service. The subscribers will be billed separately by the main service provider and the enabling service providers, so each service provider will need to identify the subscriber and, if possible, the user. In most cases the different service providers will not relate the instance of usage of their service to any other services used. This method has the advantage that subscribers deal with each provider separately, removing the need for inter-service provider reconciliation.

An example is the Viewdata service (Prestel in the UK). This is a data information service accessible over a public communication network. Information is provided by third parties who rent Viewdata pages from the communication supplier. Here, three services are involved but the subscriber generally perceives only two of them. These are the enabling communication service and a main service (which is also a compound service with two components – the Viewdata service and the information provider's service). The user receives separate communication service and Viewdata bills. No attempt is made to relate the enabling service to the main service. The Viewdata bill, which may or may not be itemized, is based on both a charge for connection time and charges for specific pages of information. This requires two separate metrics to be handled in accounting management. The Viewdata service collects the charges due to information providers from users, but charges information providers for rental of pages on the system. The information provider has no direct charging interface to the subscriber and all charges are collected via the Viewdata service provider.

Influencing and controlling the behaviour of users

Service providers and users view demand for services differently. The service provider wishes to have a uniform demand for service throughout the service provision period, whereas users want to have timely service when they need it. These goals need to be reconciled. A passive method is to provide users with feedback on their usage (and its effect on the system) and trust that this will influence users to behave in a manner which would benefit the whole user community. The alternative is to implement a policy where higher charges are incurred for peak periods of usage. This may be a straight monetary charge or it may be combined with access controls and represent a portion of the subscriber's budget. Both these methods require accounting management to supply the usage information.

A more restrictive method of influencing behaviour is to implement access controls based on budgets. Subscribers are allocated a limited quantity of service as a quota to be used in a given period. On each occasion that a user uses the service, the quantity of service used will be recorded. When the quantity of service used in the period becomes equal to the quantity allocated further use is prohibited until there is a further budget allocation. This provides a specialized form of access control (see Chapter 5), though one whose motivation is for accounting purposes rather than for security.

Quota control policies may be motivated by commercial goals; for example, to ensure that users get only as much service as they have demonstrated that they can pay for. This is a similar concept to a credit limit on a credit card. These forms of quota control policy may also encourage off-peak working by setting lower tariffs. Users who take advantage of such inducements may then be further rewarded by being assured of dependable usage patterns by having their (off-peak) budgets increased. This is not just kindness on the part of the service providers, for they can use accounting policies to assist them to make better usage predictions. Their benefit is that they can operate their services more efficiently. Quota control policies may also be motivated by altruistic goals; for example to ensure that the services of the system are divided fairly among the users of the system. The latter is typically the motivation for accounting in academic institutions, which often levy only notional charges upon their users.

In summary, it can be seen that accounting can be used as much as an instrument of policy as a mechanism for recovering cost. In fact, it can be counter-productive to attempt to recover full costs during service start-up. At these times, there may be few subscribers. If they were to bear the full burden of costs, they would be deterred from using the service. Without encouragement, they would seek cheaper alternatives so that the service might never achieve a critical mass of users.

4.9 Name management

Names, in a system, are used to enable users and processes to refer to, and to communicate with, the entities on which they operate. Three different concepts are covered under the broad topic of **name management**:

- **Symbolic names**: these are ordinary names through which users identify the entities on which they wish to perform their operations. It is convenient for human users to use symbolic names for these purposes, rather than the string of letters and numerals used within the computer systems. The symbolic name could indicate location information (for example, laser__printer@Computer__Room) or may be location-independent (that is, it could be a person's name) (Sloman and Kramer, 1987).

- **Unique identifiers**: these apply to persistent entities in a system. They provide an immutable identifier, which is efficient for system use and need not be the name used by a human user.

- **Addresses**: these enable a support system to locate where an entity resides.

4.9.1 Symbolic names

Because symbolic names permit human managers to refer to entities by meaningful names, they are part of the human interface to management. Therefore, they may not be needed by automated management tasks. Symbolic names can be of two sorts: local names, unique within a context; and distinguished names, which are globally unique.

Local names are context-dependent: that is, to refer to someone unambiguously it may be adequate to call the person 'John' within his family, 'John Smith' at his workplace, but 'John Smith, 12a Railway Cuttings, East Cheam' when identifying himself to his bank. A person may also have multiple names; he may be 'Jack' to his friends, 'John' to his mother-in-law, and 'Daddy' to his children.

The same principles are applied to entity names: they need only be unique within a context, and there may be multiple names for an entity. As the above example shows, local names are used hierarchically. An entity may have a name by which it is known locally within a context. This context may be a directory or some other element of a hierarchy. This element is informally referred to as a naming *domain*, without making the detailed assumptions about domains that are discussed in Chapter 8. The local name need only be unique within the domain.

Each domain also has a local name in its superior domain. The local names of each domain from the top level domain downwards may be concatenated into a hierarchical *path name*. In any distributed system, all that is necessary is to ensure that top level domains are named uniquely (for example, the name of a country) and any full path name is then unique. This approach is used in the UNIX directory system and the Domain Name Service (Mockapetris and Dunlop, 1988).

For most purposes, an entity may have multiple names and these may be either local names or distinguished names. For example, users may allocate their own *aliases* to entities. However, when it is necessary to ensure that two references are to the same thing, then the name used must be unique. The full path name discussed above can serve as a distinguished name for some purposes, but if an entity is capable of being moved to a different domain, its full path name is changed.

4.9.2 Identifiers

An identifier is sometimes needed to resolve doubts about the identity of a particular person. Is this 'John Smith' the same one who is recorded by the tax man as 'John Smith, 17 High Street, Newtown'? He may have moved house, but he will have retained his social security number, which identifies him uniquely.

For a system to refer to persistent entities unambiguously, each entity requires an immutable, globally unique identifier. The identifier need not carry any meaning, and should not carry information such as its current context or location. In this way, an identifier does not change when it is moved from one context or location to another.

There are at least two methods of achieving uniqueness:

- A central naming authority allocates ranges of identifiers to subsidiary naming authorities who can associate the identifiers with either a class of entities or specific instances of physical entities, as appropriate. An example of this approach is the allocation of identifiers to individual Ethernet units. Xerox licenses manufacturers of Ethernet interfaces, who then assign these identifiers to the units which they manufacture. This method is not suitable where there are multiple independent authorities. Another example is the registration of unique *object identifiers* for items of management information that are specified in standards.

- Use a hierarchical system whereby top level domains are allocated unique identifiers, for example, 'top_ID'. Each domain is responsible for allocating unique identifiers to domains or entities within it. One such way is to use a monotonic clock with a suitable number range. A globally unique identifier for an entity instance is formed by concatenating the superior domain's identifier - 'host_ID - with the allocated identifier. The resulting unique identifier is 'top_ID.host_ID.creation_time'. Note that if the entity is moved to another host or organization the identifier will remain the same; it is not derived from its new host's identifier. If a wider global context has to be recognized, then it is necessary to prefix the identifier with a further distinguishing identifier. (Social security numbers identify uniquely only within a country, and a world-wide unique identifier for a person requires a nationally unique identifier to be prefixed with a country identifier.)

4.9.3 Addresses

Addresses are needed in any communication system in order to identify a location at which to deliver messages directed to named entities. An address is not necessarily unique to a single entity, since there may be several entities at the same location. One of the functions of naming services is to provide a means of obtaining addresses from entities' names or identifiers. However, the service may not necessarily be required. In the Ethernet example above, the identifiers are also treated as data link addresses within the domain of Ethernet local area networks and no address service is required.

4.9.4 OSI names and identifiers

It is clear from this discussion that there is a close connection between names and identifiers. In the OSI model for management information (ISO/IEC 10165–1) the entity's distinguished name is used as its formal identifier for the purposes of communication protocol. A containment relation between entities is defined, which provides a context. There are two main restrictions: one, an entity can only be contained in one other entity, so that the distinguished name is unique at any one time; two, an entity cannot be moved from one container to another, so that its distinguished name does not change over time. It can therefore act as a unique identifier for the entity also. The penalty paid for using the distinguished name as the identifier is that it is impossible for entities to migrate from one containing relationship to another while retaining their identities. This has been recognized as a constraint and many of the entity specifications also allow an entity to have a private identifier as a convenient label for the entity. This label can either be a number or a string of text and graphic characters. Because this identifier is not used to gain access to the entity the standards do not require it to be unique.

4.9.5 Name services

There is a need for mapping between names, unique identifiers and addresses. This mapping is performed by name servers or an integrated directory service. A name server usually knows about only a part of the symbolic name space, whereas an integrated directory service is more generalized and can deal with different name space mappings. It can also deal with the class of services which map from a generic name to any instance of a server. A **generic name** is one which is applied to a class of services, for example, the class 'file services'. (This service is often referred to as a 'yellow pages' service by analogy with the familiar service of that name provided by some telephony suppliers.) To provide facilities to locate a named instance requires that a network provides an address service. This performs a mapping from an entity name to its address. Note that the actual name mapping function is not considered a management function but rather the normal service provided by a directory server. (See Section 6.5 for a further discussion of directories and related information services.)

4.9.6 Name management functions

Names, unique identifiers and addresses each require management. They can be treated uniformly, each within its own **name space**, and require the following management and administrative functions:

- **Name space structuring**: the structure of the name space must be defined as a design decision, and this reflects the naming policy adopted. Hierarchical structures are common for both names and addresses (for example, country.network.organization.subnet. computer.port).

- **Name allocation**: at some level or in some context, a name must be unique. For example, an address on a local area network must be unique within the network. Name management includes the activity of administering and allocating the unique part of a name to a particular entity. The name space may be partitioned so that names can be independently allocated by multiple management agents without clashing. This can be illustrated by reference to the familiar concept of names in a hierarchical filing system, which is an example of a partitioned name space. Users can assign names to files within their own directories.

- **Name registration**: this is a function of directory service management. Directory service management includes the activity of maintaining the information which permits mappings between names at different levels. An example is name to address mapping. This is critical information, so has to be complete, accurate and highly available.

There may be several authorities which provide names within an organization, each supporting name services within its own domain. Where entities are referenced from more than one domain, those entities may have many symbolic names, which are aliases for each other. Unless management discipline ensures that each domain provides unique naming as described above, name clashes will arise. This was (and still is) a common occurrence when early networks, with rudimentary naming schemes, became joined to create more extended distributed systems. The consequent ambiguity of names could result either in entering into communication with the wrong entity or, in a broadcast network, in several entities receiving (and replying to) the communication. Only when the name clashes were detected were managers forced to take steps to resolve the naming problem by ensuring proper negotiation of name spaces for interacting domains. This problem can also extend to addressing clashes and some communication protocols (for example, Fiber Distributed Data Interface, FDDI) make provision for detecting address duplication. Even then, the resolution of address clashes is a matter for management intervention.

4.10 Interrelationship of functions and services

The various management functions are closely interrelated. A monitoring service is required to determine the state of components for configuration management, fault handling, and performance optimization and to perform accounting. Name allocation may be performed at configuration time and hence be part of the configuration management process. Reconfiguration services will be used to recover from faults or re-dimension a system to optimize performance. An illustration of some of the interrelationships is shown in Figure 4.7. This shows primary and secondary management functions and their supporting services, with arrows to indicate where one service or function uses another.

   The ability to control components and perform configuration changes can give a user considerable power over a distributed system, which may have strategic importance to an organization. The monitored information on performance or usage of a distributed system may be commercially sensitive if it is disclosed to unauthorized users. Security is therefore of prime importance for all aspects of management. Security is needed not only at the human interface but also at the program interface to distributed systems to prevent malicious or incorrect programs from accessing unauthorized services.

Summing up

- Management's primary task is to maintain the operational state and ensure that the distributed system provides an agreed quality of service.
- Monitoring is the most basic of the management activities.
- Effective monitoring needs additional supporting services which add value to the basic monitoring process.

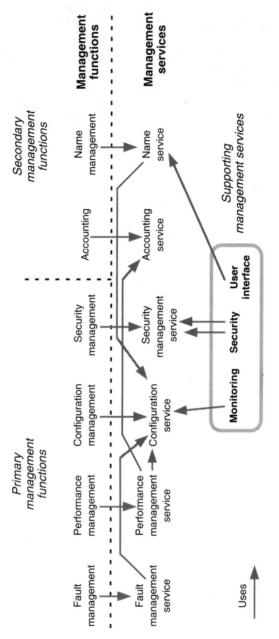

Figure 4.7 Management functions and services.

- A managed approach to fault handing involves the four phases of fault detection, fault recovery, fault diagnosis and fault resolution.
- Performance management is concerned with meeting performance related objects as defined in a QoS agreement. It requires performance measurement, performance planning (using modelling techniques) and performance optimization to achieve the QoS objective at minimum cost.
- Configuration management functions are concerned with installing and interconnecting hardware and software components.
- Accounting is a special form of monitoring whose purpose is to assign costs to resource and service usage.
- Name management is the activity of identifying and naming objects in the distributed system and mapping from identifiers or names to addresses in order to locate services and resources.
- Monitoring and configuration services underlie most of the other management services.

References

Birrell A.D. and Nelson B.J. (1984). Implementing remote procedure calls. *ACM Trans. on Computer Systems*, **2**(1), 39–59

Bratley P., Fox B.L. and Schrage L.E. (1983). *A Guide to Simulation*. London: Springer-Verlag

Casavant T.L. and Kuhl J. G. (1988). A taxonomy of scheduling in general-purpose distributed computing systems. *IEEE Trans. on Software Engineering*, **14**(2), 141–54

Chu Y.S. (1969). *Digital Simulation of Continuous Systems*. New York: McGraw-Hill

Eager D.L., Lazowska E.D. and Zahorjan J. (1986). Adaptive load sharing in homogeneous distributed systems. *IEEE Trans. on Software Engineering*, **12**(5), 662–75

Goldberg A. and Robson D. (1983). *Smalltalk-80: The Language and its Implementation*. Wokingham: Addison-Wesley

Holden D.B. (1989). Predictive languages for distributed systems management. In *Proc. IFIP Sym. on Integrated Network Management*, Boston, MA, May 1989 (Meandzija B. and Westcott J., eds.), pp. 41–60. Amsterdam: North-Holland

ISO/IEC 10165–1: 1992. *Information Technology – Open Systems Interconnection – Structure of Management Information – Part 1: Management Information Model*.

Kramer J., Magee J. and Young A. (1990). Towards unifying fault and change management. In *Proc. 2nd IEEE Workshop on Future Trends of Distributed Computing Systems in the 1990s*, Cairo, September 1990, pp. 57–63

Mockapetris P.V. and Dunlop K.J. (1988). Development of the domain name system. In *SIGCOMM '88 Sym. on Communications Architectures and Protocols*, Stanford, CA, August 1988

Sloman M. (ed.) (1984). *The Management of Local Area Networks*, Part 2. Final Report of Cost 11 Bis LAN Group

Sloman M. and Kramer J. (1987). *Distributed Systems and Computer Networks*. Englewood Cliffs, NJ: Prentice-Hall

Terplan (1982). *Performance Optimization of Computing Systems and Communication Networks*. Graenau: Expert Publishing

Wegner P. (1984). Capital-intensive software technology. *IEEE Software*, (July 1984)

5

Security and distributed systems

Objectives

- to describe the special factors for security in distributed systems
- to outline the objectives and mechanisms of security in distributed systems
- to discuss security policies, illustrated by the example of the practical application of security policies to a hypothetical company, ABC Ltd
- to discuss risk assessment and its management
- to describe the management functions of security
- to discuss the requirements that security itself has for management, considering the necessary functions and mechanisms
- to give an outline of international and other standards which affect security

5.1 Introduction

Although security management has been identified as one of the five functional areas of management, security and its management are of such significance that they deserve a chapter to themselves. The foundation of security in distributed systems is the security policies of the organizations responsible for the systems. Where these policies demand that data is retained, processed and transmitted so as to preserve confidentiality or so that their integrity is maintained, the security of the whole distributed processing environment needs to be managed in a coherent manner. Even if an organization's security requirements are minimal, it may still rely upon its information processing and communication technology for the efficient prosecution of its business. Even in this simple case the management of its information technology environment should be protected. Security breaches in the management of its supporting information technology system could have disruptive consequences for the effectiveness of computer and communication operations.

5.2 Special factors of security in distributed systems

It is assumed that the reader is generally familiar with the risks which can compromise data integrity, allow unauthorized disclosure of information or lead to denial of service, in non-distributed systems. However, there are special factors in distributed systems. These affect both the risks and the characteristics of security management for distributed systems.

5.2.1 Security risks of distributed systems

Existing distributed systems offer significant opportunities for the introduction of insecure or malicious software. They also permit hacking and browsing. Even those distributed systems that are intended to support a low or medium risk area of business still have to be careful today not to leave themselves wholly unprotected. Vigilant management is required against attacks leading to denial of service. Even where these attacks do not compromise data integrity, they may be both inconvenient and expensive. The experience of people affected by the 'Internet Worm' (Spafford, 1988) illustrates this. A deliberately created program propagated itself across several networks, especially in the USA. Although it did not itself cause any damage, it reproduced itself continuously until it had absorbed all the resources of the computers it had invaded and brought them to a halt. The cost of recovery was estimated at millions of dollars.

Similar effects can be caused accidentally. In particular, the incorrect handling of error reports in electronic mail systems can cause 'mail storms' which swamp the network. This can be caused if a message which is broadcast to multiple sites contains errors. If each receiver site reports the error back to the originator and separately triggers off a retry of the entire broadcast, the number of messages grows exponentially until the network halts.

Another risk is that unprotected systems may be used as an entry point into other inadequately protected but sensitive systems. The case of the German hackers who obtained access to many sensitive systems illustrated this risk (Stoll, 1988). They used unprotected systems as bases from which to probe systematically for security weaknesses in other more sensitive systems, with a surprisingly high degree of success. This resulted not only in the exposure of confidential information, but also in high costs for several sites who only discovered that they had been penetrated when their bills for communication were unexpectedly high.

There is a direct risk of exposure of confidential information in the uncontrolled, unprotected use of public networks between nodes of the system for information transfer. There are many opportunities for network staff to gain access to transmitted information but, in addition, any satellite or point-to-point radio link may be intercepted with the appropriate equipment. If a secure network is required, encryption and access controls are essential.

Distribution not only introduces additional risks to computer systems but also adds complications to dealing with the risks. For example:

- Communication may introduce significant time-lag into the system in respect of security-related information; this may make it difficult for the security management system to correlate information which, taken together, would indicate a security breach.
- Splitting the system into different geographical, political, technical or administrative domains complicates the setting and management of a coherent security policy; it also adds to the difficulty of tracing those security breaches initiated from a different domain.

5.2.2 Security strategies for distributed systems

Management can provide the means both to maintain a secure environment and to identify when attempts are made to breach security. In considering security risks in the managed distributed system, the first consideration is to establish what is to be protected. The appropriate level of protection is desirable at three points:

- Access to corporate data
- Access to the system's processing and communication capability
- Access to the management system

In discussing the ways in which protection may be applied, it will be seen that, as well as the down-side of introducing distribution-specific risks, distributed systems can exhibit compensating factors that can be exploited to enhance system security.

Unauthorized access to corporate data can provide the intruder with valuable strategic information. The advantage of distribution in this case is that it allows sensitive data to be distributed throughout the system. Thus, only by knowing the way in which it is distributed and accessing it at all locations is it possible to make a full reconstruction.

The damage that can result when the processing capability of a system is disrupted can be very high, particularly when a high premium is placed on the ability to process information. Distribution can provide alternative locations from which to acquire processing resources. Accidental failures typically occur at one site at a time. Deliberate attempts to deny a service require interference with a large number of processors simultaneously.

There may be a variety of security requirements within a distributed system. One advantage of distribution is that it does not constrain all components of a system to accept the same security rating. If the environment is partitioned into separate security domains, each domain can reflect an aspect of the organization's policy concerning security as well as possibly being related to a partitioning on functional grounds. Whereas some domains require the introduction of more stringent security policies than others, overall management is obtained either by negotiated security interaction policies between the managers of domains or by a hierarchical structuring of domains with one manager taking responsibility for coordinating the interactions of all. The choice depends on the organization's management style and the system's security requirements.

5.2.3 Security of management functions

The security policy and the way it is implemented must be capable of evolution in the same way as the other features of the distributed system. This requires that the capability for managing reconfiguration must itself be secured to the same high standard as other components. In other words, securing data and processing capability are of limited value if the management system is not equally protected. All management agents need to hold and manipulate information in order to carry out their functions. Normally this information needs to be kept secure in the same way as user information. Management functions such as configuration management have implications for the basic security of the system and so control of access to management operations is needed. Distributed systems management needs to make use of security facilities to ensure its own security.

Distributed systems management gains some security advantages from the security it brings to other distributed processing activities. Giving security to corporate data automatically provides the mechanisms which will safeguard the data used to control and monitor the network. Likewise, control of access to processing capacity ensures that only those who have the authority to manage the network are in a position to do so.

If a management facility is intended to extend across a number of domains which it will actively control, it will need to be as well secured as the most secure domain to be managed. Even if it will only exercise control of its own domain, this may be via a number of uncontrollable intervening domains because of the method of distribution used. Where this is the case, it will need to have security measures for its own protection and for the protection of its communication with the (distributed) domain of its resources.

Having reached an agreed basis for implementation, it is vital to support system security policies throughout the lifetime of the system. This necessitates a secure configuration management system, which employs techniques for the secure distribution of software either by manual and/or encryption-based schemes of tokens, seals and digital signatures. Even if the software has trusted functionality, it should receive, as a minimum, independent inspection and test. This may justify the use of a formal method of verification and validation, especially in those instances where the system is intended for sensitive or safety-critical applications.

5.3 Security framework

The objectives of security within distributed systems can be defined at a number of different levels, from a high-level objective such as 'to safeguard the organization's assets' to a low-level one such as 'to ensure that no dictionary words are used as passwords', with a hierarchy of objectives in between. Each level helps to achieve the objectives of a higher level. These objectives may be achieved by mechanisms at several different architectural levels within a distributed system. An example of this, mentioned in Section 5.4.5, is the protection of data in transmission. This can be achieved by link protection, by end-to-end protection, or at an intermediate level. The combination of security objectives and the architectural levels at which they may be supported together form a framework in which to describe security.

The International Organization for Standardization (ISO) security architecture (ISO 7498–2) defines a set of security services based on generally agreed objectives and sets out the options for the architectural levels at which these may be provided. The objectives are described in more detail in the ISO security frameworks overview (ISO/IEC 10182–1). Section 5.8.3 gives a summary of the ISO approach to security standards.

5.3.1 Security objectives

It is helpful to distinguish between the primary and secondary objectives of security. The primary objectives correspond to threats such as disclosure, corruption, loss, denial of service, impersonation and repudiation. The secondary objectives lead to the specification of services to support the primary ones.

There are three primary security objectives which apply to both stored data and messages in transit. They are:

- **Data confidentiality**: maintaining confidentiality of information held within systems or communicated between them. This typically means the prevention of unauthorized access to stored data files and the prevention of eavesdropping on messages in transmission. However, in high security applications there may also be a requirement for protection against revealing information which may be inferred merely from the fact that data is being transmitted and not from its contents. Such information can be derived from an analysis of communication traffic, noting the source and destination of messages. A classical case of traffic analysis is a military one in which preparation for troop movements could be revealed by the increased volume of communication between units.

- **Data integrity**: maintaining the integrity of information held within systems or communicated between systems. This prevents loss or modification of the information due, for example, to unauthorized access, component failures or communication errors. In data communication, it may also be important to prevent the repetition of a message. For example, a message in an electronic funds transfer system authorizing the transfer of funds from one account to another must not be sent and acted on twice. Protection from this risk is known as prevention of replay. Integrity can be achieved in two different ways: either preventing the occurrence of failures at all, or detecting the occurrence and recovering from it. Prevention may be achieved by a number of means: physical protection, access control against unauthorized actions, and procedural measures to prevent mistakes. Detection and recovery require timely detection, combined with back-up facilities which make it possible to start again from a situation of known integrity.

- **Data availability**: maintaining the availability of information held within systems or communicated between systems, ensuring that the services which provide access to data are available and that the data has not been lost. Threats to availability may exist at a number of levels. A data file is unavailable to its user if the computer which provides the service is physically destroyed, for example, by fire, or if the file has been irretrievably deleted, or if the communication between user and computer has failed. As with integrity, two different modes of protection are available: prevention, and detection and recovery using back-up facilities.

Two other primary security objectives apply specifically to communication between users and/or programs:

- **Authentication**: authenticating the identity of communicating partners and authenticating the origin and integrity of data which is communicated between them. It is important for several purposes. Authenticating the identity of the originator of a message gives confidence, in electronic mail systems, that messages are genuine. It also provides a basis for audit and accounting. It is a requirement for access control systems based on the identity of users of the system. Authentication of message contents enables the detection of integrity failures in messages.

- **Non-repudiation**: this is the prevention of a user wrongly denying having sent or having received a message. The first of these is known as *proof of origin* and the second as *proof of delivery*. Non-repudiation is important in any situation in which the interests of the sending and receiving parties may be in conflict, for example, in a stock transfer system where it would be in the financial interest of the sender to repudiate a selling order if the value of the stock subsequently rises, and in the interest of the receiver to repudiate it if it falls. It is a key issue for contractual systems based on EDI, for example, purchase and supply systems.

The secondary security objectives identified by the security architecture are as follows:

- **Access control**: providing access control to services or their components to ensure that users can only access services, and perform data accesses, for which they are authorized. Access control is one means which is used to achieve confidentiality, integrity and availability. It can be provided by physical and/or logical mechanisms. Unauthorized access to a personal computer may be prevented by a key lock disabling the keyboard. Access to a shared system may be controlled by a logical access control system using access rules based on the authenticated identity of users.

- **Audit trail**: providing an audit trail of activities in the system to enable user accountability. An audit trail provides evidence of who did what, and when. Auditing and accountability are discussed in detail separately, in Chapter 6. The important special case of audit of access control systems is discussed in Section 5.7.1.

- **Security alarm**: the detection of occurrences indicating an actual or potential security failure should raise an alarm and cause the system to operate in a fail-safe mode. Some security failures are not detected at the time, and cannot be reported on, like the failure of the access control system to detect an unauthorized access because of its own weakness. Other activities may be indicative of possible security failures, and need investigation; for example, a changed pattern of access by a user. The objective in this situation is to minimize, simultaneously, the risk of loss if there really is a security failure and the inconvenience to the user if there is a false alarm.

The security objectives outlined above are interdependent, and should not be taken in isolation. Authentication is the basis for achieving many of the other objectives. Authenticated user identities are needed for identity-based access control, for non-repudiation and for an audit trail. But password-based authentication requires both access control to protect the password file and encryption-based confidentiality for further protection if the access control fails. Access control, as well as requiring and supporting authentication, is a basis for confidentiality, integrity and availability. Audit trails and security alarms both depend upon and support the other objectives.

5.3.2 Architectural levels of security services

The ISO security architecture identifies the possible communication protocol layers of the Open Systems Interconnection (OSI) basic reference model at which each security service could be provided. A security service, such as confidentiality, can be applied to communication at different layers in the model but it is not sensible to apply the service at all of the layers. For instance, a user who is obtaining end-to-end confidentiality through encryption at layer 6, the presentation layer, has no need of data link encryption as well (see Figure 5.1). Further standards work will identify appropriate profiles of security services for particular applications.

5.4 Security mechanisms

A number of different mechanisms are used to achieve security objectives. They include:

- Physical and electronic security of components of the system
- Authentication mechanisms
- Access control mechanisms
- Communication security mechanisms

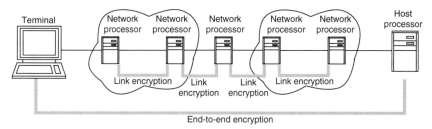

Figure 5.1 End-to-end versus link excryption.

They are described briefly here. Interested readers are referred to Davies and Price (1989), Denning (1982) and Muftic (1989) for more detail.

5.4.1 Physical security mechanisms

Physical security mechanisms are used for protection of equipment and for access control outside the scope of logical access control or encryption. They are necessary for protection against risks such as fire, tempest, terrorist attacks and accidental or malicious damage by users and technicians. Physical security requires a variety of mechanisms:

- **Preventive security**: strong construction, locks on doors, fire resistance and waterproofing.

- **Detection and deterrence**: movement detectors and door switches linked to alarms, security lighting and closed circuit television.

- **Recovery**: the provision of a back-up site, with alternative computing and communication arrangements.

A basic level of physical security is always necessary even in the presence of logical access control and encryption. In some situations physical protection may be simpler and more secure than a logical solution; for example, by controlling physical access to terminals and personal computers and their data and by storing sensitive data on demountable media.

Figure 5.2 illustrates a situation in which encryption needs to be supplemented by physical line protection if complete end-to-end protection is to be achieved. It is necessary because the encryption unit is not an integral part of a secure terminal.

5.4.2 Electronic security mechanisms

Electronic security mechanisms may be needed for protection against interference from static electricity and radio frequency (RF) interference, both of which can cause computer and communication equipment to malfunction. They are also required for radiation security to avoid the passive

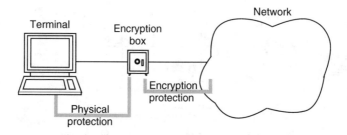

Figure 5.2 Encryption versus physical protection.

eavesdropping made possible because visual display units, printers and processors can emit electromagnetic radiation modulated by their internal electronic activity. The modulated signals can be detected by nearby radio receivers and analysed to reveal the data being displayed, printed or processed. Preventive devices are commercially available, and there are also military standards of protection known as **Tempest** proofing.

5.4.3 Authentication

Personal authentication

The aim of personal authentication in computer systems is to verify the claimed identity of a human user. There are a number of different mechanisms for it, all based on one or more of the following principles:

- a personal characteristic of the user (fingerprint, hand geometry, signature, etc.) which is unique to the individual;
- a possession of the user, such as a magnetically or electronically coded card, which is unique to that person;
- information known only to the user, for example, a secret password or encryption key.

Secret personal passwords are the simplest and cheapest method to implement, and they provide an adequate level of protection for medium and low security applications. They need a number of supportive measures if they are not to be undermined. The measures include: regular change by the user, one-way encrypted storage, minimum length and controlled format (such as no dictionary words), limited number of permitted attempts and logging and investigation of all failures. They can be reinforced by restricting users to logging in at specific physically protected terminals; for example, payroll clerks may only log on in that capacity using one of the terminals sited within the payroll office.

The use of passwords across open communication channels in distributed systems is a particular problem because the password can be discovered by eavesdropping on the channel and then used to impersonate the user. One solution to this is the use of one-time passwords, described below when discussing smart cards.

Magnetically coded cards have some advantages over passwords – they cannot be copied so easily and are less easy to forget. However, they also suffer from the potential exposure of their contents in open communication channels.

Smart cards offer increased security because they can be programmed to provide variable information. There are several methods in which they can be used for personal authentication. Two of these are:

- One-time password generators which generate a different password each time they are used. One commercial product changes the password every minute. In all cases the computing service must synchronize with the password generator.

- Challenge-response devices. The host sends a challenge number and the smart card has to calculate the correct response, including input from the user.

Smart cards are becoming cheaper and easier to use and they promise to provide a satisfactory way of overcoming the problems of personal authentication in distributed systems. However, any authentication system must cope with the problem of protecting the secure information upon which it is based. This is an aspect of security management (see Section 5.7).

Message authentication

The aim of message authentication in computer and communication systems is to verify that the message comes from its claimed originator and that it has not been altered in transmission. It is particularly needed for electronic funds transfer (EFT). The protection mechanism is the generation of a message authentication code (MAC), attached to the message, which can be recalculated by the receiver and will reveal any alteration in transit (see Figure 5.3). One standard method is the American Bankers Association message authentication standard ANSI X9.9 (ANSI, 1986). Message authentication mechanisms can also be used to achieve non-repudiation of messages.

5.4.4 Logical access control

Logical access control has to be used when physical access control is impossible, as is the case in multi-user systems. A model for logical access control is provided by a **reference monitor**, which intercepts all access attempts and

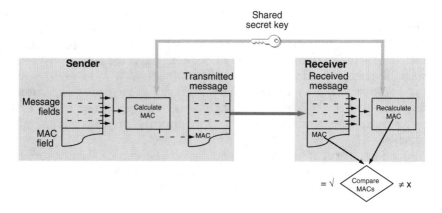

Figure 5.3   Message authentication code (MAC).

allows them only if the access is authorized. Otherwise the access is blocked, an error message is returned to the user and appropriate logging and alarm actions are taken.

There are two main forms of logical access control: **mandatory access control,** based upon fixed rules; and **discretionary access control,** which permits users to share and control access (see Section 5.8.1). The recommended discretionary access control approach is identification/authorization. The system ensures that users have authenticated identities, and the reference monitor makes a decision based on access rules which relate the user, the entity being accessed, and the operation the user is attempting to carry out.

There are two main implementations of access rules:

- an access control list (ACL) is attached to the target entities, defining the users who are authorized to access them and the operations that they can perform;
- users obtain authenticated capabilities, which act as tickets authorizing them to access defined resources.

Many personal computing systems provide only access control based upon file passwords. These provide a minimal, easy-to-use level of protection which is adequate for low security systems.

5.4.5 Communication security mechanisms

There are two main mechanisms in ensuring communication security, in addition to physical protection of the lines and equipment: traffic padding and encryption. The purpose of traffic padding is to conceal the existence of

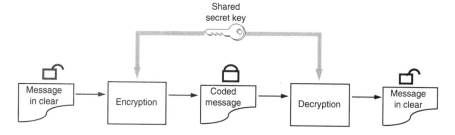

Figure 5.4   Secret key encryption.

messages on a communication line, by inserting dummy messages on the line to ensure that there is a uniform level of traffic at all times. It is mainly of interest in a military level of security.

Encryption can be used for several purposes: the prevention of eavesdropping; the detection of message alteration; and, in conjunction with the use of unique message identities, the detection of message deletion and replay.

Link or end-to-end encryption

Encryption may be used on individual links or on an end-to-end basis. These options are illustrated in Figure 5.1. **Link encryption** covers only the communication links, and the information is **in clear** at each communication processor. By contrast, **end-to-end encryption** is carried out directly between the initiating and target systems. An intermediate level is network encryption, where encryption spans an entire network, but not the gateways between net-works. In all cases where encryption is carried out by a separate hardware unit, the link between the terminal and the unit is not covered by encryption, and physical protection is required in addition (see Figure 5.2).

Encryption algorithms

There are two main types of encryption:

- **Secret key encryption**, which uses a single secret key shared between sender and receiver (see Figure 5.4).
- **Public key encryption**, which uses a related pair of keys. One key is publicly available and may be used to encrypt messages, while the other key is secret, known only to the receiver, and may be used to decrypt messages (see Figure 5.5).

Secret key encryption is available in a number of proprietary algorithms, and in the Data Encryption Standard (DES) which is an American, but not

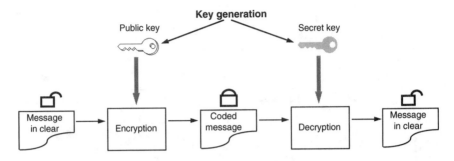

Figure 5.5 Public key encryption.

an international, standard. This is described in a number of text books (Davies and Price, 1989). The DES algorithm is available in software and also in hardware, as a semiconductor chip, where good performance must be provided. It is subject to export restrictions from the USA, and the hardware is therefore not suitable for multinational applications. Any secret key algorithm suffers from key management problems, because of the need to transport secret encryption keys securely. There is a standard method of key management, described in ANSI standard X.917 – key management (ANSI, 1985), which covers key generation and distribution; protection of the key management facility; and protocols for the cryptographic service.

The most widely accepted method of public key encryption is the Rivest, Shamir, Adleman (RSA) algorithm (Rivest *et al.*, 1977). Its performance is much poorer than the DES algorithm, but key management is easier because there is no need for secrecy of the key used by the sender. Some mixed-mode systems use RSA for key distribution and DES for message security, thus gaining many of the advantages of each method.

5.5 Security policies

Policies are the plans of an organization to meet its objectives. Within the context of security, a security policy defines the overall objectives of an organization with regard to security risks, and the plans for dealing with the risks in accordance with these objectives. Policies are usually hierarchical; the plans of a high-level policy are the objectives which a lower level policy must address.

All organizations should have a high-level security policy, defining the overall security goals of the organization and setting out a framework of plans to meet the goals. These high-level objectives vary substantially from organization to organization. Military organizations place a high value on secrecy, in contrast to academic institutions, which value openness of information. Financial institutions are concerned above all with maintaining the integrity of data and messages, which represent money. The default for simple social organizations is to have no security policy at all.

Security policies are not always precisely formulated or written down, but an effective computer security policy requires that the following questions are answered:

- What are the assets to be protected, and what is their value?
- What are the threats to these assets?
- Which threats should be eliminated and by what means?

The security policy for a distributed system should reflect senior managers' expectations of the organization's security objectives. Often, just as an organization's security objectives may not be precisely formulated, those in a distributed processing environment are unstated and they must be extracted from other documents, or identified and agreed by persuasion and discussion with the staff of the organization in question.

A high-level security policy can make general statements about the goals of the organization, but in order to be effective it requires a risk analysis to be carried out so as to understand the vulnerability of the organization and the consequences of security breaches. Risk management, discussed in Section 5.6, is required because of the possible trade-offs between the anticipated cost of threats and the actual costs of security measures. The security measures taken to counter a threat should be commensurate with the threat itself. The results of a risk analysis may help to redefine or focus high-level policies, as well as defining the lower-level policies for managing the system in a secure manner.

5.5.1 Security interaction policies

It is possible to create a distributed system in which all aspects of security are centrally managed to a common standard. However, a distributed system is more likely to evolve from a number of existing different (and heterogeneous) systems that may have previously operated to a variety of security policies. It is always possible that these may be incompatible, either because the policies of the systems differ in the level of security they provide or tolerate, or because there is technical incompatibility, for example because different encryption algorithms have been selected.

ISO has recognized this problem and has introduced the concept of a **security interaction policy** as part of the security frameworks. This is a policy which is acceptable to all parties in an interaction. It has to be negotiated between them before they can communicate. The issues that have to be resolved between them are the level of security and the technical compatibility of their security mechanisms. So far as the level of security is concerned, this is not limited to the security parameters relating to their communication. The security policy of one organization may insist that compatible standards of security are in force at the other organization's computing facilities before an interaction is permitted.

An inter-organizational security interaction policy, agreed and committed to by all parties, may be difficult to negotiate because of the need for more widespread compatibility than simply that of communication security standards. For example, there may be incompatibilities in the levels of security of their operating systems. If a common security policy cannot be agreed it is unwise to join up with the dissenting elements. Either side may run an unacceptable risk or require the imposition of unacceptable or uncongenial security practices on the other. For example, most organizations that are running their installations to government military security standards do not allow electronic mail to run on any of their networked computers, because of the known security exposures associated with it. They have to use a special free-standing electronic mail, which is disconnected or buffered from the rest of their systems.

A security interaction policy in a distributed system should lead to the generation of an agreed schedule of required security services and their supporting mechanisms.

5.5.2 Choice of security services

The choice of security services will have to meet a number of conflicting objectives, which include the following:

- Security policies are often defined centrally but applied locally, or in each application, and at many intervening points in the communication between each user. There are therefore practical difficulties in ensuring that a security policy is met.

- Design of existing standard communication products and many operating systems has avoided or neglected considerations of security. Security requirements therefore have to be negotiated separately with system suppliers, requiring much greater effort in procurement than if they were defined as part of a standard or an intrinsic part of the operating system.

One way of simplifying the range of security services needed (and hence of avoiding unnecessary cost) is to identify groups of similar operations and functions within the system to which the same security approach can be applied. For example, one group may be the set of activities needed to sign on to the system whereby each entity (be it user or system component) is required to be authenticated and the scope of its permitted activities identified. A second group could be concerned with the data transfer between systems to ensure that it is not susceptible to intrusion or eavesdropping. A third group is related to maintaining the security of user data; this covers data access and storage, and includes file and database security services. A fourth group relates to program execution and is concerned with safeguarding data processing, the integrity of processing elements and the task of managing the distributed system itself.

5.5.3 The practical application of IT security policies

To illustrate the practical application of IT security polices in a distributed processing environment, some of the policies that could apply to the company (ABC Ltd.) illustrated in Figures 5.6–5.8 are described. Figure 5.6 shows that ABC has a central corporate network, with local connections to systems operated by Corporate Planning and Sales, and remote connections to Manufacturing and Stores/Despatch. In addition remote information services, such as Reuters wire service, are used, Sales allows dial-in access by its salesmen, and a partner company DEF Ltd has a remote connection. Figure 5.7 shows part of ABC's and DEF's organizations. The IT Security Administrator in ABC has to take account of the joint research venture between the two companies, and cooperate with DEF's IT Security Administrator. Finally, figure 5.8 shows that, in addition to the expected directory tree structure for ABC's computer file, it is also necessary to take into account files which are specially grouped together for security management, such as those files which are subject to data protection legislation.

The IT security policies have to take all these complicating factors into account. They are divided into the following areas:

- Security administration policies
- Security levels
- Communication security
- System access control
- Data access control
- Disaster planning
- System auditability
- Legal and regulatory policies relating to security

Note first of all the extent and limits of these policies. They include the areas needed to ensure the confidentiality, integrity and availability of information, with two notable exceptions. First, they do not cover the back-up and recovery procedures which are part of normal day-to-day IT operations. It is assumed that, in addition to an IT security policy, the organization has an IT computer operation policy which covers day-to-day computer operating procedures, including recovery from incidents such as system failures and

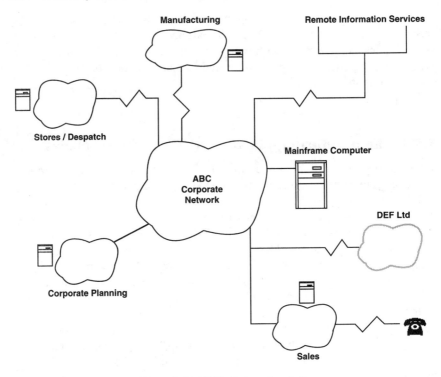

Figure 5.6 ABC's Systems (partial).

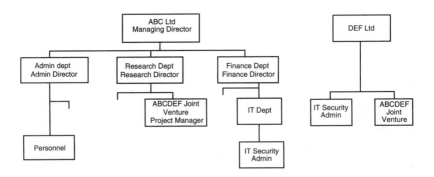

Figure 5.7 ABC Organization (partial).

disc crashes; and also an IT communication management policy covering procedures such as alternate routing in the event of line failures. The exclusion of these areas from security policies is to some extent arbitrary, but is common to many organizations, which prefer to regard them as aspects of system and communication operations. It is of course essential to ensure that these subjects are covered in one policy document or another.

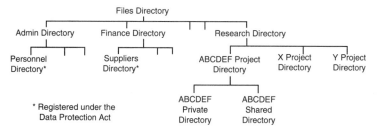

Figure 5.8   ABC's File Structure.

Second, these security policies also exclude system change control. This too may be regarded as arbitrary, but the justification is again that it should be covered in other policies. Those aspects of change control relating to reconfiguration of the system by changing hardware components such as processing systems and networks should be covered by IT computer operations and communication management policies. Software change control should be covered by polices for IT computer operations and development.

Issues relating to day-to-day recovery and system change control are discussed in Chapter 7 and Section 4.7.

In an organization such as ABC Ltd., security will make little or no direct contribution to each department's achievement of its immediate goals (until something goes wrong), while costing a substantial amount of effort and money. Therefore if the security policies are to be effective they need to be endorsed at the highest possible level of management, usually Board level, and included in the targets set for each department. Only then will business managers regard them as an integral of their goals.

Further, they must be communicated effectively. Many organizations have informal security policies that can be deduced from other policy documents and from management decisions which may be buried in internal memoranda and difficult to find. Effective security policies need to be separately and clearly documented, preferably as a security policy document or as a section in an IT policy document. It is then possible for IT and user personnel to find out easily what the policies are; there is no possibility of effective implementation of a policy that nobody knows about.

The first recommendation for ABC Ltd. is therefore that the director responsible for IT obtains Board approval for the creation and enforcement of IT security policies, as set out in an IT security policy document.

Security administration policies

The foundation of the security policies of the organization will be an effective organizational structure. While information processing is centralized, it is sufficient to put someone in charge of enforcement of IT security throughout the organization. However, as soon as it becomes distributed it is necessary to have a two-tier organizational structure: a central security coordinator; and security administrators covering every department of the organization. So as to respect the autonomy of distributed systems, direct responsibility for security in each system should be held by its security administrator, but in order to ensure that the level of security is consistent throughout the organization the security coordinator should have the goal of ensuring that each system is working to compatible standards and procedures. Since ABC Ltd. takes autonomy seriously, power and responsibility stay with the autonomous departments, but the security coordinator has two tasks: ensuring that each security administrator is aware of the standards and procedures; and helping departmental business managers to ensure that they are adhered to.

The main concern of ABC Ltd., apart from setting up its IT security organization, must be to ensure that the net is spread widely enough; every independent system that has eluded the control of communication or systems management is a potential security risk. The personal computers that have 'gone independent' may or may not be operating to ABC's standards of security. Each must be brought in under the umbrella of the appropriate security administrator.

Security levels

One of the themes of this book is that management policies should be made about groups of objects, rather than individuals. Most organizations will need to apply this concept to security measures also. If just a few levels of security can be identified, and a package of security measures defined for each level, then detailed decisions about individual objects can be avoided.

ABC Ltd. is likely to define two types of security level: for data and for users. Most commercial organizations aim to give the same level of protection to all their data, so there will be only one security level defined for data. This is much easier to administer than multiple levels, and accords with the usual requirement, that sharing and mobility of data must be enabled but controlled. However, there may be a requirement to treat some data especially securely, either because its confidentiality is critical to the success of the business or, more commonly, because of the terms of a government contract.

On the other hand, it is quite common to wish to make distinctions between categories of users, especially when outsiders are given limited access to the system for special purposes, or when insecure dial-in access is permitted. So ABC may have a policy to treat three categories of user differently: normal users, who have the least restricted access; the same users when they dial in, who are to be allowed access to specific, pre-defined data; and outsiders, with a similar restriction. Note that this concept of security levels has similarities to the military-type security levels of mandatory security (DoD, 1985), but is much less formally defined.

Physical security

Physical security is the basis of all other system security. ABC needs a policy that requires an appropriate level of physical protection for all physical assets within its control.

Communication security

ABC's communication security policies will typically define the levels of confidentiality, integrity and availability. They will be divided into two categories: the security of the corporate networks; and the criteria for applications to provide a higher level of security on an end-to-end basis. Based on today's technology, the policy is likely to require assured integrity and a defined percentage of availability from the network, in the absence of deliberate attacks on the system, but not to insist on assured network confidentiality. Within a few years, with increasing availability of cheap encryption products, the policy is likely to be upgraded to insist on network confidentiality also.

Assuming a relatively weak network security policy, an additional policy is required to ensure that applications requiring a higher level of security are provided with it by means of application level security measures. Note that user authentication policies are dealt with below.

System access control

Perhaps the most important security measures to be taken in an organization with open distributed systems are to do with controlling the access of users to the system. There needs therefore to be a policy about system access control. It will have two main parts, the first to do with user identifiers and the second to do with user authentication.

The first part will state the requirement for unique user identifiers and the need for users to respect them. The second will define the strength of authentication which must be applied to users who attempt to log on to the system. Typically there will be two levels of authentication:

- Normal users logging in from terminals and workstations within ABC's premises. The policy will state the standards for passwords, such as the minimum length and required format, and the frequency of change.
- Users, whether company staff or external, who log in from outside ABC's premises. There will be a much higher level of authen-

tication, probably using smart cards or other one-time password generators.

Data access control

The policy for data access control will contain the following elements:

- Ownership of all elements of ABC's data should be defined, with the owner being responsible for decisions about the use of the data;
- All of ABC's data should be protected, and access should only be permitted when authorized by its owner;
- All systems should have access control systems which protect data to a defined standard. Typically, the 'Orange Book' C2 level of protection (see Section 5.8.1) is suitable for a commercial organization such as ABC.

Disaster planning

ABC is critically dependent upon the working of many of its communication and computer systems. If any one of them fails, the business will have difficulty in functioning at all. There needs therefore to be a disaster planning policy which requires each system to be considered for its criticality and defines how any critical system is to be recovered. It should define what is the maximum recovery time, and how all data, communication and processors are to be backed up to enable rapid recovery in the event of any conceivable disaster. For distributed systems, the problems of back-up are eased by the existence of compatible systems at several sites.

System auditability

There are several reasons for ABC having a policy requiring the auditability of all systems; that is, the ability to trace any action that has taken place in the system. It gives a greater ability to control systems, it is usually a requirement of the auditors and it enables the company to demonstrate that it is complying with legal requirements. It is normally impractical to log all actions all of the time, so there should be a policy dividing systems and applications into three categories: events, such as security administrators' actions and financial transactions, that should be logged all the time; events that can be logged whenever necessary; and events that are so trivial that they never need logging.

Legal and regulatory policies relating to security

A policy is needed which makes it clear to all staff that all legal and regulatory requirements are to be complied with.

Use of external organizations

There are many applications in which external organizations are used for processing an organization's data, for example EFT and EDI. The policy should require that an appropriate level of security should exist on the systems of any external organization which processes ABC's data.

Concluding comment on the security policies

The security policies outlined above are a minimum set for an organization such as ABC. Most of them 'state the obvious', but it is notable how often obvious security needs are ignored. A comprehensive set of policies, on the lines outlined above, at least ensures that the appropriate questions are asked, and that no part of the organization can claim to be immune from the need for security.

5.6 Risk assessment and management

The concept of risk was introduced in Chapter 3. It is characterized by a concern for uncertainty about the future and the possibility of some form of loss. The two different forms of risk are security risk and business risk. Security risk is concerned with future events, in which an occurrence leads only to loss. Examples are the risk of loss through fraud, breach of confidentiality or equipment failure. This is the type of risk dealt with in this section. Business risk, on the other hand, which may result in either loss or gain, is discussed in section 6.2.

Risk assessment and management is an activity which takes a rational view of the assets of an organization and the risks they face, and then makes decisions about the protection they are to be given. An essential element of the decisions is that the cost of protection should be commensurate with the expected costs arising from security losses.

There are several computer-related security risk management methodologies available (Gilbert, 1989). They all have the following tasks in common:

- Identification and valuation of assets
- Construction of security risk scenarios
- Assessment of the probability of the scenarios and the losses that would ensue
- Identification and costing of possible security measures for each scenario
- Selection of a portfolio of security measures

Risk analysis is at its most effective when carried out during the specification and design phases of a distributed system development. In these phases the risk implications of design decisions (identifying where the design shows its least robust characteristics) and the security requirements can be established and their consequences identified. However, this ideal policy is seldom practical for distributed systems since one of their characteristics is that they have often come into being by a process of evolution. For a system already in operation, risk analysis can help to identify where corrective action needs to be taken to remedy any vulnerabilities which had not previously been noted or had not been properly understood. And the analysis, once made, provides a baseline from which subsequent analyses can be conducted as the distributed system continues to evolve over time.

5.7 Managing security

Security management is the activity of managing the functions and mechanisms used by the various services in a distributed system to implement security policies. The main security management functions include:

- The management of encryption keys (ANSI, 1985) and other secret information such as passwords. This involves generation of keys as required and distribution of the keys to the relevant components in the system, storing keys and archiving keys. Keys should have a limited lifetime and so should be regenerated at regular intervals.

- Managing the registration of users and the information used to check their identity (encryption key or password).

- Managing access control information relating to users and servers. This includes access control lists, capabilities, privileges and multilevel security labels.

- Providing security audit trails. These record all exceptional events (attempts at unauthorized access, etc.) and selected normal events such as log-ons and file accesses. Their purpose is to enable investigation of security breaches and audit of a security administrator's actions.

5.7.1 Audit of access control systems

Whatever the organization for security and wherever the perceived threat, one vital aspect of distributed systems management is the ability to maintain an audit trail and to relate the security audit to other events taking place within the distributed processing environment. In this way the system can not only carry out security management, it can also be seen to be carrying out security management. Indeed, maintaining a security audit trail where a system requires access through public communication services can help to meet legal requirements for demonstrating data protection.

It is virtually impossible to guarantee that unauthorized access or viewing of sensitive material will never occur. At best, it may be possible only to limit the potential size of an authorized access group and place its members under legal or contractual restraints over use or disclosure of the information. If the use of due legal process is seriously contemplated as an option, it is essential to maintain an effective audit trail of accesses. That in itself implies the need for a high level of security for the access control mechanism and its associated audit trail. These must be sustained at the expense of performance and in the event of multiple failures if any real value is to be gained from them.

Making the record is insufficient; a prompt and effective audit analysis mechanism must be supplied. If on-line analysis tools are permitted they should be able to act to isolate sources of malpractice and warn managers. Off-line methods of analysis are usually inadequate for a preventive stance and should be used only to verify that on-line systems are working or to carry out damage assessment if they fail.

5.8 Security standards

Network management standards are considered in detail in Chapter 9. However, having singled out security for special consideration in this chapter, the standards that are relevant to distributed system security are presented here.

There are three main categories of security standards which concern distributed system management. The first are standards related to the security of individual computers. These have been in existence for some time, and are quite mature. The second are standards for the protection of communication transmission and remote authentication. These too are quite mature. The third, still under development, are those which integrate computer and communication security standards to provide distributed systems security standards.

The standards do not generally prescribe physical or procedural mechanisms, nor do they prescribe risk management or risk assessment procedures or requirements for their use. These are all necessary elements to be considered and resolved for the resources that comprise the whole distributed system. Therefore, although security standards are an important support to distributed system security policies, they have to be viewed in the context of an overall security policy which uses other measures as well.

5.8.1 Computer security standards

The USA Department of Defense Trusted Computer System Evaluation Criteria (TCSEC; the Orange Book) (DoD, 1985), deals with access control to individual systems. It defines a number of possible levels of trust which may be placed in a system, ranging from the certified high security of the A1 level down to a low level of informally defined security at the C1 level. It is in common use as a means of indicating the level of security required or supplied in computer systems.

Section 5.4.4 identified that access control is divided by the TCSEC into two categories: mandatory and discretionary access control. The former enforces policies that are built into the design of the system and cannot be altered except by installing a new version of the system. An example is the policy that in multi-layer security systems data cannot be read by a user with a lower security clearance then the classification that has been assigned to the data. Discretionary access control mechanisms are defined as those which allow users to specify and control sharing of resources with other users. For example the C2 level discretionary access control policy is defined as requiring mechanisms that ensure that information and resources are protected from unauthorized access and that access permission is assigned only by authorized users.

The Trusted Network Interpretation of the TCSEC (DoD, 1987) (the Red Book) extends the criteria of the Orange Book to networks. It is chiefly concerned with the security criteria to be met when accessing remote hosts.

The Red Book is now quite old and it has always been more orientated to military type security than to commercial security. A standards effort which is now under way is the Information Technology Security Evaluation Criteria (ITSEC, 1991). This is a joint undertaking by the UK, Dutch, French and German governments. Its aim is to take into account the needs of commercial users and improve on the Red Book by separating concerns about security levels from the way in which the security is evaluated. In the UK, the Department of Trade and Industry and the Communications-Electronics Security Group have established the UK IT Security Evaluation and Certification Scheme (CESG, 1991) which evaluates and certifies products using the criteria of ITSEC.

5.8.2 Communication security standards and encryption

Transmission security

Transmission security standards are mainly concerned with encryption methods. One algorithm in particular has been the subject of standards efforts: the DES algorithm for secret key encryption which is an American, but not an international, standard. The RSA algorithm for public key encryption is the subject of USA patents. It has become a *de facto* standard for public key cryptography but because of its patented status is not currently defined as a national or international standard. These two algorithms were described briefly in Section 5.4.5.

Encryption depends for its strength upon the security of the hardware used. Standards for the physical security of cryptographic equipment are described in BSI (1986).

The basic standard for DES is NBS (1977), supplemented by ANSI (1981). There are supplementary standards describing its modes of operation (NBS, 1980), and guidelines for installation and use (NBS, 1981). The management of keys in banking applications is described in ANSI (1985), but this standard is rather generally expressed and would apply to other applications also. A detailed discussion of DES standards is given by Davies and Price (1989).

Authentication standards

A number of standards have been developed for banking applications for peer-to-peer communication and message authentication. They too are quite general in format and could be used for other purposes. They include ANSI (1986) for message authentication and ANSI (1982) for personal authentication using a personal identification number (PIN).

5.8.3 OSI security standards

Network security was not a primary concern when the OSI effort first got under way in the late 1970s. However there is now a series of ISO standards under development which aim to add security to OSI. The standards define the security services which the partners in a communication could agree upon, and the protocols to be used in setting up a secure interaction.

The security services that may be required for the communication facilities have been defined in the ISO 7498-2 Security Architecture (ISO, 1988). The protocols for their provision are still largely under development and are not yet available in OSI products.

The security services described in the security architecture are described in more detail in a series of security frameworks currently in production. They will eventually appear as international standards 10181-1 to 10181-8. The planned framework parts are:

(1) Overview – a general introduction
(2) Authentication
(3) Access control
(4) Non-repudiation
(5) Integrity
(6) Data confidentiality
(7) Audit framework
(8) Key management

Many other standardization efforts have security implications, and therefore have security-related standards. The following are particularly relevant to distributed system security:

- The OSI Directory standards (the ISO 9594 or CCITT X.500 series) include a scheme for access control in parts 1 to 4, and part 8 is the directory authentication framework.
- The OSI Systems Management Function standards (10164 series) include as parts 7, 8 and 9 schemes for security alarm reporting, security audit trail and objects and attributes for access control.
- The Common Management Information Services Definition and Protocol standards (9595 and 9596 series) describe availability of access control when communicating management operations.
- Amendments are proposed to the File Transfer Access and Management standard ISO 8571 to deal with authentication and access control.
- Electronic Data Interchange (EDI) Security standards are under development by ISO and CCITT.
- Remote Operations Service (ROS) Security standards are under development by CCITT.

Several similar and related efforts are in progress, including profiles to describe the security characteristics of selected applications.

Summing up

- Distribution introduces additional risk and adds complications in dealing with risk.
- Conversely, distribution can enhance security by enabling high security computing and communication activities to be handled separately from low risk applications.
- Primary security objectives concern unwarranted disclosure, corruption and loss of data, denial of service, repudiation of action and impersonation.
- Secondary security objectives provide access control, audit trails and security alarm services.
- Organizations should have a high-level security policy, defining the overall security goals and setting out a framework of plans to meet the goals.
- Although security standards are important, their use has to be in the context of an enterprise's overall security policy.

References

ANSI (1981). (X3.92). *Data Encryption Algorithm*. American National Standards Institution.

ANSI (1982). *Personal Identification Number Management and Security*, ANSI Standard X9.8, American National Standards Institution

ANSI (1985). *Financial Institution Key Management* (Wholesale), ANSI Standard X9.17, American Bankers Association, Standards Department, 1120 Connecticut Ave NW, Washington DC 20036, 4 April

ANSI (1986). *Financial Institution Retail Message Authentication*, ANSI Standard X9.19, American Bankers Association, Standards Department, 1120 Connecticut Ave NW, Washington DC 20036

BSI (1986). *Physical Security of Cryptographic Equipment*, British Standards Institution document 86/67937, 10 December

CESG (1991). *UK IT Security Evaluation and Certification Scheme*, Issue 1.0, 1 March 1991. Communications-Electronics Security Group, Cheltenham, UK

Davies D.W. and Price W.L. (1989). *Security for Computer Networks*. Chichester: John Wiley

Denning D.E. (1982). *Cryptography and Data Security*. Workingham: Addison-Wesley

DoD (1985). *Department of Defense Trusted Computer System Evaluation Criteria*, Department of Defense (USA), DoD 5200.78 – STD, December

DoD (1987). *Trusted Network Interpretation of the Trusted Computer System Evaluation Criteria* NCSC-TG-005 version 1. Technical Guidelines Division, National Computer Security Center (USA).

Gilbert I.E. (1989). *Guide for Selecting Automated Risk Analysis Tools*. NIST Special Publication 500–174

ISO (1988). *ISO/IEC 7498–2: 1988 Information Technology – Open Systems Interconnection – Basic Reference Model – Part 2: Security Architecture*

ISO/IEC 10182–1: *1992 Information Technology – Open Systems Interconnection – Security Frameworks – Part 1: Overview*

ITSEC (1991). *Information Technology Security Evaluation Criteria (ITSEC), Provisional Harmonised Criteria*, Version 1.2, Office for Official Publications of the European Communities, L-2985, Luxembourg, June

Muftic S. (1989). *Security Mechanisms for Computer Networks*. Chichester: John Wiley

NBS (1977). *Data Encryption Standard*, FIPS Publication 46, National Bureau of Standards, US Department of Commerce, January

NBS (1980). *DES Modes of Operation*, FIPS Publication 81, National Bureau of Standards, US Department of Commerce, December

NBS (1981). *Guidelines for Installation and Use of the Data Encryption Standard*, FIPS Publication 74, National Bureau of Standards, US Department of Commerce, April

Rivest R., Shamir A. and Adleman L. (1977). *A Method for Obtaining Digital Signatures and Public-Key Cryptosystems*, MIT Laboratory for Computer Science, memo LCS/TM82

Spafford E.H. (1988). *The Internet Worm Program: An Analysis*. Purdue Technical Report CSD-TR-823, Department of Computer Sciences, Purdue University, West Lafayette, IN 47907-2004, 29 November

Stoll C. (1988). Stalking the wily hacker. *Comm. ACM*, **31**(5), 484-95.

6

Supporting services

Objectives

- to identify services which support distributed systems management
- to consider the management of business risk
- to examine auditing in distributed systems
- to discuss the particular characteristics of 'help services' and note their value
- to examine directory services and user-related management tools
- to consider operating system and language support for distributed systems management

6.1 Support service characteristics

There is little value in monitoring and controlling the operation of a distributed system, however efficient and secure, if it is unattractive or even hostile to its users. This lack of user friendliness has, in the past, been a familiar feature of stand-alone computing systems. These failings have often stemmed from over-emphasis by the operations team on the technology rather than on the computing service to be supplied. It is a problem that has been recognized and to a considerable extent countered by the improved user interfaces of workstation and personal computer based systems. But in a distributed system, where operations teams are remote from both users and their equipment, it can still be a major problem. The risks associated with poor usability can be avoided by ensuring that there are adequate supporting services.

Some of these supporting services can be provided as extensions of the tools and services required for management operations. For example, a distributed system which offers the facility for maintaining libraries of software, can down-load that software to local systems and to users' workstations, as and when required. As discussed in Section 4.7, it can be used for configuring and updating the system components. Users can take advantage of this facility to draw upon libraries of applications software. Both users and system managers require the support of version control disciplines to ensure that they are not attempting to configure interactions with and between incompatible versions of software. This compatibility can extend to ensuring that they are not surprised by unexpected changes in the configuration of their user interfaces.

Closely allied to software management and maintenance are the support services for licence control. Distributed systems offer the potential for all system users to share common code (as well as access common data) as corporate resources. However, the suppliers of that code (or data) are less enthusiastic about such open access. Their need is to derive income from their products through licensing and this income should be commensurate with the use of the software. There are two extreme solutions. One is to provide only a set of single licences assigned either by user or by processing element. This is a regime which fails to capitalize on the merits of distribution. The other is to offer a corporate licence. If the licence price were to be determined by the number of employees who could potentially use the software, it could make some specialist packages appear prohibitively expensive. Distribution is leading to software providers offering access control software to limit the number of licensed users or the number of concurrently operational copies of the software.

There are other system support tools and services that are not strictly part of management tasks associated directly with system operations, but whose availability and use can make a dramatic difference to the efficiency

of the system's users. They can add materially to the quality of system operation and hence to its cost-effectiveness. They include user support services
such as help services and directories which are of direct value to those whose
business activities require them to employ information technology systems
as a feature of their normal daily activity. They are of equal value to those
whose task it is to operate, administrate and manage the information
technology environment. These supporting tools are especially needed in the
distributed processing environment with its added complexity. Some management and operational situations will occur sufficiently rarely that a measure
of support will always be welcome. The services are of particular value in
minimizing the impact of staff turnover. Changes of task responsibilities and
exposure to different experiences within different parts of the distributed
system cause managers and operators to be unfamiliar with the system as a
whole.

In addition, there are supporting services that are specifically of value
to managers in helping them with the organization and planning aspects of
their work. They include:

- Performance measurement and its modelling
- System audit and accountability
- Risk assessment and management
- User administration

together with the general system support for management available from
operating systems platforms and the languages used to effect system control.

The purpose of this chapter is to describe these supporting services to
show how they make for effective management. Although support for
modelling and measuring performance is regarded as a supporting service,
the reader is reminded that, because of its relevance to the topic of performance management, the tools which support performance measurement and
modelling were discussed in Chapter 4. The remaining supporting services
discussed here fall into three broad categories. In the first are the services for
risk analysis and auditing, which are needed as part of the planning and
organizing aspects of management. In the second category are help and
directory services and those features which configure the user's interface
and generally support the user and the manager's operational needs. The third
category includes the support provided at the system level and is generally of
value to system programmers.

6.2 Business risk management

When the subject of risk, its assessment and management, was introduced in
Chapter 3, two types of risk were identified, *security* risk and *business* risk.

The former was considered in the previous chapter, which looked at security risk resulting from failures of system availability, integrity or confidentiality, all of which can affect an operational system. This section considers business risk.

Business risk may result in either a loss or a gain to the enterprise. It is a matter for investigation whenever an enterprise considers whether to procure a new system or to enhance an existing one. There is a risk resulting from uncertainty in the cost of procurement or, even, that the system will fail to function according to specification. This may be offset by the possibility of gain through savings and increased productivity.

There are two main components of business risk management as they relate to the procurement or enhancement of distributed systems. They are benefit related and cost related. A project, however successful it might be technically, could fail to deliver the benefits which were projected. The effect on the projected net benefits caused by factors such as lower (or higher) projected gains in productivity has to be analysed to establish the level of benefit-related risks and to determine their sensitivity to perturbations and to critical factors in any project.

Cost-related risk is concerned with such issues as whether a project will overrun its schedule or budget. It is affected by three principal factors: size, structure and degree of technical complexity. Size, whether measured in person-hours, the number of intended users, the number of separate organizations and their locations, or the number of systems with which the system under consideration is to interface, is relatively easy to quantify. Structure concerns the qualitative aspects of a system. For example, is the system novel or is it an upgrade using existing and familiar technology? Are there new functions to be performed, requiring system users or operators to make procedural changes? How strong is user commitment to the project? What degree of flexibility has been given to the project team? These and similar questions can be readily asked and sometimes the answers can be straightforward. However, the greater the structural change, the greater the risk of failure. Risks associated with technical complexity relate to the type and mix of system hardware and the range of interfaces that have to be supported within the system. They also relate to the types of system and application software, the range of programming languages in use and the technical competence of the users and their support organizations.

All these are examples of factors which management must consider. They can be developed as a questionnaire (or checklist) to which managers should respond in order to make at least a rough estimate of the level of risk of technical failure. A risk assessment questionnaire, based upon these factors is provided as part of the management checklist in Appendix A. It is derived from a similar questionnaire devised for centralized computer systems (McFarlan, 1981). Its aim is to help the user to look objectively at the risk of failure of a project resulting from the above factors (size, structure, and technical complexity). If there is a mismatch between any of these factors and the capability of the enterprise, then there is a significant risk that the project will fail. The questionnaire can be tailored according to the specific characteristics of a given enterprise. In practice it has been found particularly useful in pinpointing likely risk areas and in ensuring that the relevant risk factors are considered methodically.

Whereas the introduction of distributed systems increases the cost-related risk because of increased complexity combined with technical innovation, some aspects of distribution actually reduce risk. After it has become operational, a distributed processing environment provides the flexibility with which to respond to changing technical needs by allowing the introduction of additional resources when demand grows. It allows alternative components to be introduced and assessed, often at relatively low cost, before the enterprise commits itself to their general use. Pilot schemes, introducing single components, can easily be extended if successful or withdrawn if they fail. The introduction of additional resources is typically achieved by adding system components. This carries lower risk than adopting a policy of outright replacement. It has the further advantage that the facilities provided by the existing component can continue to be provided during a period of transition to the modified system. As a result, system users can be encouraged to make a progressive change over to the updated working environment.

6.3 Auditing and accountability

An audit is an independent examination of an enterprise's records and procedures to verify its state. The term originates from the examination of a company's financial records and procedures by an independent auditor on behalf of the shareholders. The objective of the audit in that instance is to express an opinion on the fairness with which the records represent the actual position of the company. It has been extended to include other kinds of independent examination, e.g. efficiency audits, security audits and energy use audits.

There are two main kinds of audit procedures. The first studies and evaluates internal controls. The second carries out substantive tests which validate individual transactions and records. One method of testing the validity of transactions is by examining an audit trail. This is a set of records which contains details of all the transactions affecting the organization's assets.

The term **accountability** has already been used in this book. It is now appropriate to be specific in the use of the term. Accountability is the principle that individuals should be liable to show how they have acted as stewards for assets within their control, as part of an audit. In computer systems, accountability represents the requirement that, for example, it should be possible to trace transactions back to their origins in order to verify that they were carried out by someone who was properly authorized. Accountability is a principle of internal control.

There are several legal requirements for auditing and accountability. Examples are:

- Limited companies are required to keep accounting records which give a true and fair statement of the company's position. These records are liable to inspection by external auditors.

- The UK Data Protection Act requires personal data to be protected and accesses accounted for.

- US multinational companies are subject to the Foreign Corrupt Practices Act, which requires them to demonstrate that proper internal control is being maintained.

- Contracts between companies often have audit clauses which give one company the right to audit another's records in defined circumstances relating to the contract. One such contract is a multiple user software licence agreement.

For all user actions that are subject to audit, whether they be computer transactions or requests for processing or information, there are practical consequences. For example:

- The identity of the person carrying out the action, together with the date and time of the action, must be recorded.

- A system of authorization of user actions must be in operation, backed with the assurance of system integrity.

- A long-term audit trail of the actions must be kept.

Ideally the audit trail should be immune to change. Such immutability is an aim that cannot always be achieved in practice. However, precautions can lessen the likelihood of change or loss. These can include such simple techniques as physical protection of the media and keeping back-up copies, securely stored in different locations.

Distributed systems add specific practical complexities to auditing and accountability. These include: the identification of users, most of whom will be remote from the system where the audit records are maintained; the selection of audit trail information; the integrity of accounting records; the authorization system and the audit tools themselves. Both the authorization system and the audit tools may be distributed. In the remainder of this section each of these issues is briefly explored.

The authentication of users and services was discussed in Chapter 5. In relation to auditing and accountability, user authentication must be adequately secure for the purpose of an audit trail. Where a remote system allows users to log in under a group identity, adequate information must be provided for the purpose of the local system's accounting. Most importantly, the auditors from one system must be able to recognize and understand the identities of another system's users.

Where the application user is also operating the system, the decision about what information to record can be made by him or her alone. But, there are costs involved in keeping permanent records and it is necessary to be selective. In distributed systems, the user who is required to record the information may be remote (both geographically and managerially) from the operator of the system holding the information. It is then necessary to negotiate what information will be recorded and reach binding agreements about those negotiations with all parties concerned in the audit.

Mention has been made above of the simple approaches available for preserving the immutability of audit trails and so ensuring the integrity of the records. Accounting records, as a specific example, are required to be held unchanged for long periods. The length of the term depends upon the law or contract defining the minimum retention period. In virtually all cases it is years rather than months. There are many ways of preserving the integrity of audit records from destruction or modification. Depending upon the application, paper, microfilm, magnetic media or optical recording media may be used. Factors to be considered are ease of access and security. Both access and security may be out of the direct control of the distributed system user and, in this instance, it is also necessary to negotiate about, and ensure conditions for, the integrity of stored records.

Material being archived will rarely require access and may be kept on paper or manually handled microfilm. Material requiring regular access will benefit from being held on-line with automated access. Confidentiality requires protection from modification and protection from destruction. Paper, microfilm and WORM (write once, read many) devices are difficult or impossible to modify, at least without leaving a detectable trace of the modification. They have an inherent advantage for audit records over magnetic media, which can potentially be altered whenever it is accessed.

So much for obtaining and retaining auditable data. What are the issues faced by the auditor? Auditability requires data to be retrievable and the necessary retrieval tools to be available on all systems where transactions have been recorded. Auditors need to be certain that the tools perform their intended task and this means that the tools themselves need to be tested to demonstrate their correct operation. Where the system of authorization is under the control of remote management rather than the auditor, such control must meet the quality requirements for the audit and this quality also needs to be assured.

In summary, auditing and accountability depend upon facilities such as user identification and authorization, upon audit trails and audit tools. All of these need to have assured integrity and availability. But they are not necessarily under the direct control of the organizations which depend upon them. At a minimum, it is necessary to negotiate adequate provision of these facilities and tools with every relevant agent in the system. At worst, it may be impossible to achieve an adequate level of assurance for a particular application. If this is so and audit and accountability are significant enterprise requirements, then the responsible manager must prevent use of such a system.

6.4 Help services

The principal objective of help services is to provide information to users while they are working. Help services take a number of forms. There is user support documentation in the form of user manuals. There are user advice notes, possibly about changes in system configuration or operation. Larger systems may support a help desk with staff who note users' requests and respond, either directly or by putting the user in contact with the right specialist. As systems have become more interactive, the users' support documentation can be found on-line and can be directly interrogated by the user while working at the keyboard.

6.4.1 Forms of help information

Help information may be in the form of general advice, providing a system overview and tutorial material. Alternatively, it may take the form of detailed explanations of operating system commands with examples of the use of system command languages. In an environment where there is a significant amount of program development, this latter form of help can extend to help in the use of programming languages. Help services can provide system status information, advising users of impending shutdown of system facilities and the provision of new features. Yet another use of help services is to provide a checklist, for use by help desk operators so that they can structure the advice they give to users.

Each sort of help facility has its own requirements. The facilities which the help service must support are determined by the frequency of demand for each service and by the specific selection of options which the system provides. The list of help facilities (as has been hinted above and illustrated in Figure 6.1) may include:

- An on-line manuals service
- A tutorial or training system
- Context-sensitive help
- User-sensitive help
- Expert system help for technical users
- User extendable help systems

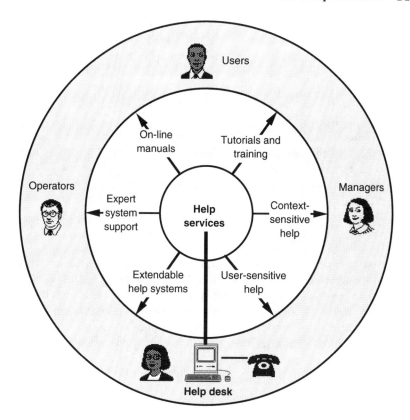

Figure 6.1 User, operator and manager help services.

Examples of these are given below.

The on-line manuals service is perhaps the simplest form of help service. Yet this should not be treated as just a direct transfer of the written manual to the user's terminal screen. The structuring of the help information is significant. Older on-line manuals services used tree structures which matched the command structures for which they were providing help. The drawback to this approach was that common commands could be buried deep within the tree and therefore hard to find. Also, items logically related to each other in some specific context can often be distantly separated in a static tree of documentation. In order to gain help on a particular topic in such a hierarchically structured help system, the enquirer needed to know (or guess) the command required with all its sub-commands. This problem is bad enough in isolated systems but becomes acute when different systems are interconnected and the range of applications and commands increases. Better techniques are becoming available. These are based upon advances such as hypertext styles of information organization; multi-level help services where users select levels appropriate to their experience; and full text databases of help information. These last named come complete with indexes and concordances backed up by an information retrieval system (Horton, 1991). An extension of the on-line help desk is the on-line expert system, which can provide specialist support for the user's on-line query. It is currently available only in specialist systems but surely set to become more widely available.

Tutorial and training systems have long been regarded as of importance to users of information technology systems. Now they can be provided on-line as extensions to on-line help. They provide structured walk-throughs of typical user activities. Smart training systems can score the user's progress and offer advice, at least when common difficulties are encountered.

6.4.2 User factors

The best sort of help systems are those whose response is sensitive to the context in which the user is operating when help is sought. These systems have an awareness of the user's current purpose and provide help in terms of what the user is trying to do. This is not easy in a distributed processing environment and it is important to temper euphoria generated by some well chosen examples in the technical literature with the realization that user context may be difficult to maintain when interacting across several systems. It can be virtually impossible for a help system to detect some semantic mistakes even when the statements are syntactically correct.

Different users have different levels of experience. A helpful reminder to the expert may be incomprehensible to the novice. At the other end of the scale, the detailed explanation available to the novice may be so voluminous that the expert feels that the help so provided has become a hindrance and is taking up valuable time. The answer is user-sensitive help. Different levels of detail are available depending on the level of experience of the user. These may be parameterized so that the user can set the level of help that is sought. They may be organized hierarchically so that initial help is terse (benefiting the expert) but successively more detailed levels of assistance are provided by continuing a series of help requests. The really smart help service will respond to the user by judging the level of expertise from noting requests for assistance and recording the accuracy of user actions.

Not all user problems can necessarily be identified when a help system is first set up. As novel problems arise they need to be solved by recourse to experts. The users themselves can become expert in some aspect of the system. There are therefore benefits to be gained from user-extendable help systems. And where the help system can be customized and extended by the user (e.g. to add comments relevant to the user's own experiences), then means must be found to publicize these extensions for the benefit of other users in the community.

6.4.3 Problems of distribution

There are many help services available, usually provided as support applications in commercial systems. Most provide on-line manuals but few of the other possible facilities are listed here. Some systems address the requirements and provide solutions separate from the help system, for example, sharing experiences among the user community by conferencing. What is relevant to the argument of this chapter is the particular value of and necessity for such services when the information processing system is distributed. Distribution creates several problems for the designers of help systems, particularly when trying to provide help across heterogeneous systems. A user running an interactive session from one system to access the resources of another system will need access to the help services of both systems and of the intervening communication environment. This need can generate particular difficulties where the style of help service supported by all these systems is radically different. At the simplest, the user may only be using facilities on a remote system as if making a (remote) procedure call. When help is needed, it has to be obvious to the distributed system, that help information has to be imported from the remote system in a form recognized and handled by the local help service. Where one help service provides a degree of sophistication, for example by offering user-sensitive or context-sensitive help, the other must be able to respond with a matching level of context or sensitivity to the user's expertise. Even this simple illustration shows the value of help services agreeing to common standards. As a minimum they should use a standardized document interchange format.

Where a number of (remote) services are being used together to accomplish an information processing objective, there may be local knowledge of a user's interactions but the local help service will be sensitive only to the context of the local interaction. It may be unable to relate to what the user is doing elsewhere or to the overall context in which the user is operating. To provide context sensitive help in a truly distributed processing environment is possible if the local help service is supplemented with specific, distributed application help support and the local help service is provided with a reference to the application's overall context.

One major complication, when operating in a world-wide distributed processing environment, is the language barrier. International networked services need multilingual help facilities, able to be selected by the user. Another complication is that not every user can be an expert in using every one of the distributed systems that are accessible. Thus, even if a user is an expert in the use of some of the systems, that user may well be a comparative novice when, very occasionally, using another system. Management activity is no exception. Some components of the distributed processing environment will be extremely familiar to systems programmers, operators and their managers. Yet interaction between systems will require these people to be aware of what is happening in remote systems, some of which could fall within the responsibility of other parts of the management hierarchy or even reside within other business enterprises. In all these cases, the level of user expertise should not be treated as a global parameter but should be dependent upon the users who are using the distributed system and upon their activity history in using the system.

One help feature that has proved its value in computer networks is **help shadowing**. This is a labour intensive service in which a human operator watches everything done by a user, steps in to comment when errors are made and explains what might be wrong. An example of this occurred during the Apollo 11 moon landing, when the system programmer for the lunar module, shadowing the actions of its crew, was able to help them override false abort signals generated by a programming mistake, thus avoiding mission failure. This technique was available in the ARPANET from some participating networked computer systems. Its availability, even as a gesture, proved invaluable in the early days of that network in getting people to adopt to a novel working environment containing many unfamiliar computer systems.

6.4.4 Other factors

Other features of help services which require a deeper level of appreciation in distributed systems are:

- Maintaining help information up to date
- Support of security policies by help systems
- Speed of response

It is important for management to recognize that help information needs to be thorough and up to date. This consideration impacts the way in which the help systems are designed. Information must be gathered regarding manuals, overview and tutorial material, system status information, users' experience and users' sessions. The different types of help service facilities have different timeliness requirements. Some configurations change only over periods of months, others over periods as short as a few seconds. Such considerations impact the decisions to be made in procuring and operating the system. It should go without saying that help information must be kept up to date and consistent with the documentation which is available in printed form.

The help system must not assist an intruder to compromise the security or integrity of a system. Information must be restricted to a user's authorized scope. This can be a particular problem for distributed systems when taken in conjunction with the help service requirement for remote managers and operators. Managers and operators may have a justifiable need to know significant details about the operational characteristics of systems that are remote from them. They therefore need help services that can offer a level of system insight and awareness which must be denied to the normal user.

If the help service is too slow to respond, its users will be less ready to use it. The minimum speed needed for on-line help facilities must match the expected response characteristics of other features of interactive systems. Ideally, there should be a prompt response in fractions of a second with follow-up, if required, in a time less than the order of five to ten seconds. If there is a significant amount of inter-system data transmission on slow networks, lack of responsiveness can be a serious problem. Even when data is provided quickly, the users' perceptions are of a slow response if the organization of the help service is such that it requires them to step through several pages of data to get the information they require.

6.5 Directories and related information services

The objective of a directory service is to provide information to users and applications about the location of entities in a distributed system. These entities can be hardware, software, processes, services or information. Related services provide information which is also needed by users and applications throughout the (distributed) system and which either is not or, by its nature cannot be, 'hard-wired' into the resources. Examples are hardware details, version numbers, cost of application functions and services, access methods, service descriptions and similar service-specific information.

Networked information service solutions exist as research vehicles, commercial products, and even international standards. The international standard CCITT X.500 (ISO/IEC 9594) defines a directory service for use by 'OSI applications, OSI management processes, other OSI layer entities, and telecommunications services'. It has global scope, with no consistency restrictions, and gives results that are independent of the user's identity and location. It provides user friendly naming (if desired), and name-to-address mapping. X.500 is not intended to be used for storing any other information. This is not prohibited, but the design assumes a considerably higher rate of queries than of updates and so may be inappropriate when data is changing rapidly.

It is useful to distinguish three different types of directory (or quasi directory) services. These are known colloquially as:

- White pages
- Yellow pages
- Trader services

By analogy with the familiar telephone directory, white page services provide a name-to-address mapping. Yellow page services provide a mapping between an application function (or service) and a name optionally with automatic white page addressing services appended. Several distributed systems projects have built directory or yellow pages services (though not necessarily to the X.500 specification). Examples are Athena (Rosenstein *et al.*, 1988), Amoeba (Steiner, 1987) and Mayflower (Bacon and Hamilton, 1987).

The ODP (Open Distributed Processing) standards complement the need for directories and related information services by the use of **traders**. These act as brokerage services matching the needs of clients to the services offered by vendors. They provide a sort of *computer dating* agency whereby a resource can advertise its readiness to provide a service and a client can make requests for services of identified characteristics. Traders are intended to be organized to cope with relatively frequent changes both to the availability of services and to the location of those services. Each trader is postulated as having a limited (geographic) coverage. All traders are expected to know of other traders in their vicinity so that requests which cannot immediately be matched can be passed on to others. The trader function is supported by protocols for offering and requesting services, for registering traders and for inter-trader communication. The interaction of clients and servers with traders is shown diagrammatically in Figure 6.2.

The directory service is probably the most important of the distributed system's supporting information services. The system designer must decide

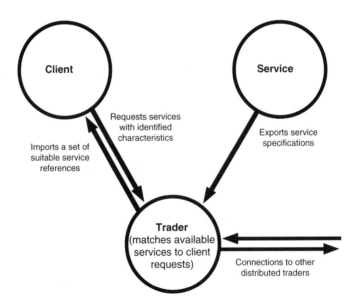

Figure 6.2   Organization and operation of the trader function.

which other services are also needed and which, in terms of cost and benefits, are merely desirable. The requirements for availability and reliability placed on each information service must be specified, together with the means by which they are achieved.

Some systems make considerable use of networked information services to provide location-independent operation and configuration data. These contain such valuable data as encrypted user passwords, network host addresses, boot information for diskless workstations, etc. A well known example is the Sun Network Information Service. Some networking systems (for example, IBM's System Network Architecture) do not need equivalent networked information services because they have centralized network management.

Even if a powerful case can be made for additional information services, it may not be easy to provide the information service to networked applications. The main problem is one of maintaining consistency. If the scope of a networked information service is purely local, then users and their applications will need some way of getting information about external systems. If the scope is global, the service could be easy to use but potentially very difficult to maintain in a consistent state. Indeed, consistency of information is always likely to be a problem. Information service users need guidance to indicate the possibility of information being out of date. One method is to provide each piece of data with a time-stamp to show when it was last updated. Where total consistency cannot be continuously guaranteed, a fall-back procedure must be used to renew information, whenever it is found to be out of date. That is, whenever an inconsistency is detected, the user or the service which recognizes the inconsistency requests the information system to perform its updating procedures. This could happen, for example, if a trader were to advise a client to use a service which the client finds is no longer available. The client would request the trader to provide better data. This sort of technique is used extensively in the Athena managed network. As with help services, security restrictions can require that some information must have its access strictly controlled.

Maintaining secure, consistent information services in a distributed system can be expensive. They are expensive in processing time to check consistency and expensive in communication bandwidth when making enquiries and distributing updates. Unless broadcast communication techniques can be employed, update becomes a combinatorial problem. Information dissemination in systems relying upon normal point-to-point and switching techniques becomes inefficient as the systems become larger. Managers therefore need to determine whether they are prepared to tolerate some inconsistency in the information and to rely on update only when inconsistency is discovered. But they must be under no illusion that it is a decision which can be deferred. Trying to retrofit consistency into a developed distributed system can prove even more expensive than providing it at the outset.

The problem is one of scaling. In a very large distributed system such as may be required by a multinational corporation, it is not efficient to maintain all the data at one location. That would result in impossibly high communication demands upon the single system, would run the risk of total failure and would, for the very remote user, generate measurable delays in the response. Nor is it possible to consider performing committed, distributed transactions. The delays of wide-area communication would generate unacceptably long periods during which the information is inaccessible for all system users.

Fortunately, and except in truly pathological cases, large organizations are rarely inconvenienced by minor inconsistencies in replicated pieces of data at the microscopic level. It is sufficient if data is maintained sensibly consistent within a given region. Indeed the ability to maintain global state in a large system must be an illusion. The time interval between sequences of events is likely to be less than the time required to propagate the information update message throughout the distributed system's communication network. Not even high performance technology can overcome the limit to signal propagation time imposed by the finite velocity of light. The consequence for management is to require that consistency is maintained with a given level of time granularity. This time granularity does not have to be the same for all items of data but can be determined by assessing the risk to the enterprise of given items being inconsistent. Whereas the safety of a chemical plant in a chemical company may be critically dependent upon the knowledge of the quantity of reacting products derived from different process streams even on the millisecond level, the same chemical company need not know the regional disposition of its workforce any more accurately than time-scales measured in hours.

Even where data is time-stamped, there are two main ways of performing update, one pro-active, the other reactive. The pro-active method employs a set of *daemons* distributed throughout the system who regularly poll data and check its consistency. The reactive method relies on the system maintaining the data to send updates whenever items are changed. Where data is found to be inconsistent or out of date as a result of either method, then modification to ensure consistency can take place. The benefit of the reactive method is that it only generates data traffic within the system if there has been change. The merit of the pro-active method is that it provides a watch-dog which can also detect when changes have taken place even if, because of local malfunction, reactive update has not been signalled.

6.6 User-related management tools

6.6.1 User and system administration

An important factor within the administrator's support environment is the ease with which new users and new resources are added to the system and how references to departed users and obsolete equipment are removed. A directory can be regarded as a database for holding data about the system resources. Other databases can hold data about users who are registered to use the system and about the resources which they can access. Access control can be implemented through the use of access control lists or capability mechanisms. (See Chapter 8 for a further discussion.)

An information base of resources can be maintained in a similar manner. Resources which provide new services advertise their availability through the use of the trader function. Where there are few access control restrictions, one of the actions of providing a service is to offer a capability for service use. Where managers seek to impose more severe access restrictions it may be more appropriate to use explicit access control, specifically identifying those capabilities which a service shall respond to and authorizing them on a restricted basis to selected customers. In these cases, the functions of the trader service can be extended to include the checking and maintenance of access controls.

The introduction to this chapter gave software distribution and also licence management as examples of support services in distributed processing environments. One specific form of access control is that which governs the availability of software. It will be recalled that the objective of licence management is to control the use of licensed software within a network. Two types of restrictive licence are possible. In one, only specified users will be allowed to load the licensed software. This approach can use the trader function in conjunction with access control in the same manner as control is exercised over the use of any other resource. If licensed, the user is supplied with a copy of the software which is down-loaded into that user's working environment. This method of providing software has the merit of always supplying an up-to-date software version, with the caveat that users may not always want the latest version if there have been changes to the user interface and they have not yet been trained in their use.

In the other scenario, the licence limits the number of users who may have concurrent access to the software. In this instance, the licence manager must maintain a count of the current number of users. Software is only down-loaded if this number is less that the number for which the system is licensed. If this number has been reached, the user can have the option of continuing the computing session without the software or else queuing for a copy to become available. When a user finishes an instance of software use, a protocol exchange with the licence manager decrements the usage count when the down-loaded version of the software has made itself unavailable for further use. If this technique were to be applied across the whole of a large distributed system, it would suffer from the same scaling problems as does the global maintenance of distributed information. It could possibly be tolerated, because the duration that users would have to wait for the count to be updated is likely to be of the order of or less than the time taken to load a typical application package. However, if there could be significant delays, it is advisable to have a number of licence controllers located strategically within the distributed processing environment so as to reduce the delay to an acceptable level.

   Naturally the licence can be modified if new users or additional users are to be accommodated. Licence managers are likely to be used in conjunction with audit trails so that it is possible to demonstrate that the terms of the licence are being honoured.

6.6.2 The presentation interface

A distributed system has many different subsystems which may require to be administered from a number of different perspectives. The information which administrators are allowed to see and their permitted control actions depend on their roles. A single administrator may even have to perform different management roles and hence require different, tailored interfaces even when these are accessed through a single terminal.

   Administrators and operators need an interface through which to access the management facilities within a distributed system. This presentation interface enables them to perform their management function, that is, obtain information about the service they are managing, make decisions and perform control actions. Good design ensures that the presentation interface is constructed so that it is separate from the managed components themselves. Interfaces internal to the system then give access to the many components that are managed by a single administrator or operator. At present, a typical computer room can have many items of equipment from different manufacturers, each with its own operator console, each of these having its own operational style. Administration is far more convenient and efficient when operators can manage all the relevant aspects of systems under their control from a single console. The number of operators' consoles required for a distributed system can then be determined either on functional or policy grounds. It does not have to be dictated by the technology. With the management interface separated from the management task, it can readily be tailored to the individual's needs.

   The overall function of the human interface is to translate management information from the format convenient for internal use into a format suitable for people to understand, and to translate commands and requests generated by a human into the form appropriate to the service being managed. The complexity of large distributed systems demands that the human interface is carefully designed to provide administrators with the assistance necessary to enable them to perform their functions.

   There is a wide range of users who need management information and there is a large quantity of information typically produced by monitoring. This information is filtered and processed into a format best suited to the needs of the particular user. Users need to select the information they require and specify how it should be displayed. The information needs to be grouped into sensibly sized 'chunks' so that it can be readily understood. Research indicates that users should be presented with no more than about seven pieces of information at any one time if they are not to become overloaded (Miller, 1975). Each piece of management information should be structured so that it provides a mechanism to access further, related and more specific pieces of information. A graphical format is well suited to humans, for displaying many aspects of management data, for example, mimic diagrams to represent physical configuration and pie charts or histograms for performance statistics. In consequence, there is increasing use of high resolution graphics workstations with a mouse pointing device for the management system's human interface.

Because many of these facilities have a very significant influence upon system operation and can result in a breach of security or system failure if misused, the human interface should make use of user authentication to control access to the management operations. Ordinary users do not need, and therefore should not have access to, the same information and functions as administrators and operators. One important security feature of the interface should be the ability to detect when a workstation, used for management purposes, has been left unattended. If this is found to be the case, the management system should be able to revoke any authorizations so as to prevent other people from masquerading as an operator or system administrator.

The speed of operation of distributed systems and the complexity of information for analysis is such that administrators can benefit from having automated tools to help them perform their management functions. Examples have already been given where expert systems can aid in decision making. Database management systems, which hold the management information about the system and upon which the manager can make arbitrary queries, provide another valuable component of the systems management tool-set. All these facilities need to offer the administrator or operator a coherent human interface. It should be based on the administrator's normal office workstation and operating system and should allow, for example, that a familiar and preferred (screen) editor be available for manipulating management data.

As the management of systems becomes more automated and more complex, there is a danger of diluting operators' skills. Operators may not be able to obtain sufficient practice in coping with problems when they do arise. It is not practical to allow them to practise on live systems as this would cause disruption. Instead they should be provided with simulations on which they can develop their skills in dealing rapidly with unusual situations. This is a similar approach to that taken by airlines, which make use of flight simulators for flight deck training. The development of the simulation may also serve to validate the operator procedures, and indicate inconsistencies in procedures or identify procedures that are inconvenient to use.

6.7 Support environments

Two features have not so far been discussed although they underpin all of system operation and are required by the system's programmers. They are the operating systems themselves and programming languages. Some of the features of the support environment considered above extend the facilities of the operating systems of the computers which are a part of the distributed processing environment.

6.7.1 Operating systems

The objective of an operating system is to provide the interface between software and hardware, and support the run-time environment of applications and their users. Hardware interfaces include disk drivers, network protocol handlers and memory managers. The operating system provides abstract interfaces to the hardware, often adding value by giving improved reliability and efficiency. Most network operating systems support concurrency, either by providing asynchronous access to system services or by the provision of suitable scheduling services for multi-tasking.

Two important requirements of distributed systems permeate right down to the operating system level. The first is that all operating system modules should provide a management interface, enabling them to be managed remotely. The second is that the operating system must be secure to the maximum level of security required in the system. As Chapter 5 insisted, it is most important that management, especially security management, is not allowed to compromise the security of the system and its information.

Operating systems in a distributed processing environment need to be flexible, to support the varied demands of the applications. They need to support published interfaces to allow interworking with heterogeneous systems. This flexibility can be obtained by having an open structure. Ideally, a small kernel containing hardware drivers, a complete set of elements providing inter-process communication, and a process scheduling capability are required. Other operational support functions are provided by configurable modules residing above the kernel (but within the operating system). If such an open structure is not possible (and many current operating systems would require extensive redesign), then it should at least be modular and extensible.

Where there are fast inter-computer communications, these operate effectively if they are backed up with simple, fast inter-process communications mechanisms. Typical of these are datagram services, which work well where communications are relatively error free and sequentiality of delivery can be assured. Inter-process communication should, however, support sufficient functionality to be usable by all applications (for example supporting the selection of incoming messages by message type or source address) and capable of interacting over long-distance networks which can be more prone to errors and even to message loss. Critical services must not only be fast from the user's perspective, allowing short response times, but efficient from the system's perspective.

A flexible scheduling scheme needs to be implemented because of the dynamic nature of the environment, and to support real-time applications. Some applications may require a distributed scheduling scheme though, in the present state of the art, these are feasible only in carefully designed, closely coupled systems. They require the support of commitment and concurrency management.

Operating systems may support various kinds of transparencies. Location transparency is commonly supported, making the user unaware of where files are located, for example. Even so, management services must be able to override transparencies if they are preventing access to specific resources or hiding information crucial to management operations.

UNIX is becoming well established as a multi-user, multi-tasking operating system which supports distributed processing activity. It is open in terms of common interfaces, but not open in structure. In spite of its virtues, this makes it somewhat inflexible and therefore not ideally suited to supporting distributed systems. Several projects have built systems retaining many of the desirable features of UNIX but with more open structures. Although many of these began as research projects (Bacon and Hamilton, 1988; Cheriton, 1984; Jones and Rashid, 1986; Mullender *et al.*, 1990) some systems are transferring to the market-place to provide UNIX-like user and programming interfaces while adding full distributed system and networking capabilities. These often offer object-oriented features and provide in-built encapsulation, protection, integrated storage and language-level invocation of distributed processing.

6.7.2 Programming languages

The objective of using a computer language is to describe something in a way that is specific, unambiguous, and can be interpreted by a computer, but which is sufficiently similar to natural language to be created and understood by a human. Programming languages are used to describe the execution of applications. They are used in distributed systems management to create manageable executing entities (often by providing libraries of management routines) and to specify the corresponding managing entities. Specification languages are needed to describe the configuration aspects of a computer system or activity. These are clearly important for distributed systems management. Specification languages may also be used to describe other system properties such as management policy, but the capture of management policy in formal language is only now being researched.

There are two main considerations in distributed systems which influence the programming environment: the need to accommodate hetero-geneous languages; and the need to accommodate changes to the system. The diversity of the software components found in large distributed systems implies that appropriate, state-of-the-art programming languages should be used. For instance, high-level procedural languages (C, Pascal, Modula-2) are used for real-time control and monitoring; object-oriented languages (Smalltalk, C++) for man–machine interfaces, artificial intelligence languages (Prolog, LISP) for the expert systems and knowledge bases needed for the advanced intelligent (that is, decision-making) components; FORTRAN and the ubiquitous (though unfashionable) COBOL for existing numerical analysis packages and data manipulation programs. Although the rewards are great, the use of heterogeneous programming languages exacerbates the problems of integration, as they may make use of incom-patible communication mechanisms and data representations.

There is the need to integrate components implemented using various programming languages. There are several possible approaches to accom-modating heterogeneity. They include:

- Use of configuration languages
- Linking mechanisms
- Shadow components
- Interface specification languages

Use of configuration languages

A recommended approach to integrating heterogeneous software com-ponents which communicate and interact in a distributed system, is the use of a configuration language. An example is provided by the Conic environment (Kramer and Magee, 1985; Magee *et al.*, 1989). Conic con-figuration facilities support both the building of a system and its subsequent dynamic modification to permit reconfiguration for operational changes and evolutionary changes incorporating new functionality. The configuration approach involves specifying a system in terms of the instances of com-ponents, the interconnection between component interfaces, and the map-ping of software to hardware. The emphasis is on the structural relationships between components. This provides an abstraction in which changes to a system, arising from adding or removing component types, instances and interconnections, can be easily understood and formulated.

A language-based configuration view simplifies the specification, validation and modification of software for operational distributed systems. Software configuration can be specified in terms of the structural relationship of components within a system. The component programming level, on the other hand, is concerned with the implementation of component types in terms of the algorithms and data structures they encapsulate and the particular programming language used to implement the component. A clear separation between these two levels is advocated. Not only does a separate configuration language provide a simplified abstraction of a distributed system for its description, construction and evolution, but it also provides a unifying framework for integrating heterogeneous software components and provides a suitable level of abstraction in which to reason about component compatibility in terms of interface types and behaviour.

Dynamic configuration permits the system to be changed without shutting it down. This facilitates incremental changes, essential for the evolution of large systems, to be applied to a running system. Support for dynamic reconfiguration is particularly important for operational systems which cannot be shut down in order to make changes. Changes to be applied to a system may be evolutionary, that is, modification of a function provided by the system or by extension and the introduction of new functions. There may be a change in implementation due to new technology, improved implementation techniques or to provide redundancy. In addition, the system must cater for operational changes such as replacing failed components or moving components to improve performance. It is certainly advantageous if the system is capable of supporting such change dynamically, without interrupting the processing of those parts of the system that are unaffected.

A configuration language should be declarative. If configuration statements are embedded within a procedural program, the current state of the configuration depends on the current state of the program and that is not easily determined. A declarative specification is more amenable to analysis and validation, with decisions about the order in which operations are performed being left to the system. There are two paradigms for configuration specification languages:

- A graphical language based on icons, menus and pointing devices emphasizes the spatial relationships between components and provides an ideal human interface for specifying configurations and topological relationships.

- A textual language (the traditional approach) is more amenable to machine manipulation. It is better for expressing very complicated interconnection patterns and repetitive instances such as arrays of identical components.

Linking foreign procedures

It may be possible to call procedures written in another language such as C or FORTRAN from a system component. This works only if the foreign language is sufficiently similar to the native language. It requires a standard procedure calling convention in terms of how parameters are passed to and from the procedure. The foreign procedures must reside in the same address space as the native component and so are linked in with the code of the component. It is not possible to call remote procedures on different machines. Another disadvantage is that parameters must have the same representation in both procedures. This approach is rather limited in its applicability.

Shadow components

Many languages and packages have a built in run-time environment, which could not easily be modified to incorporate standard communication primitives to enable components implemented in these languages to communicate with the rest of the system. Often the only interaction with the external environment is via standard operating system interfaces such as files or terminals. The solution is to provide a shadow process which translates the standard communications interface into local operating system calls.

Interface specification language (ISL)

An ISL provides a common language for specifying the interface to a component in a way that is independent of the programming language used to implement the component (Hayes and Schlichting, 1987). In general an ISL includes a data typing language to define the information transferred across the interface; a means of defining named interaction points, such as exit ports and entry ports of an interface; and specification of the interaction protocol to be used.

Although no commercial products are yet available which provide all the facilities described above, the area of programming for distributed systems is fast-changing. A more detailed discussion of the topic is to be found in Sloman *et al.* (1991).

6.8 The automation of support services

At the beginning of this chapter, the prospect was raised of management without support providing users with a sterile and unattractive distributed system. All of the aspects of support discussed above have their counterparts in centralized processing environments, but their value is particularly evident when the processing is distributed. One element of that support can be singled out above all others: it is the integrated automation of support as part of the distributed system's repertoire of services. The diversity of distributed systems coupled with their speed of operation makes it essential that as many as possible of the user and management support services should be automated. The capability to do this is just now becoming within the state of the art. It depends for its success on the knowledge and experience of managers being encoded into management knowledge bases.

Support services themselves require support and that is most easily supplied when the services are also automated. As experience (relating to a particular enterprise; to its distributed processing environment; to user needs) grows, so management knowledge can be refined and updated. This brings with it requirements for knowing where information is stored (a directory service) and for the ability to maintain knowledge consistency throughout the environment. As has been demonstrated, ensuring the global consistency of that knowledge on a microscopic level can never be assured fully. However, by recognizing the natural management structuring inherent in any large system, sufficient regional or departmental consistency can be maintained to make automated support systems viable.

Summing up

- Support services, which can readily be provided in stand-alone systems, need to have their facilities augmented to be effectively incorporated in distributed systems.

- Information which is distributed needs distributed services to maintain its consistency.

- Managers must decide the extent to which they and their systems can tolerate 'out of date' system information and be prepared to commit considerable resources as the price for maintaining consistency at all times.

- Auditing is complicated by distribution unless the auditors can have a unified view of the distributed data to which the audit refers.

- Because of the diversity of applications and systems, distributed help systems benefit users if they can be operated at various levels of expertise.

References

Bacon J.M. and Hamilton K.G. (1988). Distributed computing with RPC: the Cambridge approach. In *Proc. IFIP Conf. on Distributed Processing*, October 1987. (Barton *et al.*, eds.). Amsterdam: North-Holland

Cheriton D. (1984). The V kernel: a software base for distributed systems. *IEEE Software*, 1(2)

Hayes R. and Schlichting R. (1987). Facilitating mixed language programming in distributed systems. *IEEE Trans. on Software Engineering*, 13(12)

Horton K.D. (1991). *The Use of Conceptual Graphs to Augment an Information Retrieval System*. PhD thesis, Imperial College, London

Jones M.B. and Rashid R.F. (1986). Mach and matchmaker, kernel and language support for object-oriented distributed systems. *ACM SIGPLAN Notices*, 21(11), 67–77

Kramer J. and Magee J. (1985). Dynamic configuration for distributed systems. *IEEE Trans. on Software Engineering*, 11(4), 424–36

Magee J., Kramer J. and Sloman M. (1989). Constructing distributed systems in Conic. *IEEE Trans. on Software Engineering*, 15(6), 663–75

McFarlan F.W. (1981). Portfolio approach to business systems. *Harvard Business Rev.*, September/October

Miller G.A. (1975). *The Psychology of Communication*, 2nd edn. New York: Basic Books

Mullender S.J. *et al.* (1990). Amoeba: A distributed operating system for the 1990s. *IEEE Computer*, 23(5), 44–53

Rosenstein M., Geer D.E. and Levine P.J. (1988). The Athena service management system. *Proc. Winter 1988 Usenix Conf.*, Dallas

Sloman M., Kramer J., Magee J. and Butryn P. (1991). Software configuration techniques in operational systems. In *Advances in Manufacturing and Automation Systems* (Leondes C.T., ed.). New York: Academic Press

Steiner J. (1987). *Amoeba Programmer's Manual*. Vrije Universiteit, Amsterdam

7

Installation, operations and maintenance

Objectives

- to review the operational aspects of planning, procuring, testing and maintaining an installation
- to identify a set of pre-tender actions in drawing up a list of suppliers who could tender for the supply of a managed distributed system
- to consider the special features of acceptance tests and how the tests may be organized
- to note the value of having libraries of tests which can be used for acceptance test and, later, for operational checks
- to identify the value of documentation and of having appropriate system manuals available

7.1 Introduction

An enterprise owning a system as significant as a network of computers should always have a proper plan of campaign for its installation and continued operation. Having a plan is part of the management requirement and putting the plan into effect is part of management activity. The first step in the activity is to convince corporate management of the value not only of a distributed processing strategy but also of the necessity of ensuring that it is a managed distributed system. This aspect of management has already been covered in earlier chapters.

This chapter reviews the operational aspects of planning, procuring, testing and maintaining an installation. This four-fold set of activities presents an idealized view of the procurement cycle for distributed processing environments. It represents an approach in which systems are developed in 'green field' locations. However, distributed processing most frequently comes into being through the accretion of component parts such as networks, processing components and computing services, which are added over time. Distributed systems seldom spring into being fully formed. In this more common scenario the activities of planning, procuring, testing and maintaining happen all the time, one overlapping with another, as systems evolve and pass through the various stages of the procurement cycle. Notwithstanding this fact that systems evolve, the discussion of each aspect begins by maintaining the fiction of a 'green field' development. This allows each of the activities to be considered in turn with discussion of the management issues as the system progresses from requirement to full operation. When that has been done, the additional factors which need to be considered when a system configuration develops through evolution are highlighted.

7.2 Installation

Table 7.1 lists the main activities of the planning and procurement phases of an installation. Pre-tender action focuses on two items. The first item is to get to know what is on the market and who can supply equipment. Distributed processing and computer networking are fast-developing fields. New suppliers and new equipment appear frequently. An enterprise needs to decide whether it has the expertise and resources to undertake this survey of suppliers and their products by itself or to call upon specialist consultants. The second item is to decide whether to opt for a single system supplier or to have the various components supplied separately. Matters to consider are network design, component supply, component installation and overall project management. If a system is to be assembled from equipment supplied by a range of vendors, two factors need to be born in mind. The first is to select

Table 7.1 Planning and procurement.

Pre-tender actions
Developing a supplier short list
Supplier selection
Acceptance criteria
Planning for operation
Operator familiarization
Keeping users informed

common standards for the system and ensure that the system components conform to the selected standards so that there is an initial presumption that they can inter-operate. The second factor is to note that, where different suppliers are involved, there has to be a procedure for allocating responsibility or blame if the system does not function to specification. This is a consequence of the strong interaction and coupling between distributed system components. Contracts for this type of system require more work because they have to specify and demonstrate what is expected at the interfaces between the vendors.

With this information it should be possible to draw up a short list of vendors to whom to issue an invitation to tender. Obvious factors to consider are price and performance. With more suppliers coming into the market, competition increases, and these two factors offer less differentiation. It may be more important that one organization can supply all of the components as a package. This enables an enterprise to avoid the 'do it yourself' approach. Where there is perceived merit in placing the order with different specialists, an important factor is the ability of different organizations to interwork.

No less important in establishing a short list is to consider the experience of contractors and (in these days of mobile specialists) their staff. Questions to be asked, even at the short-listing stage, include:

- Does the supplier provide adequate training as part of the package? Distributed systems are complex to manage; they have more modes of operation (and failure) than stand-alone computers or even remote access systems.

- What approach is adopted with respect to testing and demonstrating that the system meets its specification?

- Does the supplier have adequate demonstration and test equipment to mount a convincing demonstration and provide a viable training environment?

Some suppliers will offer quality assurance to one of the recognized norms, BS 5750 or AQAP 13. Such an offer is a bonus for any installation which is to form a strategic component of an enterprise's computing inventory. This is especially the case when some of its components (particularly its networking infrastructure, that is, cables and optical fibres) will have a long in-service life. Where quality assurance is offered, the potential supplier's quality plan should identify the procedures for pre-and post-delivery checks together with provision of test plans.

Documentation is vitally important. The contract should specify full documentation as one of the requirements to be met by a supplier. This will detail documentation for cable routes, the location of equipment and its inter-connectivity, suitable component labelling for hardware, and records of all tests.

These are all matters which should influence any invitation to tender and the criteria for selection. Most enterprises are sufficiently familiar with tender specifications that legal aspects of the contract are readily covered. But distributed processing and distributed systems management are relatively unfamiliar to contracts departments and technical assistance may well be needed, including the precise technical specification of equipment. Most importantly, a condition of the contract should include a full specification of acceptance criteria. This is not trivial. The complexity of distributed processing renders it difficult to determine when a set of tests is complete. Testing each component will determine that it works in a satisfactory, stand-alone manner. However, it does not demonstrate that it works as a component of a system or that the system works as a whole. The complexity of large systems can be such that the multiplicity of system interactions make total system testing an impractical proposition within any reasonable time-scale. Therefore, it may be more appropriate to link system acceptance criteria with system maintenance. Once a system appears to be operational, any subsequent shortcoming can be handled under a suitable maintenance contract. This can be invoked to remedy defects which show up after the system has been accepted. If this strategy is adopted, the main acceptance criteria to be covered contractually are those which ensure that each component meets its specification, both in behaviour and performance, and that it interacts in a correct and consistent manner with neighbouring components. These are the minimum criteria which give the basis for a viable distributed system and allow operation to start. The subject of testing is developed in more detail in Section 7.3. The impact upon maintenance is considered in Section 7.6.

Where the system is to be composed of components from a number of vendors, the purchasing enterprise is well advised to appoint an overall management team. This may be supplied through a further contract or the team can be drawn from the purchaser's own resources. Each vendor's components can be independently subjected to acceptance tests. It is the responsibility of the overall management team to conduct the system test and to accept the system.

Many of the activities of supplier selection are similar to those of establishing a short list from the initial field of enquiries. Further factors which will influence a decision when there are a number of nearly equivalent contenders include:

- Experience of the supplier
- Availability of in-depth customer support

If possible, the intending purchaser should visit a reference site to examine the quality of the basic communication infrastructure for the distributed system and find out how smoothly and efficiently the supplier adapted to the needs of the customer, especially if there were unforeseen local difficulties.

Even if the option has been taken for the supplier to manage the installation, it is still advisable to plan for some of the purchasing organization's resources to be committed to supervising the installation. Although an external organization is going to mastermind the installation, there are some things that can be done only by the purchasing organization. Significant among these is making sure that the contractor has space to accommodate the installation team and any installation equipment. Installation requires its own equipment, which may be available to the customer or may have to be brought in. Some of it, for example, drums of fibre optic or copper cables, can be large and heavy. Suitable lifting gear is needed to unload and move them to the location where they will be required. Space is needed to manipulate this equipment.

Installation of equipment in buildings requires local planning. Other matters for local attention are to negotiate with building managers. They must plan for and confirm wayleaves for cable routes, locations for equipment cabinets and even wall-mounted termination boxes, to ensure that all can be accommodated. Those responsible for the installation should establish a proper liaison mechanism to note, respond to and resolve local difficulties speedily and as they arise. Delay during installation results in cost incurred by the supplier. If problem resolution is not expedited, these costs will eventually be charged to the customer.

An organization also needs to plan how its staff will be used to supervise the tests that will lead to acceptance. It is essential to involve those who are to be system operators and even users during the planning and installation phases. They need to be made aware of system installation plans and progress at all stages. As an exercise in public relations it has the value of accustoming users to any disruption, which is bound to occur, and so enables them to forgive small inconveniences which arise. It also encourages them to prepare to make effective use of the computing and communication capability and is a precursor to providing them with the training necessary to understand the distributed processing environment.

Figure 7.1 sums up the management interactions which take place during the procurement and installation phases.

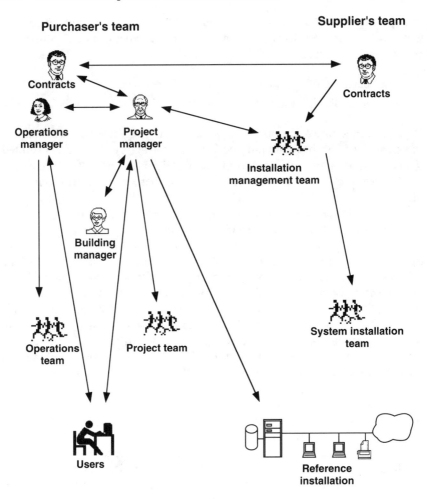

Figure 7.1   Management interactions during installation.

7.3 System integration and testing

In discussing system installation, some aspects of testing for the purpose of acceptance have already been mentioned. Those observations were primarily directed at the need for planning a test activity as an aspect of system acceptance. Testing activity and its implications are now considered in more detail.

7.3.1 Acceptance testing

Firstly, consider acceptance testing. Tests need to be performed upon system components and then upon the system as a whole. Components can be considered under the following four major headings and their sub-headings:

- The physical communication infrastructure
  - data links
  - relays, multiplexors and switches
- The communication subsystem
  - network management
  - interlinking networking subsystems
- The attachments to the communication subsystem
  - personal computers and workstations
  - departmental systems
  - specialist computers
- The distributed system services
  - the management subsystem
  - distributed applications

The above constitutes an ordered list and provides the basis for a step-by-step test and acceptance plan for system components. Computer systems can be tested in a stand-alone configuration, independently of any communication medium to which they may need to be attached. They can then be integrated and tested as components of a distributed system, once the communication attachments are made.

Distributed systems testing starts with the physical medium which will provide basic connectivity. The precise form of data link tests depends upon the physical medium used for communication. Whatever the medium, a simple connectivity test will check that there are no gross imperfections in its installation. That is, testing will demonstrate that there are no breaks in metallic conductors or optical fibres. For the latter, it will show that there are no unacceptable light losses which could have been caused by poor installation procedures leading to fibre damage.

For communication systems which rely for their operation upon the presence of active components, these components are the next to be tested. Where the topology of the communication subsystem configuration permits it, the communication subsystem can advantageously be partitioned into self-contained sub-networks. This enables testing to be simplified by attending to one sub-network at a time. A sub-network in this context is a collection of data links and their attendant interconnection components (relays, multiplexors, bridges, routers, switches, etc.) which can be configured into a network. In this way, the testing of a large communication infrastructure can be broken down into a number of more manageable sections. It has the advantage that, where resources permit, the sub-networks can be tested at the same time, so shortening the overall testing and the time-scale for acceptance.

Even these sub-networks may not be small. They may, when installed, still cover a large geographical area or occupy many floors of a large building even when the number of attached devices is not large. If that is the case then, before these components are placed *in situ*, the aim should be to gather them into one place where they can be provided with short interconnection links with all components ready to hand. They can then be given an initial test to ensure that they inter-operate according to specification. If such tests can be carried out before equipment delivery, this can ease acceptance for both supplier and customer and save long delays in testing once the components are installed. If this cannot be done, testing a local network with widely distributed components requires people to move from location to location to confirm correct component behaviour.

When the interconnection components have been tested individually they can be tested as a whole in their sub-network. Management components need to be present at this stage. Their purpose is to provide an extended test of the configuration capability of the physical communication components. During these tests, it is advisable to put only test traffic into the communication subsystem. Test traffic can be injected and monitored using one of the many test products now on the market. These cater for all of the standard data link and higher level protocols. This process is illustrated in Figure 7.2.

Once the individual sub-networks have been shown to be operating correctly (to the level possible in these tests) two options are open in the testing and system integration scheme. The first option is to add, one by one, the computing attachments that will initially reside on a sub-network, testing correct connection at each step, and treat the result as a distributed subsystem currently isolated from the rest of the distributed system. Option two is to leave the computing components unattached and join the individual sub-networks together. For the purpose of this discussion, the second of these two alternatives is selected, the addition of computing equipment being discussed later. The main issue in connecting networks in this way is to be able to demonstrate that interworking is proceeding correctly and that the sub-network segments which were managed in isolation can now be managed cooperatively. Note that some of the sub-networks which become joined in this manner may include segments of the public network. These will in general be managed by third parties. The ability to exercise (even limited) control over these third-party networks depends upon the policy of the public network supplier but it is clearly desirable if the distributed system is to be managed as a single entity. However, the communication facilities of

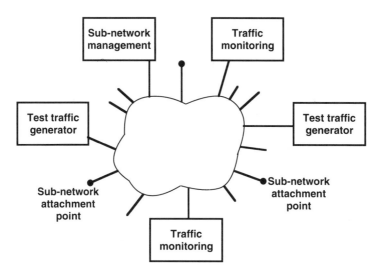

Figure 7.2 Sub-network testing.

public networks which are made available to organizations are frequently shared with other network users. In those instances, management facilities are necessarily limited to providing performance monitoring so that it is possible to check that the contracted quality of communication service is being provided.

Sub-networks should be added one at a time. Indeed, during the initial phase of interconnection it is suggested that, having checked the correct inter-working of one pair of sub-networks which are joined at a single point, the pair are then separated and a further paired testing attempted. This is because many of today's managed local networks possess considerable networking intelligence. They will automatically seek for alternative routes if they find that a preferred route is, for some reason, inoperative or an alternative route offers higher throughput. If sub-networks are joined in an uncontrolled manner, it is always possible that an alternative route exists. Under test, this can give a semblance of full connectivity even when there are faulty interconnection points. It also makes it difficult to validate the testing of the individual primary communication facilities. However, once all sub-networks have been shown to inter-operate with their neighbours, the whole communication infrastructure can be assembled, adding each tested sub-network in sequence and subjecting the entire communication subsystem to extensive monitoring. If at all possible, automatic reconfiguration of communication routes should still be inhibited during this integration phase and incrementally enabled only when the communication subsystem has been shown to be viable.

When the communication subsystem has been fully tested, it is appropriate to test the attachments of computing components. It is recommended that personal computers and workstations are attached first. This is because they place simple demands upon communication resources and because each is serving only a single user. This makes testing simple and, in the event that there are faults in the configuration, is a damage limitation strategy. These devices do, however, provide good interactive testing facilities and their use will give confidence of viable operation. Integration of departmental systems, mainframes and specialist computing systems follows. These can provide shared printing and file servers and high performance processing units such as are used in mathematical modelling and graphics design.

It should be noted that some classes of networks provide central management and that this is located in a mainframe computer. In these situations, the step by step approach to testing described above is inappropriate. Once physical connectivity has been demonstrated, it is then necessary to connect the mainframe and manage the various networking components from it, as they are attached to the network. Networks exhibiting this type of strongly hierarchical and centralized control do not scale well. They are difficult to integrate into an evolving distributed system.

7.3.2 Incremental testing

The preferred approach to acceptance testing is applicable to testing an incremental addition to an established distributed processing environment. When adding components to an existing system the approach is again bottom up, treating the new elements as modules of a system. First the communication elements are tested, then the attachments and finally any new services. The major difference in approach comes in the cut-over point at which the new components are integrated with the operational distributed system. It is vital to remember that an operational system has users and is engaged in productive work for an enterprise. It is essential to ensure that the integration proceeds with minimum disruption to the existing users. In some cases the cut-over can be performed out of normal working hours when user activity is low. But this is not always possible and some systems must always be fully operational. For this reason alone the introduction of new components into an operational distributed system must be fully monitored. Provision must be made to revert to the old configuration as soon as any hint of difficulty is detected. This degree of control requires that the appropriate distributed system management tools are available and that the management facilities for the components being added are compatible with those for the operational system.

When the decision has been made that the new components have been checked out in isolation and can now be introduced into the operational system, it is advisable to start the integration process by disabling all activity in the new components. The first elements to be introduced are then the physical communication devices. If it is intended that they shall be multiply connected to the operational system, effect these connections one at a time to ensure that the act of connection is satisfactory. Recall that, once there are multiple connections, the communication infrastructure may automatically reconfigure itself to take advantage of alternative communication routes. With connectivity and new routing possibilities checked out, the processing attachments and then the additional applications services can be brought into operation.

Although these steps appear obvious and straightforward, they are bound to be time-consuming for a system of any significant size. There is always the temptation to take short cuts. This is dangerous and should be discouraged. While tests are proceeding satisfactorily, carrying out tests upon a particular set of components within a subsystem in parallel may seem to save time. But should an unexpected situation arise, lack of integration control can render it difficult to locate the source of the unexpected behaviour. Time will be taken in back-tracking to isolate it. This time taken to locate a problem can easily exceed the time which was apparently saved by attempting the short cut. Note that parallel testing on a subsystem is different from carrying out tests in parallel on sub-networks which are totally decoupled. It is the former which is deprecated whereas the latter may indeed save time, as discussed in Section 7.3.1.

7.3.3 Test libraries

Even when the total system appears to be fully tested, management should guard against possibly misplaced euphoria. It has been repeatedly emphasized that distributed systems are complex. Some fault situations will manifest themselves only under critical operational conditions. Therefore, system monitoring does not stop at the moment the distributed system (or the addition to the distributed system) is declared operational. It never ceases but is a feature of operation and maintenance.

Therefore all tests should be planned with a view to their reproducibility. All test records of component, sub-network, subsystem and system behaviour should be retained. Doing this will enable tests to be repeated in future should it ever be suspected that component behaviour and performance has changed from that which applied upon acceptance. This same discipline should also be applied when performing acceptance tests upon component upgrades. Although first-level testing of upgraded components can be performed incrementally, the system should always be subject to acceptance tests as a whole.

The consequence of applying this policy is to maintain a library of test procedures and their results. If the tests are chosen not only for their reproducibility but also for their diagnostic capability, the test procedures have the added advantage that they can be used to demonstrate restoration of service following the repair of a failure.

7.3.4 Addressing schemes

An enterprise should adopt an agreed policy for that part of the addressing scheme which is within its own domain of responsibility. Because even an enterprise's distributed system can become attached to other enterprises' distributed systems, it is vital that its addressing domain be suitably registered at the earliest possible time. This will prevent unnecessary re-work to convert codes and directories in the event of a subsequent inter-connection between enterprises.

As networks and distributed systems have evolved, a clearer understanding has developed concerning the need for proper assignment of device addresses and the names of network facilities. Both the IEEE addressing scheme and the X.500 (ISO/IEC 9594) Directory standards set out rules for their unambiguous assignment. However, where LANs have been in use for some time, particularly if they have been operated in isolation, there will not have been the pressure to adopt these more recent, universally applicable naming and addressing schemes. It is only when confronted with their inter-connection that naming and addressing conflicts may arise. It is essential that the name and address associated with any device or service which is to be introduced into the system be vetted and approved before connection. Failure to do so will lead to multiple responses to system requests. The results are, at best, unpredictable and at worst may cause service failures. Time should be allowed to ensure that all services and facilities which depend upon knowledge of a name or an address have been checked and, if necessary, modified before integration into a distributed system is sanctioned.

7.4 Operations and user support

Operations staff have a key role to play in maintaining an information base of operational characteristics. This must include the logging of all faults and the corrective action required. Some vendors' management products already provide computer-assisted support for this type of record keeping. They allow the operator to browse through histories of past occurrences looking for similar situations so as to establish what action could be appropriate when faced with an unfamiliar situation.

As well as the operational discipline of fault logging, the installation manager should also consider aspects which affect the normal operation of the network. It is essential that good records be maintained of all cabling, where it is terminated, who is responsible for the location at which it is terminated, what equipment is connected to the network and where attachments are located. This information should have been gathered initially as part of the network installation procedure. It requires discipline to maintain it up to date.

The need to keep users well informed of the characteristics of the new technological environment was identified when installation plans were discussed. This is a desirable practice and should be continued both during and after the initial settling-down period, not least because the system can be expected to go on evolving. Decisions may have been made to phase in some services at a later stage. Although not inevitable, it is always possible that introducing new users or a new service will cause minor disruption. Hence, users need to be advised of planned changes. Where there has been lack of service, users should be informed of the reason.

One of the features of good system design and operation is that its operation should be invisible to its users. It is therefore good practice to inform users of the network's successes and not just of its operational shortcomings. Success inspires user confidence. Depending upon the type of network installation and the type of user, information can be presented through electronic mail, messages to user screens or the more conventional circular or user newsletter.

With any unfamiliar environment, however reliable, it is human nature to blame any problems upon the new technology. For example, a user has problems with a particular terminal or fails to access a particular program or database. Experience shows that faults mostly lie with the user, not the system. The operations team need to give prompt, effective and tactful support to users and to assist them in recovering from problems, whether self-inflicted or introduced by faulty operational or system behaviour. Hot-line support is particularly recommended.

Above all, the operations team must avoid a 'fire-fighting' mentality. They should anticipate requirements. Regular operations monitoring will identify situations where loadings are particularly high or frequent retrial of operations is indicative of marginal operation. A regular audit of operation (in silent hours) using library test patterns, for example, will give reassurance of adequate operation. Performing such checks and recording their satisfactory outcome are a part of internal quality assurance procedures of system operation. Thus, unless the system is small and is used by computer specialists, it is essential to have a trained operations team who can assist users in making effective use of the resources.

Some communication network systems (for example, FDDI, token ring and some X.25 products) have network management as an intrinsic part of their capability. Many of the major system suppliers are offering management systems which provide a monitoring capability and a degree of control over all the resources within a distributed system. Although these products are currently largely targeted at the manufacturers' own systems, there is a clear market perception that customers want an open capability for distributed systems management in a multi-vendor environment.

7.5 Documentation needs

The purpose of system documentation, whether for system operation, or user or operator training, is to place upon record a body of expertise which records the known facts about the system, the way in which it operates and the way in which it is to be operated. These objectives could apply equally to a stand-alone system or to a complex distributed system. What differentiates the documentation needs of a distributed system is the fact that components must be expected to be different in the various parts of the system. Consequently expertise will vary throughout the system. Yet, because all users and operators have access to and need to be aware of the system as a whole, this expertise and the documentation have to be available at all locations. This means that the documentation requirement has to be well thought through from the outset. Failure to do so risks fragmentary and inconsistent documentation.

A valuable starting point is to adopt a system standard for documentation – essentially an enterprise style – with common formats, page layout, indexing methods etc. At the very least, this measure of uniformity will make it easier for the reader to read a new document and feel that it is not totally unfamiliar. However, a documentation standard is only tackling the tip of the iceberg. Considerable thought needs to be given to content too. This section reviews some of the salient features of documentation, both training manuals for the new system and operational manuals and handbooks.

7.5.1 Training manuals

In a distributed system, users and operators have a major resource at their disposal. Training is required to help them exploit it effectively. That is, it assists in meeting the aims of the organization effectively and so justifies the investment. Training manuals aim to satisfy four objectives, both for the system's users and its operators:

- to introduce users to the basic features of the system,
- to show users how to run simple jobs,
- to show how to get assistance when things go wrong,
- to show where more detailed reference information can be found and how to structure a search for particular system features.

The term 'user' (when unqualified) is used to signify both users and operators.

Although the above list gives the flavour of getting a user started, it is a feature of distributed systems that they will evolve during the system's life. Therefore training is a continual requirement and training manuals should make a positive feature of subsystem and cultural differences which must be expected in a distributed system of any significant size. They must show how different components might react differently, to what appears to be the same enquiry. Although this looks like an admission of failure, it is most unlikely that, as a system grows and ages, it will be possible or even desirable to maintain an absolute standard at all times. Part of user training in the use of distributed systems is to assist them to adapt to system evolution and also to the evolution of training manuals.

Experience has shown that the best training manuals are backed up with tutorial software which operates on the system (or a subset of the system) about which the user is learning. Therefore the training manual should match any interactive training software which is provided. Because the interaction will be through one of a number of workstations, attached personal computers or even simple terminals, there will be a diversity of ways in which the interactive training can appear to the user. Good manuals provide examples of the screen appearance for the range of device types that are commonly supported within the system.

Because users under training will make mistakes, some of the features of training are akin to those required for providing help and on-line diagnostics. So although the primary form of training manual is a text book, the equivalent material can also be provided on-line to take the user step by step through the examples in any given training session. Because a user will be operating in a training context and a well managed system is capable of recognizing the training mode of operation, sufficient safeguards can be placed upon user activity to ensure that no permanent changes are made to critical features of the system and that, at the end of the training session, training files are restored to their unmodified form. There is a particularly important constraint which has to be applied for operator training. Operators have to interact with the highly critical system components in order to ensure their correct operation and management. But to do so while training would be a recipe for disaster. Therefore fully interactive operator training must take place upon a 'shadow' system which, while giving the semblance of real effects, does not affect the operational system in any way.

No matter how well users are trained, the extent and complexities of a distributed system render it improbable that they will know everything about the whole of the system. It is therefore essential to provide reference documentation as a reminder of how a given task is performed. Because the system is large and evolving, the form of that documentation is again equivalent to that discussed in Chapter 6 concerning on-line help.

7.5.2 Operational manuals

Operational manuals are aimed at satisfying the following objectives:

- providing information and guidance to operations staff and their immediate managers,

- providing an index and guide to the interpretation of errors and problem resolution,
- giving details of the system configuration,
- acting as a repository for statements of policy concerning the operation and administration of the system.

Again, it is important for system managers to make some strategic decisions when establishing the distributed system as to what documentation will be held on-line and what will be in the form of hard copy. If information is on-line, what mechanisms will be used (a) to distribute it and (b) to draw it to the operator's attention? An obvious method well matched to a distributed system is to use electronic mail services for urgent or transient items of information. Urgent ones can be arranged to place an attention alert on the operator's terminal screen, possibly accompanied by an audible warning. By using mail, operators will be advised of pending messages when they log on to the system at the beginning of a turn of operations duty. But, unlike some mail systems, it must be the default operational requirement that the information remains available to the operator at all times for ready reference. It should be deleted only by the authorization of the person who was the source of the information or other proper authority.

In spite of the advantages of receiving instruction on-line, the information must always be provided as hard copy as well. There are three reasons. One is that operational information is central to the proper conduct of system management. It is therefore important to ensure that information can be audited at some future date. Secondly, quality procedures can require that the receipt of significant information about system operation be acknowledged. For this to be carried out on-line requires procedures for receiving and acknowledging information in a form that cannot be repudiated. Many managements will not wish to engage in this degree of complexity. Finally, operational information and advice must always be available to the operator even when the system is faulty and the operator is trying to carry out a repair. Clearly, in such a situation, an on-line documentation system could become unreliable or even totally unavailable.

In spite of the concern expressed above about the availability of on-line data, one form of distributed system information is, without doubt, best handled on-line. This concerns the current status of the distributed configuration and the services that are operational within it. This data is being modified so frequently that hard copy could not hope to keep up with the minute by minute changes taking place. The type of configuration data that can be usefully committed to hard copy concerns the overall topology of the network to show the principle locations of activity and to provide data showing the types and total numbers of resources which may be found there. It would also show the major communication routes between these locations.

Not all operational documentation is concerned with the behaviour of the operational system. Some is concerned with the management policy relating to the action of the operators themselves. The operations manager needs to establish standard operating procedures to define the responsibility boundaries of a given class of operators, what procedures are to be followed in the escalation of operational problems and the way in which operator logs are to be maintained. These procedures need to take account of the fact that, although some procedures for handling abnormal situations can be worked out in advance, problem solving is frequently based upon hunches. One method of addressing management problems heuristically is to employ an expert system whose knowledge base is constructed from experience. An important component of the operational documentation is a repository of problems encountered together with their solutions. The latter may be built up from the combined experience of the operations team during the lifetime of this (and other) distributed systems, so adding to the knowledge base. As earlier discussion of this aspect of providing operator help has shown, this can prove invaluable to an operator who, meeting a situation for the first time, can obtain documented and authoritative evidence of how to handle it based upon a similar occurrence which could have been noted several months or years ago.

7.6 Maintenance

A new system requires a new maintenance agreement. For an extension to a system, maintenance agreements need to updated. The type of maintenance agreement depends very much upon the policy of the enterprise which owns the distributed system and whether the staff operate it themselves or engage another organization to manage the facility. But, at some level, maintenance decisions have to be made. These should take account of the multiplicity of components and, more and more, the multiplicity of vendors' equipment which will be present in the system.

Two aspects of distributed system management are usually covered under the heading of maintenance:

- The provision of support to handle equipment failure
- The provision of upgrades to take account of technical evolution

Component failure is a characteristic of all hardware. Software, embedded in communication equipment, is not always free from design faults and maintenance is a recognized means of receiving support to correct design shortcomings which manufacturers detect, often in another enterprise's systems. Technical evolution can affect all aspects of a distributed system.

Some vendors have a maintenance policy which includes system updates, while others make an explicit charge for an update service, limiting maintenance to a repair and advice service.

For maintenance purposes (as with testing) the system can be divided into its main components:

- the physical data links: these are the physical network subsystem components and the gateways, routers and bridges which interconnect them,
- the workstations and personal computers,
- departmental and specialist computer systems,
- applications.

Physical data links have a long life. If undisturbed and with robustly constructed sheathing, they are tolerant of other cables being drawn over them. Maintenance requirements are therefore long term and should not demand frequent inspection or replacement due to component failure. An annual audit of cable quality is recommended to ensure that nothing has occurred to render its characteristics marginal in relationship to its normal operating specification. For optical fibre, this means ensuring that the light budget is still adequate. For structured wiring schemes based upon metallic conductors, it means checking that connectivity and impedance are still within tolerance. Given suitable test equipment, these checks can be carried out by locally trained staff. Maintenance provided by a cable supplier then becomes a matter of an insurance policy and a means of ensuring an interest in continuing support in the event of difficulties. Enterprises should not expect to pay more than a low percentage of the installation cost as the premium for such support.

Hardware and its embedded software to supply communication needs are subject to typical hardware and software maintenance agreements. A variety of call-out schedules may be available, ranging from on-site maintenance engineers, through a 4-hour response, to next-day service. Repair is usually by component or sub-component (printed circuit board) replacement. Since it is likely that the communication subsystem will have been configured to provide a degree of resilience, with alternative routing or (for some types of network technology) built-in resilience, an enterprise may be prepared to risk single failure and opt for a 24-hour response. They may rely on their own staff to diagnose the fault and even maintain a stock of spares so as to effect a repair by replacement. On the other hand, the smaller organization may opt for this specialist support to be externally supplied. It means that they do not have to maintain a stock of back-up spares, nor do they require to hold specialist network test equipment. It is a company policy decision, influenced by staff availability and the size of distributed systems, as to which approach is adopted. Maintenance contracts are typically in the range 7% to 15% of equipment cost, depending upon service response required.

Attachments, whether workstations and personal computer systems or departmental and specialist computer services, will be subject to their own maintenance contracts. These will have their own interfaces to the communication subsystem and this is a boundary which has particular significance for maintenance since the computing equipment will, in many instances, be from a different manufacturer and available through a different vendor from the equipment of the communication subsystem. Where this is the case, the enterprise must expect to take up some of the burden of locating faults which affect the boundary between these two classes of equipment and of resolving boundary disputes. The alternative is to negotiate a maintenance contract with a third party, covering the equipment at both sides of the interface. This should be organized to guarantee to resolve any dispute as to the location of faults and their rectification. Because analysing distributed systems faults is a specialist activity, such support will carry a premium and require the availability of suitable test and management equipment. As distributed systems increase in number and complexity, this activity (going under the name of **outsourcing**) is increasingly offered by specialist organizations.

The application software which provides distributed processing services to users should not be forgotten. Many common applications have been extended to operate in networked environments. Sometimes these networked environments prove, upon investigation, to be communication technology specific. Although the move towards OSI standards ought to ease the problem of inter-communication between the parts of a distributed application package, application installers are well advised to check carefully any operational guarantees that are associated with the package and its maintenance. This warning is of particular significance for applications which support multiple concurrent transactions. There is a need to check that the application is not dependent upon specific aspects of a presumed underlying communication protocol which, as the system evolves, may not be supported or may be in conflict with some later distributed system addition.

Section 7.2 identified that it may not prove possible to devise acceptance tests for every aspect of a system. Acceptance tests will be sufficient to demonstrate essential system operation but may be expected not to reveal obscure incompatibilities or failure to meet certain performance criteria. These may become manifest only during operation. Such potential deficiencies have therefore to be covered in a maintenance contract which recognizes the incompleteness of system tests and requires that deficiencies, discovered in operation, be rectified under maintenance. This influences the approach which should be taken to a maintenance agreement and biases the organization towards taking out a maintenance agreement with the equipment supplier.

Summing up

- Distributed systems seldom spring into being fully formed.

- It is essential to maintain good documentation from project inception through to, and during, system operation.

- Documentation, whether of the system configuration or operational manuals, needs to be readily available at all times; this is best handled by maintaining the documentation on-line.

- Because of the complexity of the distributed processing environment, it is difficult to determine when a set of tests is complete.

- Testing several sub-networks in parallel can save time but a total system test is still needed.

- Because some fault situations only appear under critical operational conditions, system tests continue to be required as features of operation and maintenance.

- Acceptance and subsequent maintenance agreements must make allowance for the fact that a complex distributed processing environment cannot be completely tested for all possible types of interactions.

- Many of the factors which influence installation, testing, operations and maintenance of distributed systems are common to stand-alone systems and to small computer networks.

- *Ad hoc* or centralized management approaches that are often adopted for small systems do not scale to larger distributed systems.

- Independent of whether specialist external management or management from enterprise resources is preferred, a disciplined approach to monitoring and control, backed up with adequate monitoring equipment, test libraries, system and user documentation, is essential.

- Users need to be kept informed of systems changes and system performance.

- Every distributed system manager's budget should make provision for acquiring and maintaining the above list of facilities.

Reference

ISO/IEC 9594:1990 *Parts 1 to 8: Information processing systems – Open Systems Interconnection – The Directory*

8

Distributed systems management concepts

Objectives

- to formalize managers and resources using an object model
- to explore domains as a general concept for structuring management
- to formalize policies as objects and relate them to management domains
- to apply the formalism of policy to security models and access control mechanisms

8.1 Introduction

This chapter presents some of the basic concepts of distributed systems management in a more formal manner than has been the style of earlier chapters. The starting point is the reminder that there are two distinct generic management activities:

- Creating, interpreting and monitoring *policies* to organize management activity. Large scale systems may have millions of resources so it is impractical to specify policies for individual resources. Policies need to be specified in ways which enable them to be applied to sets of resources.

- Performing *management operations* for monitoring or controlling the behaviour of resources related to a management function such as configuration or accounting. A managed resource must provide a management interface as well as supporting the operations related to its normal functionality. Management operations are different from policies. A management operation is an instantaneous activity, whereas a policy is intended as a persistent means of influencing operations.

The reader is further reminded of the discussion on modelling the management of the distributed processing environment first introduced in Chapter 1. The themes of this chapter are how resources and policies about them relate to those models, how resources and policies are formally represented and how resources may be grouped into sets.

8.2 Objects and object models

The approach taken to formalizing the concepts of modelling distributed systems is object-based. That is, all entities are defined as computational objects whether they are managers, users, or resources (both logical and physical resources). This approach is becoming widely adopted and, as shown in the next chapter, is the model adopted in developing international standards for distributed processing and for management.

The significant feature of an object is that one can distinguish the external perception of the operations an object performs and its visible attributes from the internal activity of how the object's operations are implemented and how its attributes and internal data are maintained. The object is said to **encapsulate** its data and operations. It presents an external interface which, together with a specification of its behaviour for each operation, characterizes all that needs to be known about an object.

There are many texts which develop the object modelling paradigm (see, for example, Wegner, 1990), and it is not the purpose of this chapter to repeat their contents. Some features of object models should be mentioned for their relevance to distributed systems management. The first is the distinction between **class** and **instance**. Many objects have common properties and the generic definition of those properties constitutes a class definition. Actual realizations of individual members of the class are termed instances of the class or just **objects**. Another feature is **containment**. One instance of an object is said to be *contained* within another if the contained object is not visible when operations are directed towards the containing object. The contained object is visible only when, for example, a system implementer is concerned with the internal behaviour of the containing object or operations are directed specifically to the contained object. Other features, such as inheritance of properties through a class hierarchy, are not important for this discussion.

8.2.1 Managed objects

An object may exhibit several different aspects of its external interface, depending upon the role it is called upon to play at any one time. In the context of management, a resource will exhibit a set of operations and their associated attributes that are concerned with the normal operation of the resource and a (possibly) distinct set of operations concerned with its management. For example, a data communication router will exhibit its normal switching function by routing its input data to desired destinations. Management will be concerned with the operations that enable and disable the operation of the router or control its routing algorithm. Similarly, clients of a computer system will be seen to perform application-specific computational activity yet, for management purposes, have their behaviour constrained by specific management policies.

Any entity which is subject to management is termed a **managed object**. That is, it supports a management interface. Management entails obtaining information on the current state of a managed object, making decisions and performing control operations on the object to modify its behaviour, as shown in Figure 8.1. Note, the definition adopted here is subtly different from that adopted by ISO for Open Systems Interconnection management (ISO 7498–4) and the management standards for communication systems. That definition of a managed object is limited to the characteristics of the management interface alone. There is no definition in Open Systems Interconnection object modelling terms of the normal (communication) interface which the entity exhibits although open distributed processing standards are taking a broader perspective of objects (see Chapter 9).

A managed object may be a real-world entity such as a workstation, terminal, software process, file or person. A computer is an example of a real-world entity. It is also a managed object when it is directly managed by

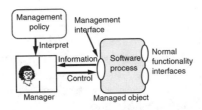

Figure 8.1 Manager interactions with a managed object.

a maintenance engineer who is performing diagnostic tests as part of fault management.

In some cases, a manager does not interact directly with the real-world entity it manages, but rather the managed object is a representation of the real-world entity. A resource scheduler has a 'processor' object which is a data structure representing a computer, which it manages for work allocation. The same computer may also be represented by a second 'maintenance' object managed by a configuration manager. This example illustrates that there can be several different types of objects being managed, for different purposes, which nevertheless represent the same real-world entity.

The model recognizes three types of *interaction* between managers and managed objects:

- *control* actions directed by the managing object to the managed object,
- *requests* for information by the managing object which result in a reply from the managed object,
- *notifications* of events by the managed object.

An object interface specifies a named set of operations and attributes. The object oriented database approach (Peckham and Maryanski, 1988) of defining **attributes** which are internal variables or constants visible at the interface is used here. It can be regarded as 'syntactic sugaring', which avoids the need to specify a read or write operation upon externally accessible data. Typical attributes include instance identifier, template identifier (from which the object is created) and management-specific information such as error statistics, performance information or maximum number of buffers. An attribute may be a simple data type (for example, integer or real) or structured data type such as a record, array or set. Note that some attributes may be read-only from a manager's viewpoint, that is they are changed only by the object itself, as a result of changes in the internal state of the object. Others, such as instance or template identifiers, are constants. Attributes are analogous to set points and state variables found in control systems.

The following minimal set of management interactions is needed for the management of objects.

- *Read attribute*: this request operation permits a manager to obtain information on the current state of an object in order to make management decisions.

- *Write attribute*: this control operation permits a manager to modify the behaviour of an object, for example by changing a set-point or error limit. There will be application-specific constraints on what values can be written to an attribute. The input parameters specify the attribute name and corresponding values to be written.

- *Application-specific operation*: this control operation may alter an object's state, trigger off further interactions with other objects, and then return a response to the initiator. It may reference multiple attributes. For example, a Boolean expression involving some attributes may be used as a guard on changing the values of others. When an application-specific operation can also be considered as an operation on the object as a whole it is termed an *action*.

- *Notification*: this interaction results from a managed object generating an unsolicited report, for example notifying error conditions or giving regular reports on the state of the object. It is directed to a manager object.

In addition to these basic interactions there will be others that are dependent on the particular type of object and its particular activity, such as configuration or fault management. Some interactions with an object may affect the real-world entity that it references whereas others affect only the managed object itself.

8.2.2 Managers

The management model must cater for both human and automated managers. Managers can be both *managing objects* and also *managed objects* able to perform in both a manager and managed role. That is, a manager may itself be a resource managed by a higher level manager, so facilitating the formalization of a hierarchical management structure.

The model for a manager used here derives from the modelling discussion of Chapter 1. The manager is constructed from four different types of entities, as shown in Figure 8.2.

The model has four main components:

- *Human manager*: usually specifying policy but may implement the decision making for simple functional managers. The decision making loop could be closed within one of the functional entities to provide automated management, with the human manager as back-up.

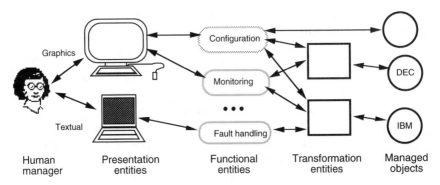

Figure 8.2 Example manager structure.

- *Presentation*: providing an input interface for people to access computer based management activities, typically including graphical or textual output.

- *Functional*: implementing the management functional operations, which may be partitioned according to the main management functions: configuration, security, monitoring, accounting etc. Automated management would typically be implemented in a functional manager object.

- *Transformation*: permitting the transformation of an interface provided by a managed object into one expected by a manager. For example, there will be transformations for managing components compatible with standards and other transformations for non-standard (proprietary) components. The transformation may not necessarily be between different protocols. For example a management activity may act as an interface to a set of objects and transform a single interaction into an interaction with each member of the set (compare OSI management agents (Chapter 9), which transform remote operations into local operations (ISO 10040)).

This approach permits a distributed implementation of managers and there may be multiple instances of any of the manager entities. It is very flexible and permits one functional management component to use the services of another. Failure of any one of the above components should not affect the normal functionality of the managed objects but may prevent them being managed.

8.3 Domains

The rationale for structuring management and grouping objects for management purposes is:

- to *modularize* management so as to provide the basis for coping with the complexity of managing large scale distributed systems,
- to permit multiple co-existing views of the managed objects,
- to permit a group of managed objects to be treated as a single entity for the purposes of specifying policy.

A set of objects that have been explicitly grouped is termed a **domain**. A grouping for the management purpose of applying a common policy to the objects is termed a *management domain*. Domains provide a flexible and pragmatic means of specifying boundaries of management responsibility and authority.

Formally, a domain is an object representing a collection of managed objects that have been explicitly grouped together. The objects may be resources, workstations, modems, processes, etc., depending on the purpose for which a particular domain is defined. A domain has an attribute called a **policy set**, which identifies the set of member objects to which domain policies apply. (Some authors use the phrase *object set* with the same meaning as the phrase *policy set* as used here.)

Generally, identifying a management domain is a response to the requirement to control a group of objects in order to manage them. Management of unidentifiable sets of objects is obviously impractical, so every object in a domain must have a unique identity. Sets of objects which have some arbitrary attribute in common are not management domains, unless each is identified as a member of the policy set. Thus, the set of all the people in the world over 65 or even the more limited example of the set of blue cars in London are not suitable for grouping as domain members because a manager could not identify the objects in the domain. However, a particular manager need not know the identifiers of the objects in a domain. The manager could interact with the domain as a set of anonymous objects. This could be implemented, for example, using multi-cast addressing or using a manager's agent to forward interactions to individual managed objects. The minimum representation of an object in a domain is a unique identifier which can be used to locate the object by means of a location service, although the domain may optionally hold a local name for use by human managers to refer to an object.

An object is referred to as a **member** of a domain if its identity is a member of the domain's policy set. Objects may be a member of more than one domain at any one time. Domains are persistent even if they do not contain any objects. It must always be possible to create an empty domain and later include objects identities in it.

Because the rationale for grouping objects in domains is to make them manageable, managed objects must exist within a management domain. That is, they are always created within a domain. If an object were created outside the domain framework it could not be managed, and hence could not be controlled. Objects in a domain do not all have to be of the same type. For instance a maintenance domain may have workstations, computers and terminals as objects.

Domains do not encapsulate the objects themselves, the relationship being by *reference* and not by *containment*; that is, managers or external objects can interact directly with an object referenced in a domain. Even so, it is sometime a convenient convention to speak or write of an object as being in a domain when it is the object's reference which is held as a value within the domain object.

Examples of domains include:

- workstations connected to a local area network for which an operator has maintenance responsibility;

- a subset of the above workstations, managed by a scheduler process which allocates background jobs to idle workstations;

- a set of files in a directory which is managed by the owner of the directory;

- a distributed application such as an enterprise-wide mail service in a company, which is managed by a number of systems programmers who are responsible for configuring and maintaining the service;

- a set of objects within the scope of a security administrator, who gives access rights to users;

- a naming context in which all names of objects are unique such as in the Domain Name Service (Cheriton and Mann, 1989);

- a management position in an organization with access rules defining the management rights for the domain. (An individual is appointed to the position by including the object representing the user into the position domain.)

8.3.1 Operations on a domain

Domains are themselves managed objects on which operations can be performed. They may be referenced from and be members of other domains. The following is the minimum set of operations required to manipulate objects within a domain:

- *Include object in a domain*: this includes an object into a domain by adding its identity to the policy set of the domain. It does not affect its membership of other domains. The effect is to make an existing object a member of an additional domain without creating a new instance of the object.

- *Remove object from a domain*: this removes an object from a domain without affecting the state of the object. Removal of an object from a domain is carried out by removing its identity from the policy set.

- *List objects in a domain*: this enables managers to determine the members of the policy set of a domain.

- *Create object*: this creates an object in a domain from a specified template, and sets its attributes according to specified parameters or default values.

- *Destroy object*: this removes the object from the system and recovers any resources allocated.

Operations, such as *move* objects between domains, are performed by including them in the destination domain and removing them from the source domain. They can be constructed as compounds of the above basic operations, *include* and *remove* in this example.

Because domain objects can themselves be included in other domains this enables structures of subdomains to be created. The fact that a subdomain may be a member of more than one domain results in potential cycles of domain membership. This can be very difficult to prevent as domains may be distributed over many computer systems and networks. Management applications which trace through domain structures need to implement loop detection algorithms.

Management of objects in domains requires that all objects, except for one or more root domains, should always exist in domains. Therefore creation of an object (or domain) consists of the composition of the object creation and inclusion operations; it both creates an instance of an object and adds it to the policy set of a domain. Similarly, destroying an object instance entails removing the object's identity from the containing domain's policy set.

Constraints on domain operations

Constraints on domain membership are of two kinds. The first kind constrains operations which affect domain membership, typically the *create* and *destroy* operations on any object and the *include* and *remove* operations on a domain. These add and subtract objects to and from the policy set. The predicate defined by the constraint has to be evaluated once only, when the operation is performed. Limits upon the number of members, and on any read-only attributes of objects in a domain, can be enforced by constraints of this kind.

The second kind of constraint is a general predicate, which the system is required to maintain, about the attributes of members of a domain. This is potentially very difficult to achieve because every time any function attempts to change an object's attribute, the system is required to verify that the domain constraints are not violated for each domain of which the object is a member. Constraints of this kind should therefore be excluded from the domain model.

The following are examples of application-specific constraints on domain operations.

- The objects created in or included into a domain must satisfy a constraint in terms of the minimum management interface expected by the domain.

- For a specific domain, only objects which implement code for a particular processor type, for example, the 80x86 processors, may be created or included in that domain.

- As the result of a policy decision, there is a limit on the number of members of a domain, for example, a limit which permits only a single manager in a manager domain in order to prevent any problems from having multiple managers (see Section 8.5.5).

- Attempts to destroy an object are to fail if the object is still a member of another domain.

- An object may not be removed from the last domain in which it is a member, but the *destroy* operation must be used instead.

Operations on a domain's members

The interactions defined so far are between a manager and an individual object. One of the objectives of the domain concept is to manage objects as a group. Complex operations may be defined as part of a functional manager object which determines the members of a domain and then performs an operation on each object in the set.

There may be requirements to select objects on which to operate by means of arbitrary expressions involving predicates on object attribute values and set expressions, for example 'all processes in domain X with core image greater than one megabyte except compiler servers and printer servers'; or 'all workstations of type = Y in LAN1 domain and in B3 operator domain'.

8.3.2 Example domain structure: ABC Ltd.

The following example will help to illustrate the discussion thus far. Consider the commercial organization, ABC Ltd., whose research department is engaged in a joint venture with an external organization, DEF Ltd. There is a need to organize access control for ABC itself, and also to allow limited access for members of DEF staff to research department files. DEF staff gain access from terminals in their own research laboratory by means of a communication network. After an audit of the security arrangements at both sites, ABC have selected a policy to allow DEF limited security administration rights to control the users who can access ABC.

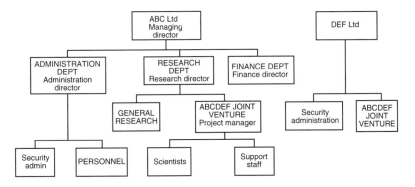

Figure 8.3 Conventional organization tree.

ABC's system consists of a number of computers connected by a company network. The example makes no assumption about what resources are located on what computer, but requires a global identification scheme so that all objects may be identified uniquely.

Figures 8.3 and 8.4 show the organizations (as viewed from ABC), presenting an organizational chart and the domain representation, respectively.

It will be seen that there is a close correspondence between the conventional and domain representations. However, management relationships representing authority in the organization chart are lost in the domain diagram. From the organization chart it is possible to infer directly 'who manages whom' (the administration director manages the security administrator). This information cannot be derived from the domain

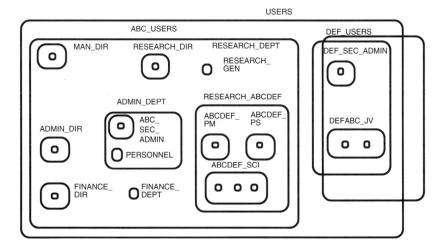

Figure 8.4 Domain representation of organization.

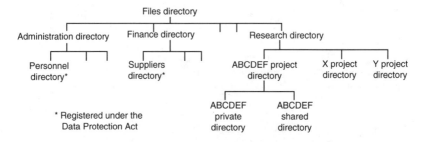

Figure 8.5   Directory structure for ABC files.

diagram and it could be perfectly consistent with that diagram for the security administrator to manage the administrator director. Simple domain diagrams only provide data about their membership and not about the authority relations between domains. The extra information is added in access rules and the management role domain diagrams, to be described in Sections 8.6 and 8.8.

Figures 8.5 and 8.6 show a part of organization ABC's file structure and its corresponding domain representation. The personnel and suppliers directories contain data which is registered under the United Kingdom Data Protection Act. Unlike the organization structure, no information is lost in the translation between the tree structure and the domain diagram.

A domain which spans the domains of two departments, such as 'DPA_DOM' in Figure 8.6, may be required for specific purposes. In this case it is assumed that members of 'PERSONNEL' need to be able to *read* the contents of all files containing personal data, so that they can monitor compliance with the Data Protection Act. The domain cannot be set up by one user but requires cooperative activity. 'ABC_SEC_ADMIN' will have to create access rules which allow a suitable member of 'ADMIN_DEPT'

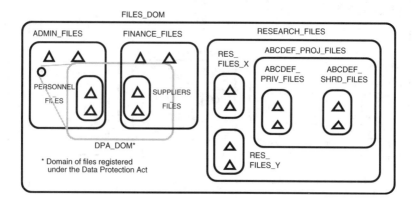

Figure 8.6   Domain representation of ABC file structure.

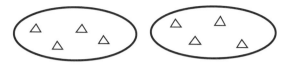

Figure 8.7 Disjoint domains.

to create an empty 'DPA_DOM' domain within 'ADMIN_DIR' and include 'PERSONNEL_FILES' into it, and a suitable member of 'FINANCE_DEPT' to include 'SUPPLIERS_FILES' in it.

8.3.3 Domain relationships

Because the main motivation for domains is their use for structuring management, this section discusses the requirements for structuring management and how this can be achieved using domains. Three types of mathematical set relationships are distinguished in this section, *disjoint domains*, *overlapping domains* and *subdomains*.

Disjoint domains.   Two domains are defined to be disjoint if their policy sets are disjoint (see Figure 8.7). Mechanisms are needed to permit interactions between disjoint domain hierarchies representing different organizations to allow inter-organizational cooperation (see Section 8.3.4).

Overlapping domains.   Two domains overlap if there are objects which are members of both domains (Figure 8.8). One example is a gateway interconnecting two networks whose management is shared by the management centres of each network.

Overlap is contentious in that it may result in the problems of multiple managers of an object. It may be a policy decision to exclude overlaps, as is the case in organizations which insist on a single manager being responsible for people in a department. In many cases, the problems of overlapping management are avoided by creating a new management domain with a single manager and moving the objects which would otherwise have been in the overlapping domains into the new domain. However, the organizational transitions that are likely to occur as distributed systems evolve are sufficiently complex that it is always worth considering that instances of overlapping domains, and hence manager conflict, may occur.

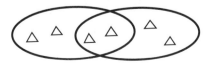

Figure 8.8 Explicit overlapping domains.

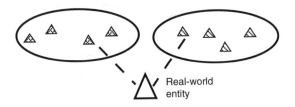

Figure 8.9 Implicit overlapping domains.

Implicit overlap may occur between two domains containing managed objects created from different templates but referring to the same real-world entity (Figure 8.9). In the example given above (Section 8.2.1), putting a maintenance object out of service makes the computer, which it represents, unavailable for scheduling. However, there is no means by which the scheduler can be informed because the two managers operate upon different managed objects. Implicit overlap can therefore give rise to serious problems. It is likely to occur where there is a functional partitioning of management into different domains. Careful design is needed to coordinate management operations in implicitly overlapping domains.

Subdomains exist if one domain object is a member of another domain. The first is referred to as a subdomain of the second.

Creating a subdomain enables a management policy to be applied to the subdomain which is different from that of the enclosing domain. This is the main method of structuring management. In Figure 8.10(a), D2 is a **direct subdomain** of D1, and D4 is an **indirect subdomain** of D1; D1 is a **superdomain** of D2, D3 and D4. An object is a **direct member** of a domain if it is in the domain's policy set. An object is an **indirect member** of a domain Dx if it is a member of a domain Dy which is a member or indirect member of Dx. Note that indirect members of a domain are not in the domain's policy set.

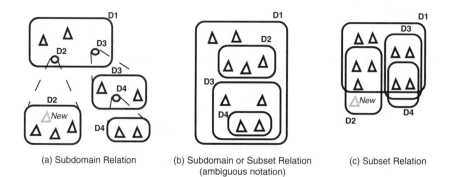

(a) Subdomain Relation   (b) Subdomain or Subset Relation   (c) Subset Relation
(ambiguous notation)

Figure 8.10 Subdomains and subsets.

An alternative notation for showing a subdomain relation is shown in Figure 8.10(b). It is simpler, but ambiguous, as it can also be interpreted as a subset relation, as in Figure 8.10(c). However, the notation of Figure 8.10(b) is often used as a shorthand to denote the subdomain relation, for compactness.

In a static situation the evaluation of the indirect membership of a domain hierarchy such as is shown in Figure 8.10 would yield the same overall set of objects whether the domains were subsets or subdomains. However, the effect of removal or inclusion of an object in D2 will have different results for the evaluation of the membership of D1, depending on the sort of relation. If D2 is a *subset* of D1, as in Figure 8.10(c), then the addition of object *New* to D2's object set does not affect D1 in any way and there is no resulting relationship between it and D1. After the operation, D2 is no longer a subset of D1, but D1 and D2 overlap. If D2 is a *subdomain* of D1, as in Figure 8.10(a), then *New* becomes an indirect member of D1 and of all super-domains of D1.

8.3.4 Domain expressions

Domains and subdomains are a powerful means of expressing hierarchical membership and set union, but provide no means of expressing other basic set operations such as set difference and set intersection. Set difference can express sets of objects such as 'all files in Payroll_Files except Payroll_Master'. Set intersection can express sets such as 'all files which are in Payroll_Files and also in Personal_Data'. Domain expressions provide a way of formulating policy using standard set operations – union, intersection and set difference – as well as membership enumeration and subdomains.

It would be possible to use domain manipulation operations to create a new domain with the required membership e.g. create DomainA with the same members as (DomainB ∩ DomainC), and refer to DomainA in the policy. However, the policy then applies to membership of DomainB and DomainC at the time DomainA is created and not at the time that its applicability is checked. Static enumeration of objects at some point in the past is not usually what is required in evaluation of policies, and domain expressions in a policy are evaluated at the time the rule is checked.

8.3.5 Positions

In most cases policies should be expressed not in terms of individual users but in terms of the **positions** which they occupy. As an example, the organizational hierarchy in Figure 8.4 is expressed in terms of positions. Since positions are 'occupied' and domains have members, it is useful to represent positions by domains, with constraints on membership operations to ensure that only user objects can be members and that there are the appropriate limits on the number of members.

Note that there is a distinction between a position, which simply defines a named set of users, and a **role**, which is a relation between a position or user and other sets of objects (see Section 8.8). One position may be associated with a number of roles, for example, the manager of Northern Sales Division has the roles of 'Staff Supervisor' for his sales staff and of 'Sales Manager' to customers in the North.

8.3.6 User and mechanism views of objects and domains

It is worth while at this point in the chapter to identify one aspect of distributed systems management that has only recently become apparent in technical work on domains. That is the importance of distinguishing between the view of the user managing a system and the underlying mechanism(s) used within the system for implementing this view. Some examples, taken from the researches of the Domino project (Moffett & Sloman, 1992), illustrate this.

(1) In the user's view, objects are referred to by names. In the mechanism view they are referred to by unique identifiers, through addresses. An object identifier (OID), consisting of its address and identifier, is associated with each object.

(2) In the user's view, the members of a domain's policy set are named objects. In the mechanism view the members of the policy set are OIDs. This approach avoids possible inconsistencies when an object is a member of several domains. There is only one copy of the object upon which all operations are performed. The approach achieves consistency at the cost of having to perform remote accesses when, say, the object is remote from one of its parent domains.

(3) The mechanism view uses domains to provide a naming service. Each OID in the object set of a domain has a local name associated with it, by which the object can be referred to by users. The user only sees local and hierarchical names, while the implementation mechanism provides the translation between these names and OIDs.

(4) The grouping of objects into domains is essentially determined by policy. In order to determine the policies which apply to a particular object, it is necessary to know the domains of which it is a direct or indirect member. These are termed its *ancestors*. It is impractical to inspect all domains for this purpose, so implementations arrange that each object has an attribute called the *parent set*, which is a list of the domains of which it is a direct member, enabling derivation of its ancestors. The parent set is not visible in the user view.

This relationship between the user and mechanism views of objects and of domains is illustrated in Tables 8.1 and 8.2.

Table 8.1 User and mechanism views of objects.

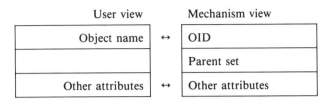

User view		Mechanism view
Object name	↔	OID
		Parent set
Other attributes	↔	Other attributes

Table 8.2 User and mechanism views of domains.

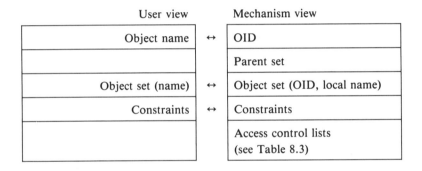

User view		Mechanism view
Object name	↔	OID
		Parent set
Object set (name)	↔	Object set (OID, local name)
Constraints	↔	Constraints
		Access control lists (see Table 8.3)

(5) The user view of other users is as *user objects*. There are substantial advantages to be gained from a mechanism in which user objects are implemented as a special kind of domain, a *user representation domain*. The domain represents the persistent aspects of a user from one logon to the next. When the user logs on, process objects which temporarily represent the user become members of the user representation domain and gain the privileges and authority which belong to that user. When the user logs off, the processes cease to be domain members and no longer have the user's privileges. In this case the user view of user objects does not use the concept of a domain at all, but the system uses the mechanism view of a domain.

(6) *Access rules* are objects which specify discretionary access control policy in terms of the set of operations which any of a set of users is authorized to perform on any of a set of target objects. Although it is a concept which managers find intuitively easy to deal with it is one which does not implement efficiently. Unreasonably long searches would be needed to evaluate access requests if the system had to search through all access rule objects in order to decide whether to allow the request. Therefore, the mechanism implements the access rules by means of **access control lists** attached to target object domains. See Section 8.6.3 for a further discussion.

It is important to maintain both a distinction and a relationship between the user and mechanism views of management concepts. As with any system, the user requirements must drive the mechanism, but it must be subject to the condition that it can be implemented efficiently. Users and users' managers have to be able to work with objects which are implemented in accordance with their view, while the underlying system has to be able to use a mechanism which provides an efficient implementation of the functions seen by the user.

8.4 Management policies

All formal organizations have policies ('the plans of an organization to meet its goals') with two related purposes: to define the goals of the organization; and to allocate the resources to achieve the goals. The policies are used as a means of management, often in a hierarchical fashion. A high-level policy guides a manager, who may achieve its goals by making lower-level policies, which apply to other managers lower in the hierarchy.

Most organizations issue policy statements, intended to guide their members in particular circumstances. Policies may provide positive guidance about the goals of the organization and how they are to be achieved, or they may set constraints limiting the way in which the goals are to be achieved. Other policy statements may allocate (give access authorization to) the resources which are needed to carry out the goals. If they allocate money they are typically called *budgets*.

Management control activities are determined by the response of managers to policies. Management domains provide a valuable structuring construct for grouping objects to which a common policy applies. However, domains neither define policies nor specify how they shall be manipulated. Furthermore, experience has shown that formalizing policy and relating that formalism to everyday experience does not always come naturally. Therefore, the following sections make extensive use of examples.

Some general characteristics of policies are defined below in order to give a working definition which is more precise than simply to regard them as 'plans for action'. The starting point is the assumption that policies are intended to influence actions. There is a distinction between policies which are intended to motivate actions to take place and policies which give or withhold power for actions to take place. **Actions** are operations which are performed by agents provided two preconditions are satisfied: motivation and power (see Figure 8.11):

- **Motivation** implies that the agent wishes to carry out an action, and will do so if endowed with the power to do so.
- **Power** implies that if an agent attempts to carry out an action, it will succeed.

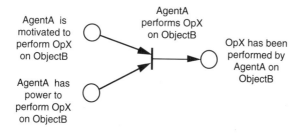

Figure 8.11 Preconditions for action.

One method of acquiring power is through delegated **authority**, that is, legitimately acquired power. The very concept of a policy implies a well-ordered world in which policies are rarely concerned with unauthorized power. It is therefore reasonable when considering the management of distributed systems to take the simplifying view that all policies giving power can be viewed as giving authority so, for the remainder of the chapter, policies are characterised as either *motivation* or *authorization* policies.

Agents may be people or computers, so it is convenient to extend the concept of 'action' to include computer processes. A process's motivation is represented by submission of a command to the computer system. The authorization may be represented by mechanisms of the type:

- *access control* to authorize use of named resources,
- *accounting* to authorize use of quantities of commodities such as file store and central processor time.

Policies are not concerned with decisions to carry out an action instantly. When a manager specifies that something is to be done once only, and instantly, this does not imply that a policy is to be created. It simply causes the action to take place. Whether the policy defines a single future action to be carried out, or requires repeated actions, or relates to the maintenance of a condition, it needs to have persistence. Ex1 is a command which is to be carried out immediately and has no persistence. By this definition it is not a policy.

> Ex1　The system administrator is to back up department D's disc files to tape now.

Policies are about organizational goals, which need someone to achieve them. Policies have **subjects**, the people to whom they are directed, although in some cases the policy applies to all members of an organization. Ex2 has no subject to which it is directed. It is a goal but not a policy.

> Ex2　It should always be possible to recover from media failure.

It is a fundamental characteristic of policies that they are organized in a hierarchical fashion. Examples Ex3, Ex4 and Ex5 illustrate this:

> Ex3   The manager of department D is to ensure that the department can always recover from media failure.

> Ex4   The system administrator is to back up department D's disc files to tape once a week.

> Ex5   There is a system command (which was input by the system administrator) to run a job which backs up department D's disc files to tape each Friday at midnight.

In this example, the source of policy Ex3 (perhaps a director of an organization) has given responsibility for it to the manager of department D. The manager has made policy Ex4 and given responsibility to the system administrator to carry it out, which leads to the creation of policy Ex5. Policies are being made at a high level by a manager and the responsibility for achieving their goal is assigned to other members of staff, who may in turn do one of the following:

(1)   Create a lower level policy which will achieve the policy goal they have been assigned, and assign responsibility for it to another member of staff. This is what the manager did in the policy statement Ex4.

(2)   Achieve the specified goal themselves by carrying out actions which achieve the goal, for example, by the system administrator manually running a job each week to back up the files.

(3)   Create a lower level policy which applies, not to another member of staff, but to a computer system which will carry out actions which achieve the goal. This is what the system administrator has done in Ex5.

The examples also show that a policy at one hierarchical level may be considered, at a different level, as a plan of how to realize the policy.

It might appear that the distinction between authorization and motivation policies is artificial. Since no action can be performed without the agent having both authority and motivation, there is no point in having separate types of policy. However, there are cases where it is valuable to distinguish authorization and motivation policies because it is sensible for a manager to have the authority for some action without the immediate motivation to do it. Conversely, the manager may have motivation but no direct authority. Examples Ex6 and Ex7 illustrate the situation by having separate policies for authorization and motivation:

> Ex6   X has authority to create access rules for the entire organization. Other managers motivate him to create access rules according to criteria which they specify separately.

Ex7 X is responsible (that is, *motivated*) for getting the office rewired, even though not an electrician and not authorized to do rewiring. However, X has an adequate budget, and pays an electrician to do the job.

8.4.1 Interaction between managers: the need for policies

A common theme in distributed systems management is the need for independent managers to be able to negotiate, establish, query and enforce policies which apply to a defined general set of situations. Consider the example of an interaction between independent managers which arises from the interconnection of two network management domains, one a public network (PN), the other a private business network (BN). Communication is needed between the PN and BN network managers in order to exchange management information and establish access authorization. Suppose that there are two relevant policies in force: PN policy gives the PN Manager the authority to carry out all relevant management operations on the network, and BN policy requires the BN Network Manager to report regularly on the status of the business subset of PN nodes. These managers are the *subjects* of the policies. In the absence of any other policies, then the PN Manager has the authority to provide the regular status information, but no motivation to do so, while the BN Network Manager has the motivation to obtain the information but no authority to do so. The initial situation is shown in Figure 8.12a.

An additional policy has to be established by the PN Manager to meet BN's requirements. One approach is to create a policy which motivates the PN manager to generate the status information and provide it to the BN

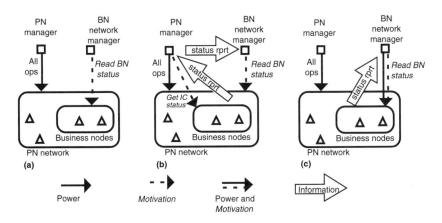

Figure 8.12   Policies for PN and BN managers. (a) Initial situation; (b) PN management operation; (c) IC management operation.

network manager regularly, as shown in Figure 8.12b. An alternative approach is to create a policy which gives the BN network manager the authority to perform the operations needed to obtain the regular status information, as shown in Figure 8.12c.

This example reinforces one of the main points in the model, that policies which *motivate* activities and policies giving *authority* to carry out activities can exist independently from each other. If only one of the two kinds of policies exists in relation to an action, the action will not be performed. Although the value of distinguishing the two types has been shown, there needs to be a manager who is the subject of both the policy authorizing the activity and the policy motivating it, in order for management activities to be carried out.

The example also shows that there is a need for a means by which independent managers can query, negotiate, set up and change policies. It can, of course, be done by the well-tried method of telephone calls and the exchange of paper. But, with the automation of many aspects of management in distributed systems and computer networks, there are potential benefits in using the distributed system itself to communicate and store policies, particularly with respect to automated management. Storing an organization's policies in a database permits staff to search, using keywords, for policies relevant to their proposed plans. To do this requires a way in which to represent and manipulate policies within a computer system. Converting policies and plans into sets of rules, with each set subject to controlling predicates, provides a declarative specification for interpretation by a supervisory function and hence a policy driven mechanism for control over managed objects. In distributed systems, it is preferable that the representation of policies and the protocols used to negotiate them should be uniform across management applications.

8.5 Policies and objects

The object-based view is that an operation is performed by a user object on a target object by sending a message to it. This view can be extended to distinguish between an operation and an *operation request*. This is a message which is issued by the user object as a result of being motivated. It will be delivered to the target object only if it is authorized. This observation and the preceding discussion show that it is useful to view many policies as objects which can be created, destroyed and queried, particularly those which motive or authorize management actions. Where there is a risk of ambiguity, these policies are referred to as **management action policies** but, where there can be no ambiguity, 'policy' is used for brevity. A policy, whether concerned with motivation or with authorization, is an object having at least the following attributes:

- **Modality**: a policy has one of the following modalities: positive authorization (*permitting*), negative authorization (*forbidding*), positive motivation (*requiring*), and negative motivation (*deterring*). Other modalities may be possible but the above have thus far proved adequate for the analysis of distributed systems management.

- **Policy subjects**: this attribute defines the user or process objects to which the policy *applies*. That is, it defines who is authorized or motivated to carry out the policy goal within the limits defined by the policy constraints. It is an expression that defines an explicit set of subjects or a predicate which a subject may satisfy (see Section 8.5.1).

- **Policy target object**: this defines the objects at which the policy is *directed*. It is also an expression which defines a set of objects (see Section 8.5.1).

- **Policy goal**: the goals or actions defined by the policy. Actions are modelled as *operations* to be performed on the target object (see Section 8.5.2).

- **Policy constraints**: predicates which must be satisfied before the policy is to have any effect (see Section 8.5.3).

8.5.1 Policy subjects and target objects

Policy subjects and target objects may each be specified either as a set of objects which can be enumerated or by means of a predicate which is to be satisfied. Example Ex3 is an example of the former. Ex8 and Ex9 show policies where the subjects and target objects, respectively, are defined in terms of predicates:

Ex8 Any user who is an owner of an object may delegate manager authority of the object to any other user.

Ex9 All users must apply encryption to the transmission of any financial transaction which is over £20,000.

Enumeration of policy subjects and target objects is normally not in terms of individual users as policy subjects or individual target objects but as organizational positions and domains of objects.

One essential characteristic of management domains is that their membership can be evaluated at any time. Some policies, however, such as Ex8 and Ex9, are general principles which can be stated without necessarily being able to state at any moment the set of objects to which they apply. The predicate may be expressed in terms of an attribute such as financial value, or a role such as ownership.

8.5.2 Policy goals

Policy goals may define either high-level goals or actions. Example Ex3 illustrates a high-level goal 'recover from [media failure]'; it does not prescribe the actions in detail. A number of different actions could achieve the goal. On the other hand, example Ex5 illustrates an action 'run the BackUp job [on department D's disc files]'. Note that the distinction between high-level goals and actions may depend upon the context. In an environment in which there is one standard 'back-up' operation defined, example Ex4, 'back up [department D's disc files]' might be regarded as an action, while in other situations it might be a high-level goal in which the system administrator has several options for action. Where there is no risk of ambiguity 'high-level goal' can be abbreviated to 'goal'.

Generalizing, any goal which is expressed purely in terms of operations is an action and any other goal may be regarded as a high-level goal. *Procedures*, often found in organizations' policy manuals, can be regarded as a sequence of actions.

Although examples Ex3 and Ex4 are motivation policies, the distinction between goals and actions is equally valid for authorization policies. There may be a high-level authorization policy, such as Ex10:

> Ex10   No one is authorized to carry out any financial transactions without specific authorization.

In this model this policy would be written as 'All users (*subject*) are not authorized (*modality*) to carry out any financial transactions (*goal*) [on accounts (*target objects*)] without specific authorization (*constraint*)'.

Actions represented by operations naturally have three components: the target object on which it is performed, the operation performed on it, and one or more *parameters* to the operation. Policies may relate not only to the operation name, but also to parameters of the operation. In example Ex9, the amount of the financial transaction is a parameter of the operation and forms a part of the authorization policy.

8.5.3 Policy constraints

The policy constraints component of a policy object places constraints on its applicability. Constraints are predicates which may be expressed in terms of general system properties, such as extent or duration. An example of constraints in authorization policies expressed by access rules is the limitations placed upon the terminal from which the operation may be performed, and/or limits on date or time, as shown in Ex11:

> Ex11   Members of Payroll Department may read Payroll Master Files, *from terminals in the payroll office, between 9 a.m. and 5 p.m., Monday to Friday.*

Policy constraints may be also be expressed in terms of events, as in Ex12:

> Ex12 is responsible for backing up the department's files *until Susan returns*.

8.5.4 Ordering of policies

Precedence ordering of management action policies is required either when they conflict or when two actions are incompatible, for example, if there is competition for the allocation of scarce resources. There are a number of ways in which policies can conflict. The simplest is when there are two policies, one of which motivates or authorizes a subject to perform an operation on an object and the other deters or forbids it. In this case precedence ordering can determine which is to have priority. Current security models assume mandatory security policies have precedence over discretionary security policies. If a discretionary policy authorizes an action and a mandatory policy forbids it, it is forbidden. A similar approach can be taken in respect of other policy conflicts.

Policies defining priorities state an explicit precedence order, in Ex13 for example:

> Ex13 The following priority ranking will be given to requests for [purchase of] hardware or software resources: (1) Mainline teaching resources. . . . (2) Equipment for support staff. . . . (3) Equipment for optional courses. . . .

A set of priorities is a set of interacting policies; the policy subject is motivated to perform the first priority action unless there is no longer any requirement for it, in which case the second one is chosen, and so on. The concept of *satisfaction* of a policy is needed to deal with prioritized policies. When high ranking policies are satisfied, policies with a lower priority may be addressed. Regrettably, these observations cannot be discussed further within the framework which has been presented thus far. To do so requires the exploration of the concepts of 'policies about policies' and how policies are to be manipulated. Although people have informal and intuitive perceptions about such policies, their formalization is still a subject of research.

8.5.5 Multiple management

The issue of multiple management has already been identified in discussing objects which are referenced from two or more domains. Now that a more formal view of policies has been presented, it is possible to analyse this further. Multiple management of objects arises because:

- there are multiple managers in a domain of policy subjects;

- domains explicitly overlap, each domain being the target object of a policy with a different set of policy subjects;

- there are implicit overlapping domains containing target objects of different types which refer to the same real-world entity. This can result in conflicting management operations which affect the real-world entity;

- two policies with different policy subjects apply to a single domain of target objects.

When more than one manager controls an object, potential conflicts may occur which are similar to those found in multi-user databases, which result from having multiple writers to shared data. Two managers may attempt to perform conflicting operations on an object or one manager may change the state of an object without the knowledge of the other. Concurrency controls such as locking provide mechanisms to serialize the operations and prevent interference between simultaneous operations on an object. These are familiar distributed database techniques for handling concurrency control and atomic transactions, which can be applied to management operations. However, concurrency controls on their own may not be sufficient. Managers need cooperation protocols to ensure that they do not issue inconsistent operations which are applied sequentially to an object. These prevent one manager enabling an object and another immediately disabling it. Concurrency control cannot prevent this. These types of cooperation protocols are application-specific.

8.5.6 Operations on policy objects

The minimal set of operations that can be performed on policy objects is:

- *Create* a policy
- *Destroy* a policy
- *Query* a policy

These operations on policy objects may or may not require authorization. If the computer system were used passively, say as a documentation aid, it might be acceptable to have no restrictions upon its operations. At most there could be a warning if an invalid policy object is created. An example could be the system detecting that a filing clerk appeared as the policy subject for the company's corporate strategy! On the other hand, if the policies are actually used to influence system actions as in the case of access control policies, restrictions on operations are certainly required. Authorization policies are discussed in Section 8.6 and a similar approach is taken in discussing responsibility in Section 8.9.

Although all policies are regarded as objects, some are *fixed policies*, fixed for the life of the system, while others may be altered dynamically. Example Ex14 illustrates a fixed policy.

> Ex14 The system coding shall ensure that it is impossible for a user to be logged on at two terminals simultaneously.

An object which expresses policy Ex14 will typically be separate from the coding that implements it. But a system could use the same policy object as part of its implementation, for example, by representing it as an object with a read-only attribute stating the number of terminals at which the user could be logged on, which the system queries when appropriate. Registering it as a persistent object ensures that it is not removed as an undesirable restriction at the next software release, that is, the intent is deliberate. Using it as part of the implementation enables systems with differing policies to be generated more easily.

8.6 Authorization policies

The most common form of authorization policy is access control. Very large distributed systems typically consist of multiple interconnected networks which span the computer systems belonging to a number of different organizations. Authority cannot be delegated or imposed from one central point, but has to be negotiated between independent managers. They wish to cooperate but may have a very limited trust in each other. They may wish to give each other access to their computer systems which is closely controlled both in the scope of the objects which can be accessed and the operations that may be performed on them. Access control policy relates to *authority* and to how authority is delegated. Security models of access control are first considered, followed by a discussion of one particular approach to discretionary access control.

The organizations using and managing distributed systems are hierarchical in nature and authority in them is delegated downwards from senior managers. In general authority is delegated not to a person but to a position or role within an organization. Typically the decision is that 'the payroll clerk is authorized to change the payroll master file', and that 'John Smith' should have that authority only because he occupies the position of payroll clerk.

The model for delegation of authority must reflect the organizational management structure and policy as well as providing mechanisms for the transfer of authority from one agent to another. A resource owner should be able to delegate authority over its resources to another within the mandatory constraints of the system. In addition it must be possible to delegate *the authority to delegate*, but limit the scope of this second level delegation. For example, an owner can delegate responsibility to a security administrator to give users, in a defined part of an organization, access to objects for which the security administrator has responsibility. The model assumes that there is no inherent right of access of any kind for ordinary users; if a person is not the owner of an object, and has not been given authority, then the system should refuse all access.

8.6.1 Security models

Security models, in general, do not attempt to model policies as objects. However, policies are recognized as essential to security modelling. A number of different models of security policies are discussed in (Olson and Abrams, 1990). As an illustration, consider the USA Department of Defense Trusted Computer System Evaluation Criteria (TCSEC) (DoD, 1985), which regards a security policy as a fundamental aspect of its approach. Statements like; 'There must be [a] . . . security policy enforced by the system. . . . there must be a set of rules that is used by the system to determine whether . . .' give the impression of a policy, specified as a set of rules, which guides the actions of the system. This is compatible with the policy model of this chapter if a rule is viewed as a potential system object. The definition of security policy in the OSI Security Architecture (ISO, 1988) is similar: 'The set of criteria for the provision of security services'.

Logical access control is divided by the TCSEC into two categories: mandatory and discretionary. **Mandatory access control** enforces polices which are built into the design of the system and cannot be altered except by installing a new version of the system. TCSEC does not define it formally, but an example is the policy that in multi-layer security systems data cannot be read by a user with a lower security clearance than the classification that has been assigned to the data. It defines **discretionary access control** mechanisms as those which allow users to specify and control sharing of objects with other users.

This categorization can be described in terms of the policy object model. There are in fact three different characteristics which appear in the Department of Defense definition of mandatory access control:

- the policy cannot be altered;
- the policy applies universally, that is, the sets of policy subjects and target objects are all the objects in the system;
- the policy has priority over all other policies, that is, over discretionary access control policies.

8.6.2 Access rules

Access rules are authorization policy objects whose purpose is to enable the system to determine if users are allowed to perform operations on target objects. A simple access rule is shown in Figure 8.13. It specifies a **user domain**, which identifies the set of possible users who can perform operations; the **target domain**, which identifies the set of possible target objects on which operations can be performed, and an **operation set**, which are the authorized operations a user can perform on a target. There is no default access allowed to users. An operation request is authorized if and only if an access rule exists which applies to it. That is, the user object is in the set defined by the user domain of the rule, the target object is in the set defined by the target domain of the rule and the operation is in the operation set of the rule.

Access control policy is inherited through subdomains; that is, an access rule applies to all the indirect members of the user and target domains. For example, the rule 'Members of ALL_USERS can read members of ALL_FILES' would allow any user to read any file by inheritance through the domain hierarchies.

An access rule maps on to a policy object as follows:

- the modality is always positive authorization;
- the policy subject is the user domain of the access rule;
- the policy target object is its target domain;
- the policy goal is its operation set;
- constraints, typically relating to date, time or location of user, are also allowed in access rules.

An operation may require more than one access rule. For example, the *include* operation on a domain object (see Section 8.3.1) requires permission both to add to the policy set of the domain and to use the identifier of the object to be included. Also, a compound operation such as *move* requires both the above *include* permissions for the destination and also *remove* permission for the source domain; three permissions in all.

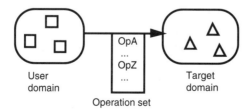

Figure 8.13 An access rule.

Access rules are not unique to managers and management interactions; they are required to enforce the security policies of computer systems with respect to what resources can be accessed by users or objects acting on their behalf. The generalized access rule is the specification of a low-level security policy in terms of what operations are permitted between two objects, which may be domains or ordinary objects. In addition to an applicable access rule, there has to be compatibility between the interfaces of the user and target objects, to permit the user to bind to the target. This is a configuration issue rather than an access control issue, and is checked by the configuration management system.

As with other policies, it is possible that there are overlapping access rules – more than one access rule satisfies the requirement. No conceptual difficulty arises from this, as it indicates that authority has been granted through more than one route, but there may be practical difficulties when attempting to remove a user's access rights. For example, if it is intended to prevent a user from accessing a particular domain of objects, it is not sufficient to remove any access rules which give the user explicit access to the domain. It is also necessary to ensure that there are no access rules which would give the user access by policy inheritance from its superdomains.

The specification of access rules will be constrained by the security policies within an organization. Where there is a need to modify access rules dynamically during the life of the system, this is modelled by treating access rules themselves as objects. Access permissions are given and removed by creating, destroying and modifying access rule objects. These operations must themselves be controlled by policy constraints. This is achieved by imposing rules for the creation, destruction and modification of access rule objects. This is discussed in Section 8.8 as one of the aspects of delegation of authority.

One way in which to enforce access control is to use the **reference monitor** concept (Anderson, 1972; DoD, 1985). The function of a reference monitor is to enforce the authorized access relationships between subjects (users) and target objects of a system. It is a trusted component of the system. All operations requested to be carried out on an object are intercepted by the reference monitor, which only invokes the operation if the access is to be allowed. Figure 8.14 illustrates that, in general, access control is carried out by the system, and not by the target object itself, although the implementation of the reference monitor by the object is not ruled out. The figure also shows that the operation of the reference monitor is transparent to the user provided the access is authorized, but if the access is not authorized the operation is not invoked and the user is informed by a failure message.

To illustrate further how access rules support authorization policies, consider the following example access rules. Both relate to the interaction of the hypothetical companies ABC and DEF and the need of DEF to access

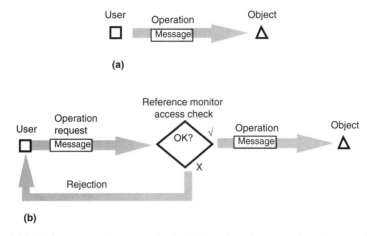

Figure 8.14 Reference monitor access check. (a) User view of an operation; (b) access checking by a reference monitor.

ABC's files. (Refer again to Figure 8.5 for a diagram of ABC's file directory structure.)

(1) Any member of DEF_USERS can create, read and write files in the ABCDEF_SHRD_FILES domain.

(2) Any member of PERSONNEL can read files in the DPA_DOM domain.

The access rules name neither the users nor the objects and so one cannot tell directly from them whether the access by a particular user to a particular object will be allowed. The domain structure, as shown in Figures 8.4 and 8.6, has to be known in order to interpret the access rule. The access rules remain valid for members of the domains, whatever objects move into and out of the domains. This achieves the requirement for maximum stability in the face of change.

8.6.3 User and mechanism views of access rules

The meaning of an access rule is straightforward. It states that any user object in the set defined by the user domain of the rule is authorized to perform any of the operations in the operation set on any of the objects in the set defined by the target domain of the rule. There is a fixed policy that in the absence of authorization by an access rule, an operation request (attempted access) is forbidden. In the user view of the system, whenever a user issues an operation request, the system must appear to search every access rule in the system, allowing the request if an access rule matching it is found, but forbidding it if none can be found. This is clearly completely impractical as a mechanism since it does not scale for use in systems with large numbers of users and objects and, consequently, large numbers of access rules.

Two implementations of access rules are therefore necessary. An **access rule object** corresponds to the user view and is the means by which users specify access control policy. The (simplified) mechanism for efficient implementation of this is by translating each access rule into access control entries (ACEs) in access control lists attached to target domains. The ACE consists of the user domain and operation set in the access rule. It is attached both to the target domain and also to all its direct and indirect subdomains. When a user attempts to access a target object, the user's ancestor domains are attached to the operation request. The reference monitor examines the ACEs for each of the target object's parents. If the user domain part of the ACE matches any of the domains in the operation request, and the operation itself is in the ACE's operation set, the access is allowed. If none of the target object's parents have an ACE permitting access, the operation request is forbidden.

The system can therefore evaluate the request by reference solely to the information in the operation request and the parent domains of the target object. The relationships between the user and mechanism views of access rules is illustrated in Table 8.3 (see Figure 8.15). (Domain expressions are discussed in Section 8.3.4.)

There is clearly a problem of ensuring consistency between the views of access rules, as the two views can become inconsistent through system errors and failures. Consistency checking and restoration tools are therefore necessary in order to diagnose and recover from any inconsistencies.

Other possible implementations are by capabilities held by the source or through an authorization server (Steiner *et al.*, 1988). The latter is queried by the destination when an operation is attempted or provides a capability to the source before an operation is attempted. This works well when the

Table 8.3   User and mechanism views of access rules.

User view		Mechanism view
Object name	↔	OID
User domain		Combined to form an access control list (ACL) entry:
Operation set	↔	{*user domain, operation set*}
Target domain		The target domain and each of its subdomains hold an ACL

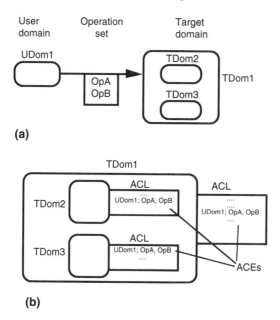

(a)

(b)

Figure 8.15 An access rule and its corresponding access control lists and entries. (a) User view: access rules; (b) mechanism rule: ACLs and ACEs.

destination has ready access to the authorization server, for example, by being in the same high speed local area network. But unless provision is made to cache authorizations at the destination in anticipation of further enquiries, it is a mechanism which scales rather poorly.

8.7 Management control concepts

This section describes the management concepts of **ownership, separation of responsibilities** and **management structure** relating to authority and its delegation.

8.7.1 Ownership

Although humans will use automated agents to perform operations in many situations within the system, they are ultimately responsible for the actions of any system and retain responsibility for the actions of the agents. They therefore require the power to control the agents. Thus one can always trace responsibility back to human users, the **owners** of the system (the board of directors of a company). *Ownership* is here intended to denote a concept as close as possible to normal legal ownership of goods and property. All computer systems in a country such as the UK process resources with identifiable legal owners who have legal powers over them. Ownership is assumed as the starting point for delegation of authority.

As an approximation, ownership of an object implies the legal power to perform any feasible operation on it, together with responsibility for the operations which are performed. There are of course limitations to this power, which act as constraints. For example, owners of personal data may not disclose it except under the terms of data protection legislation; the owner of petroleum spirit at a bulk distribution plant must ensure that an automated system dispensing it to tanker vehicles does so in accordance with defined safety regulations. Restrictions of this kind have to be represented in computer systems as mandatory constraints.

Unlike some authors, for example Lampson (1974), who have assumed that the user who creates an object automatically becomes its owner, a distinction is made here between ownership of objects and the delegated power to create them. The example of a data processing clerk who submits a job to create a new version of a file of bank accounts clarifies the argument. The clerk is not the owner of those accounts, but is carrying out the task of creating the file as an agent of the owner of the bank. When considering authority, the assumed starting point lies with an owner, who can then dispose of or share ownership, or delegate a subset of powers to another person. Provided that this is done legitimately this other person is described as having gained authority.

8.7.2 Separation of responsibilities

Separation of responsibilities is an important control concept which is familiar in the context of auditing. It ensures that no one has excessive authority. It requires that different aspects of certain transactions should be carried out by different users, so that no one person can carry out the transaction autonomously. An example is the authorization of payment of suppliers' invoices, where the input of invoices to a computer system must normally be carried out by a different user from the person who can trigger off the actual release of payments. Neither can carry out the other's function, so the payments cannot be made without their cooperative activity. Requirements for separation of responsibility have to be specified at an application level but support for it needs to be provided by the access control system. This example demonstrates that the concept of separation of responsibilities should also be modelled in computer systems (Clark and Wilson, 1987).

The separation of responsibility also manifests itself in the role of a security administrator who is often responsible for granting access authority in large organizations. Security administrators must be able to grant access authority, but must themselves be denied access to the resources under their control. That is, the concepts of having access and giving access have to be decoupled.

8.7.3 Management structure

Each organization has its own management style, which is reflected by different management structures and policies for delegation of authority. Four typical roles within an organization management structure are identified here: *owner*, *manager*, *administrator* and *user*. Owners can share ownership with other users, or can delegate manager authority. Managers can delegate authority to administrators. Administrators can, for example, create access rules which allow ordinary users to perform operations on target objects. Note that it is a policy decision whether users in a management role have authority over themselves. Administrators can also give themselves access rights. Although this can be specifically prevented as in the above case of the security administrator, it is not enforced as part of the model.

8.8 Delegation of authority using management role objects

When authority is delegated, there is a need to control to whom it is delegated, the resources over which the authority applies, and how the authority can be passed on down a management chain. The existence of an access rule allowing UserA to create an access rule object is clearly not a sufficient control by itself. It provides no constraint on the contents of the access rule object which is created. UserA would be able to create access rule objects to enable any user to access any objects. A means is therefore needed of placing controls on the contents of access rule objects.

The concept of **management role objects** (MROs) is introduced to define the range and nature of the managerial authority of the members of a domain. A management role object has a *user domain*, which defines the members of the role. It also has a variable number of scope attributes, one for each kind of authority for the role, defined by management policy. Each scope attribute is a domain expression which identifies the objects over which the role members have managerial authority. Using owner as an example, authority relationships are mapped onto management role objects as follows: a user is an owner of a target object if there is an owner MRO for which the user is a member of the MRO's user domain, and the target object is a member of the MRO's Owner_Scope attribute.

Membership of a role gives a user the authority associated with that role. If a user is a member of more than one role it has the authority associated with each role, that is, someone or something may be the manager of more than one department in an organization. A user is moved to another role object if his function in the organization changes.

The example management structure discussed in Section 8.7 can be used to illustrate typical management objects. There are managerial roles of owner, manager and administrator. Owner and manager MROs have single scope attributes: Owner_Scope and Manager_Scope. An administrator's MRO has two scope attributes: Administrator_User_Scope and Administrator_Target_Scope, one to define the users and the other to define the target objects, for which the administrator can make access rules.

An owner has authority over a defined set of objects (users and/or target objects). An owner can give away or share ownership (sharing means creating joint ownership rather than partitioning the objects between two owners), and delegate the manager authority over these objects, to other users. An owner is defined as a member of an MRO whose Owner_Scope determines the extent of owner's authority. The owner can create manager MROs, include users in them and alter their Manager_Scope attribute, within the bounds of the Owner_Scope attribute, in order to set the scope of their authority. The owner can also share the ownership.

The fact that the creator of an object is not necessarily the owner of it follows automatically from the model. If a user creates a new object in a domain, the ownership of that object, like all others in the domain, remains with the domain's owner. Indeed, the user cannot even read the object after creation unless an access rule also permits the read operation.

A manager similarly has authority over a defined set of objects. The manager can define a set of users and/or a set of target objects as the scope of authority of an administrator. A manager is defined as a member of a manager MRO. A manager can create administrator MROs, include users in them and alter their Administrator_User_Scope and Administrator_Target_Scope attributes, within the bounds of his Manager_Scope attribute. In this way administrators can be appointed and have the scope of their authority set.

An administrator can give authority to users to perform operations on objects by creating access rules, by virtue of membership of an administrator MRO. The users to whom access authority can be granted are limited to those in the role's Administrator_User_Scope while the target objects on which access authority can be granted are limited to those in the Administrator_Target_Scope.

Where one of the main aims is to allow administrators to create access rules for other users while preventing them from giving themselves access, for example, for security administrators, this is done by ensuring that the membership of the MRO's user domain and of the Administrator_User_Scope attribute of the role do not overlap. Because administrators (as members of the user domain) cannot themselves be members of their Administrator_User_Scope attribute, they cannot grant that access authority to themselves. This achieves the desired separation of responsibilities between granting access and having access. Administrators do need to have access to some objects, but they cannot create the requisite access rules. This need is satisfied by a second administrator who can allocate the required access to the first.

Many systems have an informal concept of users' personal domains, where the user is automatically allowed authority to give access for other users. A typical and quite general (mandatory) policy is that a user should be allowed to give any other user in the same organization access to resources in the user's personal domain. In terms of the model, a user should have an authority equivalent to an administrator's authority, with an Administrator_ User_Scope of all users in the same organization and the user's personal domain as the Administrator_Target_Scope. The setting of these scopes is envisaged as being done automatically by the system when a new user is registered.

8.9 Responsibility

A policy subject has been said to be 'responsible for' carrying out the goal of a motivation policy. So far this has meant that someone has the intention that the subject should carry out the action. Likewise, the policy manager, is said to be 'responsible to' someone else. Consider example Ex15:

> Ex15   The head of department decides that the system administrator shall be responsible to the administration manager for backing up the department's files.

Ex15 is represented by two policy objects, each created by the head of department. One motivates the system administrator to do the back-up actions, and report to the administration manager on their success or failure. The other motivates the administration manager to supervise the system administrator and take appropriate action, depending on what the system administrator does.

Delegation of responsibility is represented by the creation of motivation policy objects within the constraints of a hierarchy of managerial responsibility. If the policy objects are to be more than documentation aids, they must support the notion that users can create policy objects only within the scope of their responsibility. Recognizing that the development of the concept of policies as objects is still a matter for computer science research, this section sketches out a possible approach.

A manager's delegation of responsibility for a goal to a user is through the creation of a new policy object, as seen above. The creation operation is itself subject to a fixed policy. This requires that three conditions are met:

(1) The set of users to whom responsibility is delegated (the subject of the new policy object) is a subset of those which the manager can motivate to perform the goal (the set of users within the subject *user scope* of the manager);

(2) The set of target objects to which the new policy object is directed is a subset of those on which the manager is motivated to achieve its own goal (the set of target objects within the *target scope* of the manager);

(3) The goal of the new policy object is a goal which the manager is motivated to achieve by some existing policy (the goal is within the *goal scope* of the manager).

The user and target scopes are identical to those which are used in the delegation of authority – a domain expression which defines a set of users. On the other hand, definition of 'goal scope' is impossible until goals have been successfully defined. Intuitively, goals should be ordered and policy creation should be permitted only if the goal in the created policy is less (in the ordering) than the goal scope of the manager. As an example, *selling* policies may be considered of 'lesser' scope than *marketing* polices, which includes market research and product development as well as selling.

8.10 Conclusions

This chapter has shown that many features of distributed systems management can be represented formally. Most successful has been the application of the object modelling paradigm, which assists in capturing the notion that it is real logical and physical entities that have to be managed and that it is important to identify the management interfaces to those entities. It is then tempting to apply the object modelling approach to the problem of representing agglomerations of manageable entities by introducing the concept of the domain. Domains provide a useful structuring construct, enabling the system architect or designer to represent large systems at a coarser level of granularity than the object. Systems constructed to this type of modular architecture have the merit of being more scalable than systems structured in terms of their basic (object) elements. However, the value of this concept for systems implemented in the field still remains to be proved in practice. Some authors consider domains to be determined by any predicate which can lead to a grouping of objects. The approach taken here is that the natural grouping for management purposes is in terms of a common policy which applies to the group.

Much of the discussion on policies applies to management issues in general and is not restricted to information technology. However, policies are seen as being of particular significance in distributed systems management. Not only do they provide predicates for grouping objects into domains (thereby helping to reduce the complexities of scale), but their influences are recognized far from the location where management first puts them into effect. With distributed systems often being loosely federated distributed processing environments, each with its own managers and policies, there is the strong possibility of interaction between independently specified policies and, consequently, the prospect of conflicts. Therefore, if one intends to model all management activity in terms of objects, the next step is to apply the model to policies. Even though the first applications show promise, they are very much subject to further research. It could be some time before suppliers will adopt these techniques and give their products object interfaces to distributed system management policies. However, the examples given in this chapter show the value of being able to formalize policies and the relationships between policies so that deductions can be made concerning their consequences.

Summing up

- Object modelling captures the essence of management, its policies and its domains.

- The object model forms a good basis on which to describe managers and managed objects.

- Objects need to be grouped so that policies may be specified in terms of groups rather than individual objects.

- Management policies are a main driving force behind the actions of managers. They can be divided into policies which motivate them, and those which authorize them, to perform actions.

- Because policies are an important part of any management system, it is useful to model them as objects whose main attributes are: modality (positive/negative motivation/authorization), subjects (who carry out policies), target objects (at which the policy is directed) and goals of the policy.

- One important example of a policy object is the access rule, a form of authorization policy for discretionary access control.

- Management concepts, such as ownership, separation of responsibilities and management structure, are required for control of an organization.

- The orderly transfer of control in an organization, based on management concepts, is achieved by using management role objects to define the range and nature of managerial authority.

- The concept of responsibility can be analysed in terms of motivation policies, but its elaboration is still the subject of research.

- Further research on formalisms for policies is required.

References

Anderson J.P. (1972) *Computer Security Technology Planning Study*, ESD-TR-73-51, vol. 1 AD-758 206, ESD/AFSC Hanscom, AFB Bedford, MA, October

ANSA (1989). *ANSA Reference Manual*, APM Ltd., Poseidon House, Castle Park, Cambridge CB3 0RD, UK

Cheriton D.R. and Mann T.P. (1989). Decentralising a global naming service for improved performance and fault tolerance. *ACM Trans. on Computer Systems*, 7(2), 147–83

Clark D.C. and Wilson D.R. (1987). A comparison of commercial and military computer security policies. In *IEEE Sym. on Security and Privacy*, pp. 184–94

DoD (1985). *Department of Defense Trusted Computer System Evaluation Criteria*, Department of Defense (USA), DoD 5200–78-STD, December

DOMAINS (1990). DOMAINS Basic Concepts, version 1.0, November

ISO (1988). *ISO/IEC 7498-2: 1988 Information Technology – Open Systems Interconnection – Basic Reference Model – Part 2: Security Architecture*

ISO/IEC 7498-4: 1989 *Information Technology – Open Systems Interconnection – Part 4: Management Framework*

ISO/IEC 10040: 1992 *Information Technology – Open Systems Interconnection – Systems Management Overview*

Lampson B.W. (1974). Protection. *ACM Operating System Rev.* 8(1), 18–24

Magee J., Kramer J. and Sloman M. (1989). Constructing distributed systems in Conic. *IEEE Trans. on Software Engineering*, 15(6), 663–75

Moffett J.D. and Sloman M.S. (1992). *User and Mechanism Views of Distributed Systems Management* Proc. Open Forum '92 'Distributed Computing Practice and Experience' Utrect, November 1992

Moffett J.D. and Sloman M.S. (1991). Delegation of authority. In *Integrated Network Management II*, (Krishnan I. and Zimmer W., eds.), pp. 595–606. Amsterdam: North-Holland

Moffett J.D., Sloman M.S. and Twidle K.P. (1990). Specifying discretionary access control policy for distributed systems. *Computer Comm.*, 13(9), 571–80

Olson I.M. and Abrams M.D. (1990). Computer access policy choices. *Computers and Security*, 9, 699–714

Peckham J. and Maryanski F. (1988). Semantic data models. *ACM Computing Surveys*, 20(3), 153–89

Sloman M.S. and Moffett J.D. (1989). Domain management for distributed systems. In *Proc IFIP Sym. on Integrated Network Management*, Boston, MA, May 1989 (Meandzija B. and Westcott J., eds), pp. 505–16. Amsterdam: North-Holland

Steiner J.G., Neuman B.C. and Schiller J.I. (1988). Kerberos: An Authentication

Service for Open Network Systems, Winter Usenix 1988, Dallas TX, Project Athena. MIT, Cambridge, MA 02139, USA, 12 January

Wegner (1990). Concepts and paradigms of object-oriented programming. *OOPS Messenger*, **1**(1), 7–87

9

Standards for distributed systems management

Objectives

- to identify management standardization activities taking place in ISO, CCITT, IEEE and related bodies
- to note the contributions being made to the management standards by the Network Management Forum and to distributed systems management by the Open Software Foundation
- to compare the systems management approach of ISO with the Internet Simple Network Management Protocol
- to note that most of the standardization activity concerns the management of communication resources
- to consider the likely future developments of distributed systems management standards

9.1 Relevant standards activities

Standards benefit users by providing an open market for equipment. In this way users are not obliged to obtain their computing and communications products from a single vendor. Standards benefit vendors by encouraging inter-operability. This increases the size of the market and opens up new opportunities. Standards also bring the benefit of defined functionality and provide a yardstick against which to make and to judge claims of conformance. These benefits of standardization, which are familiar in programming language and communication protocol standards, apply equally to distributed systems and to their management standards.

A first significant step towards developing the relevant standards came in 1978, when the International Organization for Standardization (ISO) created a subcommittee whose task was to develop standards for Open Systems Interconnection (OSI). This move stemmed from the experience gained during the 1970s in the design and structuring of data communication networks. Although standards had previously been developed for some aspects of data communication such as the High Level Data Link Control protocol, OSI was a new direction for standardization for two reasons. Firstly, it was *prospective* rather than *retrospective*. That is, OSI standards anticipate, and so prepare the way for products rather than arise as a response to the development of products. Secondly, OSI considers the requirement for a family of related standards and provides a standardization regime so that this family can be developed in a coherent manner.

The OSI standards are targeted at the communications environment and data communication. Although they deal with some applications of communications such as file and message transfer, they are not capable of providing an integrated set of standards covering all aspects of distributed systems. They are therefore being augmented by a complementary activity to establish a regime in which standards for Open Distributed Processing (ODP) can also be developed prospectively. The main international activity for developing both these sets of standards is taking place in a Joint Technical Committee of ISO and the International Electrotechnical Commission (IEC) within its Sub-Committee 21 (ISO/IEC JTC1/SC21). This work is closely paralleled by CCITT (the Consultative Committee for International Telephony and Telegraphy), which is developing a set of technically equivalent recommendations for OSI. That is, the substance and editing of the ISO and CCITT texts are generally identical except for those stylistic differences where, for example, ISO refers to *standards* whereas CCITT refers to *recommendations*. CCITT is developing ODP-related recommendations under the title of 'Distributed Application Framework'. Further references to networking and OSI standards can be found, for example, in Waters (1991).

The need for management standards was recognized at the birth of OSI and was later identified as a significant aspect of ODP. However, the diversity of management requirements means that these standards are harder to define and to apply than those for data link control or for file transfer. The initial focus of standardization activity has limited the development of standards for distributed systems management to the management of the communications infrastructure of OSI; hence the name OSI Management. It is undertaken internationally within working group 4 of Sub-Committee 21 (ISO/IEC JTC1/SC21/WG4). There is related work taking place within other JTC1 Sub-Committees. For instance, the management aspects of protocols appropriate to networks and data links are developed within SC6. CCITT's recommendations for OSI management standards are documented in the X.700 series of CCITT recommendations. The IEEE, having developed the 802.x series of local area network protocols, is developing protocols to assist in managing these local area networks. In a separate activity, the IEEE is developing standards for managing processing systems. The work is being undertaken as part of the POSIX initiative to develop open interfaces for applications support from computing platforms.

Since 1989, the development of OSI management standards and of products conforming to those standards has been given a major impetus from the activities of the Network Management Forum (NMF). The Forum is a world-wide association of over 100 companies. They represent computer manufacturers and communication systems suppliers. Their work has contributed significantly to the development of the ISO/IEC standards. The Forum publishes its proposals for network management and, whilst there are some differences between these and the equivalent drafts for international standards, it is the Forum's policy to converge to the international standards within two years of their publication.

Whereas the Network Management Forum, as its name implies, is concerned primarily with the management of networks and hence with OSI management standards, another grouping of suppliers, the Open Software Foundation (OSF), is concerning itself with the management of open computing environments. OSF seeks to identify and endorse suitable, state-of-the-art products. It is leaning heavily towards the POSIX initiative to meet its management needs.

Whatever the source of the standards, they deal exclusively with the operational and supervisory aspect of management. There are no standards (and no proposals for standards) to support the organizational aspects of management. This chapter shows, in outline, what has been achieved so far in the development of network management standards. For a detailed exposition of OSI management standards see Jeffree *et al.* Westgate (1992).

9.2 Organization of OSI management standards

Network management, as a distributed processing activity, requires a symbiosis between people, their management activities, their computing systems and their communications environments. Three interface types are relevant to distributed systems and their management (see Figure 9.1):

- those between user and system,
- those between the application program and the system,
- those between systems.

Here 'system' is used in the OSI sense of an information processing system which, whilst it can be complete in itself, is configured to interact with other systems to meet the requirements of an information processing activity. All three of the above interfaces are amenable to standardization. The user–system interface is the domain of windowing systems and user interface management systems. That between the computer program and the system support is seen as being the provence of programming languages and operating systems platforms (e.g. POSIX). The third area is that of OSI standards and hence of OSI management standards.

The initial motivation for OSI standards was the need to develop a coherent structure for communications which could support a diversity of computing applications programs interacting over a range of communications technologies (Ethernet, token ring and bus, X.25 packet switching, frame relay, etc.). This structure is specified in the OSI Basic Reference Model (ISO/IEC 7498–1) and is independent of applications and of technology. However, the individual communications protocols to which the Basic Reference Model gives rise are application and technology specific. Whereas OSI is primarily concerned with communications, certain common applications, such as file handling, message handling and management, have

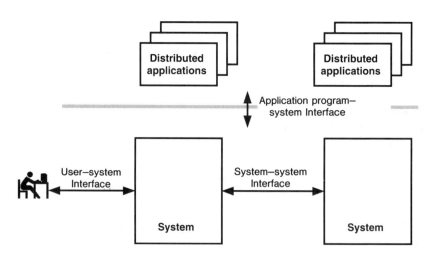

Figure 9.1 Distributed systems interfaces.

recognized that it is possible to define standards for the structure and meaning of application specific data and the operations which can be performed upon them. This has given rise to two important aspects of OSI application layer:

- standardization of open communications between systems,
- standardization of end system activity.

The former is expressed as conventional OSI protocol standards. The latter has led to the development of new techniques for documenting application specific standards. OSI management standards provide one of the best examples of this trend in needing to specify standards for distributed end system activities. They demonstrate an approach which is worthy of study because it is being refined and applied to other distributed processing standards.

This development of management standards uses an object modelling paradigm. Some of the benefits of object oriented approaches to distributed systems management have been described in the previous chapter. There are significant reasons why this is valuable and appropriate for information technology applications which are the subject of standardization as well as for management standards in particular. Object modelling identifies the interfaces to objects and the operations which can be invoked. It uses information hiding to conceal the internal structure of the object and treats separately the methods by which internal functions are to be implemented. In an analogous way, standards are concerned to specify interfaces and the functions that are accessible through those interfaces. The realization of those functions is a matter for specific and proprietary implementation.

The objects of concern to OSI management are the management view of resources which support an OSI communication environment. The resources may support several sets of functions, some of which will be concerned with their normal communications activity, others with their management activity. The management aspects of the object interface are described as a **managed object**. The term has arisen for historical reasons. From an object modelling perspective it could be simpler to regard the resource as an object and the managed object as one of a set of typed interfaces which the object presents, being the one which represents those aspects of concern only to management.

OSI management standards also relate to the processing and data storage resources which support management activity. Examples of management support are **filters**, which selectively discriminate items of management data, **logs** in which to accumulate management data records, and **schedulers**, which identify schedules for management operations. As well as performing management functions, these resources can themselves be managed. As managed resources, they too are represented as managed objects.

These factors led OSI management to be organized into four groups of standards:

- standards which relate OSI management to the OSI environment;

- standards which set out the information model for management, showing how managed object data and operations are formally defined, cataloguing common objects and their attributes;

- standards which define the semantics of certain classes of managed objects and how they can be used to support and provide management functionality;

- standards to handle communication of management data and controlling operations. These provide the conventional OSI **service** definition and matching **protocol** specification for data interchange between management applications.

These four groups of standards are discussed in turn in Sections 9.2.1 to 9.2.4, respectively.

9.2.1 OSI management in the communications environment

The architectural view of OSI management places it firmly within the context of the communications environment specified by OSI. There are two standards in this category. One, the OSI Management Framework (ISO/IEC 7498-4), extends the scope of the OSI Basic Reference Model for the purposes of management and is a part of that standard. The other, the Systems Management Overview (ISO/IEC 10040), aims to give an architectural perspective of the normal manner in which management and its communications are perceived as taking place.

The OSI Basic Reference Model expresses the concept of protocol exchange between peer entities in a seven-layer hierarchy. The service provided by each layer adds value to the communication service provided by lower layers and so provides an enhanced service to a higher layer. Because OSI management is a distributed processing application, system-to-system communications are conveyed by application layer protocol exchanges (that is, through the topmost layer of the OSI Basic Reference Model). This is termed **systems management**. However, some management information is of necessity communicated in lower layer protocols. This may occur during failure conditions, or during system bootstrap or re-configuration. To handle these management communications, the OSI Management Framework defines the concept of **layer management**. The framework specifies the circumstances when layer management is appropriate and the constraints upon its use. Systems management is specified as the norm.

The OSI Management Framework also defines the concept of the **management information base**. This provides a way to visualize the management data flow within a system. Data generated as a result of layer management exchanges or relating to the operation of the layer entities which handle communication protocols can be made available for monitoring communications or for their control. Data related to or derived from the activity of one layer can be used either by that layer or by other layers in the same system. Clearly, it would be inappropriate to pass this management related data through the service interfaces between each of the OSI layers unless the data were being communicated, through the systems management protocol, to other open systems. The management information essentially lies outside the specific context of the immediate data interchange. The information provided is often of more significance to the network operator, because it relates to the use and performance of the communication resources, the nature of faults to be rectified or equipment changes to be configured into the network. The way in which the management data is made available to and communicated between the communication and management resources within a single open system is determined by management need and realized through local implementation. The data associated with the managed objects which represent the resources constitutes the system's management information base. This is to be visualized as a conceptual repository of the management data associated with the management of the resources referenced by that system (see Figure 9.2).

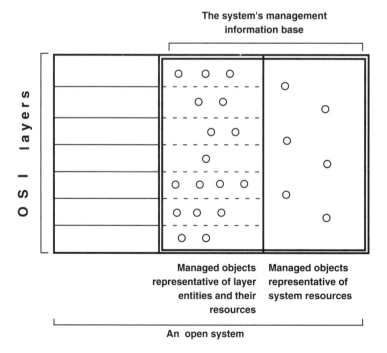

Figure 9.2 Visualizing the management information base.

The way in which systems management standards are organized is further developed in the Systems Management Overview. This standard defines how the application layer is modelled for the purpose of management. It specifies how a communication context can be established for the purpose of management. It places constraints upon conformance criteria that are applicable to systems management standards.

Systems management is described in terms of management interactions between the management process and the managed object. These interactions fall into two categories, **operations** and **notifications**. Operations are initiated by the management process and responded to by the managed object; notifications are 'spontaneously' generated by some internal event within the managed object and communicated to the management process. The management process is partitioned into two management entities. The entity concerned with initiating management operations performs a **manager role**. The other entity provides a controlled mechanism for accessing the managed object. This is termed the **agent role**. Systems management standards currently define no structure for the process that performs the manager role beyond its ability to generate operations and receive notifications. The agent role is a dual role. On the one hand it provides many of the supporting distributed processing activities of management. On the other hand, it performs the normal functions of a conventional 'layer-protocol machine'. The protocol supporting aspects of the agent are discussed further in Section 9.2.4. In supporting management, it controls the access to managed objects, handles predicates to define which operations will be performed upon managed objects and determines which notifications will be forwarded to their intended manager role destinations. These can include a management log. This two-fold character of the agent role is not brought out explicitly within the Systems Management Overview's architectural description.

In as much as the agent role provides a representative for items of management support functionality, the agent can be considered as containing resources which may be controlled and monitored for management purposes. The management interfaces to the agent's resources are also characterized by managed objects. As a consequence, the architecture of the systems management standards specifies how systems management manages itself. Thus, discriminator managed objects provide systems management with the tools to express predicates to control the flow and distribution of notifications and determine what data is to be recorded in log objects. This enables systems management standards to provide a unified architectural view of all management data and activities and to offer a valuable foundation upon which to build a more general description of distributed systems management standards.

The manager role and the agent role are represented as being embodied within two application layer entities residing in different open systems. This architecture make the interactions and the interface between manager and agent explicit. However, the standard emphasizes that the roles are characterized by the nature of the information exchange which is taking place at any instant. The distinction between manager and agent is entirely related to a given instance of management communication. A real computer system can be functioning in an agent role for one sort of management communication and also functioning in a manager role for another sort of management communication. Figure 9.3 illustrates these two roles. It shows two systems, X and Y. An entity operating in the manager role in X is shown interrogating system Y to determine the state of a resource (represented by a managed object in system Y) through an entity operating in the agent role. An entity operating in the manager role in system Y is shown receiving a notification (as an M-EVENT-REPORT; see Section 9.2.4), which identifies that an alarm has been generated in system X and has been forwarded by an entity operating in the agent role. These two communications can even be taking place at the same time. Figure 9.4 shows this interaction as a time sequence diagram to illustrate how the interrogation and the event report can overlap in time.

Whereas the systems management overview standard provides the above architectural perspective upon systems management, it does not, in its present form, provide a sufficiently detailed architecture to describe how OSI management as a whole can be envisaged as supporting the management of the communications environment. This is being addressed in further work on an **extended management architecture**. Issues which arise from the present, incomplete specification of the systems management architecture are discussed at the end of this chapter.

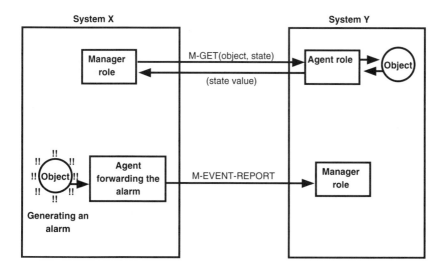

Figure 9.3 Interactions between entities in manager and agent roles.

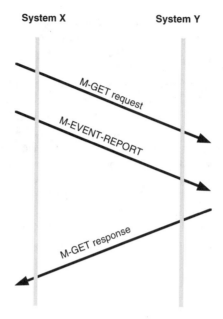

Figure 9.4   Concurrent management interactions between systems.

9.2.2 The structure of management information

A particularly important set of standards deals with the way in which management information is standardized. These are shown in Table 9.1. The first member of the set (ISO 10165-1) defines the object model used for OSI management. The Guidelines for the Definition of Managed Objects (GDMO) (ISO/IEC 10165-4) show how managed objects and their attributes, operations and notifications may be formally specified. Recognizing that many objects and operations are common to several different management functions, two further documents (ISO/IEC 10165-2; ISO/IEC 10165-5) provide sets of these definitions.

Table 9.1   Structure of management information standards.

ISO standard reference	Title	CCITT recommendation
10165-1	Management Information Model	X.720
10165-2	Definition of Management Information	X.721
10165-4	Guidelines for the Definition of Managed Objects	X.722
10165-5	Generic Management Information	X.723

The first three documents listed in the table were ratified as international standards during 1991 for publication the following year, at which time the fourth was registered as a Committee Draft for progression to full International Standard status in a further two to three years.

As well as setting out the object modelling principles being adopted by systems management, the Management Information Model identifies the operations which may be performed upon managed objects and their attributes. These are:

- *create* a managed object;
- *delete* a managed object;
- perform an *action* upon a managed object;
- *get* an attribute value;
- *replace* an attribute value;
- *replace* an attribute value with its *default value*;
- *add member* to a set valued attribute;
- *remove member* from a set valued attribute.

The Management Information Model also specifies that managed objects may emit *notifications* as a result of an event which is internal to the managed object. The standard states quite precisely that it does not constrain how that notification may be subsequently processed. Notifications can be forwarded to other open systems, submitted to a local log or to another process internal to the open system or discarded. All these options are subject to management control.

The Guidelines for the Definition of Managed Objects standard specifies a set of **templates** to be used in the formal specification of managed object classes, their attributes, actions, notifications, etc. Once the syntax of the templates has been mastered, the templates make it easy to understand the precise specification of all standard features of any piece of management information. The value of this approach is demonstrated by the fact that it is being adopted by other information technology standards. The templates have five important characteristics: registration; importation; packaging; abstract syntax and behaviour semantics. These are discussed in turn.

Firstly, every specification of a managed object class, an attribute, a notification, etc. can be registered and that registration can be referenced by means of an **object identifier**. An object identifier is a registered label whose construction is unique and unambiguous. Registration therefore provides a way to label all standard aspects of management information. If the specification is provided in a standard, the registration of the object identifier is provided in that standard. To deal with the situation that some aspects of management information may lie outside the scope of international standards, ISO has defined mechanisms whereby **registration authorities** may also provide unique object identifiers (ISO/IEC 9834-1). These can be used to register, and thereby identify, other managed objects.

Secondly, specifications of managed object classes in one standard can import specifications from classes defined in other standards. Where the class specification is refined by importing an object class definition and adding additional characteristics, this is performed through the process of class **inheritance** leading to the specification of a subclass. Classes may also *import* specifications of attributes, actions, and other parameters by reference to the standards in which those things are originally defined. The significance of these importing and referencing mechanisms from the point of view of standards is that an item of management data needs to be defined once only. Thereafter, its use elsewhere is always by reference. This has the advantage that if problems are subsequently discovered in the primary specification, only one document need be revised and re-issued. It could be argued that, had the decision been taken to provide a copy of the full specification in any standard, the standard might have been easier to read because it would reduce the need for extensive cross-referencing activity. However, the penalty would be the need to make parallel updates of all the standards whenever a single change was required. This raises the prospect of introducing unintended differences and standards modified in this way could become incompatible over time.

The process of making standards inevitably results in compromise. One set of national representatives may wish to see certain features highlighted in a standard. Others may not be concerned with those features but seek to promote an alternative. Obtaining international consensus, therefore, tends to result in choice and options within the standards. As a result, there is a kernel set of features which an implementation of the standard must provide if it is to conform to the standard, together with a range of options. Too many options can result in difficulties for suppliers who try to implement conforming products. Suppose supplier X implements a management system which expects to access subset P of the optional attributes of a managed object class. Supplier Y on the other hand decides to implement subset Q of the attributes within that class. If subsets P and Q have no common members, implementations supplied by X and Y will be unable to use any of the optional features even though both could reasonably claim to conform to the standard. In an attempt to avoid this type of scenario, systems management introduces the concept of a **package**. This is a defined subset of the full object specification. It is constructed according to the specification of a package template and can be registered with an object identifier just like any other instance of a template. Packages are of two types, **mandatory** and **conditional**. The conditional packages provide the options but constrain the way in which options are specified. Firstly, if the package is to be used, then all features of the package are to be used. Secondly, if a managed object class contains one or more conditional packages, its specification is required to say the conditions under which that package shall be present. If these conditions are satisfied, the package must be instantiated in order that the object may conform to the specification, that is, the package then becomes mandatory.

A feature of the template structure is the way in which it aids the syntactic specification of the data associated with the managed object class. Abstract syntax for OSI management data is expressed using the ASN.1 notation (ISO/IEC 8824) and the various templates provide pointers to ASN.1 definitions. This aspect of the standards is sufficiently formalized that a number of computer programs are beginning to appear that are capable of checking the syntactic specification and generating coded data structure statements in a standard programming language for embedding in a computer program.

Another important feature of template constructs is the ability to specify the **behaviour** of an object, attribute etc. Currently, this takes the form of natural language expressions of the semantics of the entity whose behaviour is being classified. If a suitable standard specification language were available, that behaviour could be defined formally. One obvious benefit of formal specification would be to provide automatic code generation using the combined syntactic and semantic specification of the managed object.

The Definition of Management Information standard (ISO/IEC 10165-2) specifies some of the managed objects which support and organize the flow of data needed to manage the open communication environment. These objects include log objects, log records and discriminator objects. The same set of standards documents also records the attributes which may be found within the managed objects (status indicators, counters, thresholds, etc.) and classifies a set of standard notification types. The more recent Generic Management Information standard is being developed to provide a common way of referencing managed object classes which are required when defining management activities associated with OSI layer entities.

All managed object classes inherit certain properties from a special managed object called **top** which resides at the top of the inheritance tree. *Top* is defined in the Definition of Management Information standard. Its mandatory package specifies two attributes. One is the *object class*. That is, every managed object has a (read-only) attribute which declares what sort of managed object it is. (Its syntax is an object identifier.) The other mandatory attribute is the managed object's **name binding**. This provides an object identifier of a name binding template which specifies the rules by which that managed object has been created and may be deleted, and the naming tree in which the object is contained. One of the conditional packages of *top* is a **packages** package. This package is present if the object instantiates any conditional package. Its single *packages* attribute lists the object identifiers of each of the instantiated conditional packages. The application of these simple standard rules, together with registration, provide a powerful mechanism by which managers can gain information about the characteristics of managed objects within an open system.

9.2.3 Management functions

Standards for network management cover the five functional areas of:

- Fault handling
- Performance monitoring
- Accounting
- Security management
- Configuration management

which were identified in Chapter 1. Although this classification has proved highly valuable in establishing management functionality, many of the elementary activities of management and many managed objects and their attributes are to be found in more than one functional area. This is particularly true of the discrimination and data logging functions, and also of the requirements to handle the management of operation schedules and timing data that provide the supporting functions for management. Therefore, the approach taken to documenting all the standards for management functions has been to break each functional area into a number of basic functions. These base standards can then be combined in whatever manner is suitable to meet the needs of a given management situation.

Agreement was reached in 1991 that the first seven of these functions should be registered as international standards. These cover some of the supporting functions and some functions relating to fault, configuration and security management functional areas. All are parts of the ISO/IEC 10164, the **systems management function standard** (ISO/IEC 10164). By mid-1992 a further eight standards had been registered for progression towards international standard status, covering other aspects of fault and security management, and also relating to accounting and performance management. These are listed in Table 9.2, which, in addition to providing a reference to the part of the ISO standard, also references the corresponding CCITT-assigned recommendation. Event Report Management and Log Control Function provide the support functions for monitoring which control discrimination and logging. Other support functions for Time Synchronization and Scheduling are under development. The Alarm Reporting Function and the Test Management Function supply some of the fault handling functions identified in Section 4.5. Also under development are standards for various categories of confidence and diagnostic tests.

Because discrimination is a particularly powerful facility for controlling the flow of management data, it is worth examining it in a little more detail. Notifications, which arise as a result of some object's internal

Table 9.2 Systems management function standards.

ISO/IEC standard reference	Title	CCITT recommendation
10164–1	Object Management Function	X.730
10164–2	State Management Function	X.731
10164–3	Objects and Attributes for Representing Relationships	X.732
10164–4	Alarm Reporting Function	X.733
10164–5	Event Report Management Function	X.734
10165–6	Log Control Function	X.735
10164–7	Security Alarm Reporting Function	X.736
10164–8	Security Audit Trail Function	X.740
10164–9	Objects and Attributes for Access Control	X.741
10164–10	Accounting Meter Function	X.742
10164–11	Workload Monitoring Function	X.739
10164–12	Test Management Function	X.745
10164–13	Summarization Function	X.738
10164–14	Confidence and Diagnostic Test Categories	X.737
10164–15	Scheduling Function	X.746

behaviour, are notionally submitted to any instances of **event forwarding discriminator** objects or **log** objects (or of objects which inherit their properties, or the properties of discriminator objects) which are within the same system. In terms of the current standards, the notifications may be thought of as **potential event reports**. Both logs and event forwarding discriminators contain a **discriminator attribute** which specifies a predicate, a boolean combination of identified attributes and the values to be associated with them. The potential event report is tested to see how the values of identified attributes compare with those in the predicate. Text strings may be tested for sub-strings. Alternatively, the test may be to check the presence of the attribute. If the predicate is satisfied, an event forwarding discriminator will arrange for the potential event report to be forwarded to a destination which is specified in another of its attributes. If the notification is being processed by a log, the event will be recorded as an **event log record**.

Handling states and relationships together with basic object manipulation (ISO/IEC 10164 parts 2, 3 and 1, respectively) provide the rudiments of the configuration management functions described in Section 4.6. Clearly, many more functions in support of configuration management remain to be developed.

The Accounting Meter Function supports some of the accounting activities specified in Section 4.8. Workload Monitoring and Summarization Functions provide two closely related standards to meet performance management requirements. They identify the concept of a **metric object**; an entity which can receive and manipulate monitoring data and provide behaviour statistics. These metric objects can have parameters through which the operation of their statistics algorithms can be controlled in the same manner as any other resources. The ways in which this control is exercised have much in common with the Accounting Meter Function.

The remaining function standards support security related activities. The Security Alarm Function, as its name implies, specifies standard ways in which alarms are communicated in the event of security violations. The Security Audit Trail Function provides the control of the special logging needed to assure managers and security assessors of a system's behaviour in a secure operating environment, as discussed in Chapter 5. Objects and Attributes for Access Control provides only the access control requirements for management and does not set out to be a general access control mechanism. It has been developed essentially as a support function for those objects which provide management with a secure networking environment.

9.2.4 Common management information service and protocol

An application layer protocol is used to communicate the data and operations relating to managed objects. This is the Common Management Information Protocol (ISO/IEC 9596). In principle, it is not the only protocol which could be used for this purpose and it has proved useful, as with other OSI protocols, to provide a description of the communication *service* which is being provided for the purpose of management communications. This is documented in the Common Management Information Service standard (ISO/IEC 9595). Colloquially, these two standards are known as CMIP (see-mip) and CMIS (see-miss) respectively. They are independent of specific management procedures and specific managed objects. They are applicable to all management functional areas. CMIP is designed to provide a mechanism for communicating between an entity operating in the *manager role* and a system which contains the managed object representation of resources and the facilities needed to support management. This latter system operates in the *agent role*.

CMIS offers the set of services which map onto the interface requirement of managed objects. That is, they provide the means for a managed object to send a notification to a managing system by means of a management event report (M-EVENT-REPORT). They also enable managing systems to communicate operations to the managed object interface. The general format of an operation is:

{operation, object reference, access right token, parameter list}

The basic operations are:

- *get* the value(s) of identified attribute(s) of the referenced object;
- *set* the value(s) of identified attribute(s) of the referenced object;
- perform an *action* on the referenced object;
- *create* a managed object of a referenced type;
- *delete* the referenced object.

It will be seen that these bear a close relationship to the operations that can be performed upon managed objects (see Section 9.2.2). *Set* is used to communicate the requirement to *replace*, *replace with default*, *add member* and *remove member*.

Additional facilities can be invoked as extensions to the basic standard. Using a concept known as **scoping**, one of these additions enables a set of managed objects, which are grouped together within some containing managed object, to be referenced within a single protocol exchange. It is then possible to manipulate the controlled object to *get* and to *set* the values of identified attributes. Another facility enables a request to be made for all operations upon objects within that scope to be performed as an **atomic** activity; that is, the operation is either successfully performed upon all items referenced or it is performed upon none of them. By using scoping and requesting a response from a managed object, it is possible to generate a considerable volume of data if the operation were, say, to *get* data from all the managed objects which it contains. Therefore, a service is provided to *cancel get* operations.

Because management operations may generate significant effects upon the ways in which systems operate, each communicated operation can be accompanied by an **access control** field. Where access control is managed using the access control attributes, an agent system importing those attribute definitions carries out only operations for which the correct access control authority is presented as part of the protocol. Another form of selection is the use of a **filter**. This operates in a similar manner to the discriminator which selectively forwards notifications. A filter uses the same set of constructs to define a predicate as does the discriminator attribute. If the predicate evaluation is satisfied, the specific operation can be performed. However, unlike the discriminator whose effect applies to all notifications, the filter applies only to the operation with which it is associated in the protocol exchange.

9.3 Conformance to OSI management standards

Standards are of real value only if artefacts can claim conformance to the standard and that conformance can be demonstrated. To avoid uncertainty,

OSI standards make explicit those features which must be implemented in order to demonstrate conformance. These items relate to the communication behaviour of application entities operating in the manager role and in the agent role as defined in the CMIP standard. The behaviour of implementations of managed objects must conform to the syntax and semantics as specified in the function and management information standards.

Thus, a system operating in the manager role must be capable of generating well formed CMIP application protocol data units (APDUs) and of accepting well formed APDUs from systems operating in the agent role. Because there are, as yet, no standards for manager procedures, no further conformance requirements can be placed upon managers. Systems operating in the agent role must be able to receive well formed CMIP APDUs from managers and generate well formed APDUs either in response to manager operations or as a result of notifications arising from within the system. The agent must be able to generate the appropriate error response if the incoming APDUs are not properly formed, or invalid operations are requested or non-existent managed objects are identified. This communication behaviour of manager and agent can be observed, at least conceptually, by detecting the data being exchanged through the connecting communication medium. Therefore, verifying that systems conform to CMIP is no different from verifying the conformance to any other OSI communication protocol.

OSI standards permit alternatives and options and this results in complex conformance requirements. In order to help both users and suppliers to derive benefit from the standards, OSI protocol standards are complemented by a series of standard proformas called **protocol implementation conformance statements** (PICS). These set out, as tables, the declarations that a supplier of products has to make when claiming OSI conformance. The supplier is required to affirm that mandatory requirements are met and to indicate which optional items are supported.

Agents provide the interface to managed objects and hence open systems claiming conformance in the agent role must be able to support the operations upon and notifications of the managed objects they contain. As a minimum, they must also be able to support the appropriate CMIS elements which enable them to communicate the data that is required according to a managed object's interface specification. Two classes of conformance have been identified. These are currently termed **dependent** and **general** conformance. However, the reader is cautioned that these terms have not been universally acclaimed and it is expected that they will be replaced over the next few years as the standards are revised. Even so, the concepts that these terms embody should retain their validity. Dependent conformance requires only that a system supports those communication services that are necessary to meet the needs of the objects it contains. That is, the communications needs of any managed object have to be satisfied.

A system which offers general conformance provides a CMIP platform. At association time, the services offered by that platform may be constrained by selection of appropriate functional units. These identify five functional categories which are indicated, in protocol exchanges, by object identifiers. A system claiming general conformance must declare which of these functional categories it intends to support. In effect, it identifies a profiled communication platform which a system can claim to make available for management purposes.

Verifying that systems conform to specified managed object behaviour is not straightforward. It is not the intent of the standards to coerce product suppliers to reveal the details of their implementations. Therefore, one cannot 'look inside' an implementation to see that any specific managed object is present and that it is likely to behave as required. Demonstrating conformance must rely on testing object behaviour from outside the system. Similar requirements exist when demonstrating that programming language compilers conform to programming language standards. Both require that tests be carried out by accredited test centres. But whereas it is reasonable to expect that a compiler implements all of the mandatory features of a programming language, there can be no corresponding requirement that a system shall implement every aspect of OSI management. It would be quite inappropriate to insist that a managed modem, for example, must operate in the manager role or that it must implement logging. Possibly its only required OSI management features are that it can identify its state and generate alarms. For this reason, OSI management standards are complemented by a further series of proformas. Analogous to PICS proformas, these provide:

- **implementation conformance statements** (ICS), which state the managed objects supported by the system;

- **managed object conformance statements** (MOCS) to identify the optional features of the managed object that are supported and any specific constraints that have been imposed as permitted by the standard;

- **management information conformance statements** (MICS) to state those features related to attributes, actions etc. which have been imported into implementations.

The guidelines that specify these proformas are documented in ISO/IEC 10165-6.

In view of the variety of options in OSI management's generic standards and the alternatives for the underlying communications support, even these statements are insufficient to ensure inter-operability. Therefore, OSI standards are being grouped into a series of **profiles**, which represent coherent sets of generic standards that have been selected to meet specific sets of requirements. Work on OSI management profiles is in its infancy.

The first two profiles relate to CMIP and its lower layer protocol support. One profile (ISP 11183-3) provides basic CMIP functionality while the other (ISP 11183-2) offers the extended functionality of access to contained managed objects with filtering and atomic synchronization of operations. Work is beginning on profiling management functions and the selection of appropriate managed objects.

The development of these profiles is taking place in three regional workshops: in North America (the Open Implementors' Workshop), in Europe (the European Workshop on Open Systems) and in the Pacific basin of the Far East and Australasia (the Asia Oceania OSI Workshop). Profiles developed through their collaboration are submitted to ISO and when approved are published as **international standard profiles** (ISPs).

9.4 Alternative approaches to management protocols

The standards for management described above are essentially those which relate to communications between OSI application layer entities. Two other approaches to communicating management data need to be considered for their position as *de facto* standards. These are the layer management protocols developed by the IEEE for local area network management and the Simple Network Management Protocol (SNMP) developed by the Internet community.

The IEEE has successfully developed a well known set of communication protocols for a number of local area network technologies (the IEEE 802 series of specifications). One member of this set (IEEE 802.1) defines how management interactions, for networks conforming to this set of specifications, shall be carried out. Because the IEEE specifications are limited to the physical and data link layers of the OSI Basic Reference Model, their management communications must take place through *layer management protocols* as defined by the OSI management framework. IEEE adopts an equivalent object model to ISO but, instead of mapping the operations and notifications onto CMIP, maps them on to the logical link layer protocol. Recognizing that this mapping could be regarded as a highly specific mapping onto an application layer protocol where the intermediate layer protocols are unchanging and implicit, IEEE have developed 802.1 to specify CMIP as communicated over a data link protocol. This approach is sometimes referred to as CMOL (Common Management Over Link-layer).

The Internet series of protocols developed through the use of ARPANET. Its end-to-end transmission control protocol (TCP) used over the Internet protocol (IP) (as the TCP/IP combination) is well supported by products. As networks grew in size and importance, the Internet community realized the need for protocols which carry management data. In keeping with the spirit of Internet protocols, which eschew complexity in order to reduce overheads, these management protocols were also to be simple, leading to the concept of the Simple Network Management Protocol (SNMP). SNMP has many of the features of OSI management. It allows operations upon attributes of a system and recognizes that systems can generate notifications concerning internal system changes. Thus, SNMP provides operations to *get* and *set* attribute values and **traps**, which, like notifications, signal events demanding management attention.

However, the SNMP data model is more rudimentary than that for OSI management. There is no equivalent concept of an object which is rich in internal behaviour. Rather, the attributes of a system are structured into a list which can be read from and written to. Also, the reports which signal events carry little information other than to indicate the event. It is anticipated that a manager will then read the attributes of the system issuing the trap to obtain more specific information concerning the event which caused the trap to be generated. The control of systems is carried out by the manipulation of attribute values rather than by invoking defined procedures like those which OSI systems management is able to do with the use of the *action* operation. The consequence is that side effects of attribute changes are less easy to specify and control. A further difference between the SNMP model of management and the ISO model concerns the presumption of where system intelligence resides. In SNMP it clearly resides within the system containing the managing activity. In contrast, the OSI model anticipates that managed objects and the systems which contain them may have sufficient intelligence that they are to some extent, self-managed. In spite of these basic differences in modelling management activity, there is sufficient commonality in the basic features of both OSI and SNMP approaches that simple systems conforming to systems management and others, conforming to SNMP, have been able to interwork through the implementation of a suitable management gateway.

It is when one considers very large networks, with thousands of attached systems, each one containing several attributes to be managed, that the limitations of SNMP become apparent. The need for the manager to know the structure of many remote attribute lists, the limitations on the ability to communicate significant management data in traps, the lack of filtering and scoping constraints all mean that SNMP does not readily scale. So although the protocol remains simple, the management task increases in complexity and the management communication traffic increases in volume to a far greater extent than is the case for OSI management.

One of the primary objectives of SNMP was to provide management over the Internet transport protocol, TCP/IP. Some consideration has therefore been given to the possibility of providing the richness of OSI management communications but using TCP/IP. Termed CMOT (Common Management Over TCP/IP) this approach introduces a lightweight presentation layer protocol so that CMIP can be carried over TCP/IP protocols.

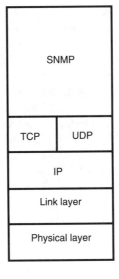
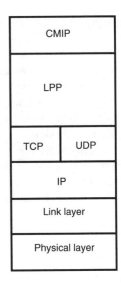

CMIP
Presentation layer
Session layer
Transport layer

OSI management

CMIP
SNMP

SNMP

CMIP
LPP

CMOT

Figure 9.5   Protocol profiles for OSI management, SNMP and CMOT.

Products are available which support CMOT though these are not as extensive as those that support management using SNMP. The protocol profiles for OSI systems Management, SNMP and CMOT are compared in Figure 9.5.

9.5 Other CCITT management standards

In addition to adopting OSI management standards in the X.700 series of recommendations, CCITT is also working on a parallel activity to develop management recommendations for telephony. It is developing the concept of the **Telecommunications Management Network** (TMN) for the management of its next generation of services, which includes frame relay and broadband integrated services digital network (ISDN) and uses the digital synchronous hierarchy of transmission standards. Whereas a management standard for telecommunications is narrower in scope that the management of distributed systems as a whole (the subject of this book), it is nevertheless appropriate to identify certain aspects of TMN, not least because the management of telecommunications is itself a significant distributed processing activity.

The TMN architecture is defined in recommendation M.3010. Because the application area is specific to wide area telecommunications, that architecture can be much more specific than it is possible for OSI management to be. TMN recognizes a hierarchy with three levels of management activities and each level of that hierarchy is associated with a particular part of the management system. At the apex of the hierarchy is the **operations systems**. This is where manager functionality is found. Operations systems communicate with **mediation devices**. Mediation devices have a role akin to the *agents* of OSI management. Communication between these two layers is specified in terms of the Q3 interface by Q series recommendations, Q.961 specifying the lower layer protocols of the OSI Basic Reference Model, Q.962 specifying the upper layers. (These references are currently subject to revision.) At the lowest of the three hierarchical levels are the **network elements**. These represent managed resources. TMN identifies two interfaces for communication with mediation devices (Q1 and Q2). TMN follows the ISO management model particularly closely when modelling the management data and operations of its resources in terms of managed objects. It uses the GDMO standard to specify its managed objects and their attributes, etc.

Helped by the specific nature of the management application, TMN is able to define an interface (the F interface) through which manager interaction can be take place. In this, it differs from ISO, which has not attempted to define such an interface in spite of its obvious importance. Any one of the architecture's components can be accessed through the F interface, thereby providing for direct operator interaction at any level in the hierarchy. The F interface is conceived as a workstation interface by which the workstation interacts with the other TMN components. It does not, however, specify the user–workstation interface, which is left as a local implementation matter.

9.6 Open issues in management standards

OSI management has successfully developed a considerable number of standards, which can support the management activities of a system which implements OSI standards. It has also developed a particularly powerful object specification method which is coming to be adopted by others who are specifying management requirements. Even so, there are a number of issues still to be resolved which affect the applicability of these standards to distributed systems. They relate to:

- Architectural issues
- Constraints in applying standards
- Limitations to the development of standards

9.6.1 Architectural issues

Although OSI management standards have the potential to evolve to include distributed systems management within their scope, it is essential that they adopt an architecture which supports a higher order structuring of management than the limited two-party interactions of the present standards. Indeed some attention to the basic architecture is also desirable and, without it, development of this large and ever-growing set of standards could become uncoordinated, with consequent lack of coherence in its components. The danger is that not only could there be irritating omissions, but there could also be conflicts where two developments provide the same functionality or the same specifications of objects in different ways. As an example, the concept of the agent does not fit well with the basic model of managers performing operations upon resources. The support functions used by managers, such as discriminators and access controls, are assigned to the agent. On the other hand, some support functions such as the ability to correlate notifications are being specified as part of the managed object interface. This is inappropriate if the managed object is intended to be a management representation of the resource because the ability to correlate data is a management property and not a property of the (communication) resource. Until the architecture of manager–resource interaction is clarified, and guidelines established to identify whether to consider management support as residing in the manager or the agent or managed object, there will be a blurring of the boundaries for placing support.

However, the more fundamental architectural change is that concerning handling the large scale of distributed systems. To date the focus, both in OSI management and SNMP, has been on the micro-behaviour of objects and attributes. Macro-constraints, such as those implied by a policy applicable over many open systems, still need to be addressed. A start has been made in ISO's extended systems management architecture studies. There are three aspects to consider. One aspect, the grouping of collections of managed objects into domains, was discussed in Chapter 8. Another is the provision of enquiry mechanisms to enable managers to gain knowledge about the structure and contents of these domains and the open systems within them. Already the concepts of the **discovery** and the **repertoire** objects have been proposed. Currently these are restricted to providing data identifying the contents of a system. However, by simple extension, they could be applied to a domain or other higher level structure. The use of these objects, coupled with the use of directory services and facilities for interrogating objects to discover their class and the packages they have instantiated, are all that is required to find out about standard objects within distributed systems. The third aspect concerns performing sets of operations upon collections of managed objects. These objects could be collocated in a single open system or they could be distributed over several open systems. These operations could be subject to constraints so that they may be scheduled to occur at given times, be subject to a system related predicate or performed as an atomic action. CMIP provides simple protocol tools to perform a single operation upon managed objects which are contained within another managed object and to arrange that the operation is performed atomically or not at all. However, there are no protocol mechanisms yet available which allow a set of operations to be performed as a single transaction. Possible protocol extensions under consideration include those for OSI transaction processing (ISO/IEC 10026). Because management is a real-time activity it may not be possible or even appropriate to recover a distributed system to its previous state if the transaction fails. More research is needed in this aspect of management before the appropriate protocol standards for synchronizing distributed systems management activities can be drafted.

Also missing are the ways to represent the activities of managers and the way that they are controlled through the rules expressed in management policies and planning statements. Whereas the behaviour of managed objects can be well specified to assert their response to operations and the conditions under which they will emit notifications, the corresponding behaviour specifications for managers are absent. What should a manager do upon receiving a notification (communicated internally or as an M-EVENT-REPORT)? Under what conditions should a manager request an operation upon an object? Clearly, these activities are governed by the rules to which the manager is subjected by higher authority and imposed by treating the manager as a managed object for the purpose of asserting those rules. Sequences of rules and their controlling predicates are expressions of management procedures. Only when there are standard ways in which to express and execute these rules will it be possible to specify management procedures and the behaviour of managers in an open manner.

9.6.2 Constraints in applying standards

Notwithstanding the uncertainties which relate to possible extensions to the architecture and the support needed for distributed processing, there are factors of a more practical nature about which managers of distributed systems are concerned. These are:

- The availability of products
- The diversity of objects
- Testing for conformance

A large number of management standards already exist and more are promised. There is a danger that the complexity of management, the range of future standards and uncertainties over product availability could act as barriers to the acceptance of management standards. To overcome user reluctance to commit to OSI management while it still under development, a number of major suppliers and user organizations have come together to specify a **Roadmap** for the standards. This specifies a phased development of the standards and the features that will be available at the completion of each phase. The concept arose within the Network Management Forum but has evolved to take account of the complementary developments elsewhere. The first phase of this work is largely complete and provides the essential components for responding to system faults. Some members of the Network Management Forum have already demonstrated the inter-operability of some aspects of the first phase at international communications conferences and exhibitions. This is an important step in establishing user confidence that the approaches to management are practical and effective.

The object modelling approach of OSI management has proved so successful that many organizations and many system suppliers wish to use the approach to develop their own object specifications. Whilst this is to be welcomed, there is a genuine concern that similar, but not identical, managed object specifications could evolve as a result of parallel activity in different areas of information technology standardization. If this occurred then, rather than easing the task of management, it would generate problems of inter-operability within open distributed systems. Those developing management standards are aware of this problem but are not constituted to police the situation and constrain proliferation of duplicate specifications. There are moves by some organizations to consider the provision of catalogues and libraries of managed object specifications. These, if developed and made readily available, will help to identify, and so possibly limit, unnecessary duplication of managed object specifications.

Management, being a complex activity, is bound to pose significant problems for those who wish to use the developing standards. This is particularly apparent when one considers that some of the management standards themselves relate to the issue of testing systems for correct (rather than conforming) behaviour. Test methods are needed to test for conformance when, for example, demonstrating the correct generation of fault reports even when the system is not faulty. When testing conformance to performance-related standards, it is important to ensure that the test itself does not compromise the performance data. Furthermore, there is a general issue of how to conduct conformance tests that are related to the management of system security in such a way that they do not compromise that security. These constraints have not been encountered in the development of conformance tests for OSI communication protocol standards. Agreed approaches are required before OSI management products can be submitted to standards test centres for certification that they conform to the standards.

Furthermore, the matter of interest for the user is not whether the individual aspects of the standard conform but whether the system as a whole conforms with the standards in a coherent manner. This requires that not only do the communications conform to the protocol specification but that the way in which managed objects are implemented also satisfies their specifications. Although the regional workshops are helping to constrain unnecessary variability in the realization of conforming products, ways to test these interfaces to determine the real effects of management controls (without having to delve into the supplier's code) are still to be examined and agreed.

9.6.3 Limitations to standards' development

In the long run, all aspects of management will have to be handled in a coherent manner whether they relate to communications objects, to processing resources and activities, or to data storage. Until this has been done, it will not be possible for managers to monitor and control their distributed processing environments effectively. This would be especially true if the computing and communications areas were to be developed, and therefore standardized, separately. When considering management standards in the context of distributed systems, two questions have to be answered. One is, can object modelling approaches pioneered in these standards be applied to distributed processing activities and not just those for management? This is the province of ODP standardization. The second question asks, what are the possible sets of management activities which may be expressed as standards? At present, most operations and most objects are very simple, as are their mappings on to management protocol. The objects of concern to the open processing environment have yet to be specified, though many types of object and attribute will be common to both the communications and the computing environments. Research programmes (such as those referenced elsewhere in this book) indicate that the principles found within OSI management are indeed applicable. The object modelling approach to management information can be extended to consider the managed objects that are to be found within the processing and data storage environments. Essentially these objects represent: physical computing resources; the logical resources of computer programs and their structured data; storage resources with their logical organization into filing systems and databases.

Finally, it is important to identify that management requirements can never be fully satisfied by standards, however perfect and complete those standards may be. There is a danger that the unwary, seeing the value of the standards and the functionality they support, may believe that standards are all there is to management. A simple example should counter this naive viewpoint. It concerns management policy. Standards can model and hence define the way in which management policy can be expressed, possibly in the form of control constructs. However, it is unlikely that standards will ever be able to specify standard policies. This is not because it may not be possible to identify a policy and then classify it; rather, it is because each enterprise has its own view about its policy and how it relates to its information processing environment. Standards can only be developed for situations that are common to many management situations and where the outcome can readily be foreseen. Yet some management situations must be expected to be too complex to be handled this way. They may be deemed sufficiently rare that it is not worth the expenditure of effort to plan in advance. That is, management, having analysed the situation, is prepared to take the risk and to adopt a policy of 'dealing with the situation should it occur'. Only one step further is the totally unforeseen situation. These must always be expected in any dynamic environment such as a distributed system. Clearly the unforeseen events cannot be codified into standards yet managers have to live with and plan for their occurrence. The best one can hope for is that standards provide the basic set of tools which enable managers to respond to the foreseen by taking appropriate action. This is the real challenge of open distributed processing management standardization, to produce the appropriate set of standard tools to support management. A response to this challenge is considered in the final chapter.

Summing up

- OSI's systems management standards are proving a valuable basis for a range of management applications.
- Systems management has the potential to scale well but it needs the augmentation of its extended architecture to do so effectively.
- Even with extensions, there will always be many aspects of distributed systems management which will not be standardized.

References

ISO/IEC 7498-1: 1984 *Information Technology – Open Systems Interconnection – Part 1: Basic Reference Model*

ISO/IEC 7498-4: 1989 *Information Technology – Open Systems Interconnection – Part 4: Management Framework*

ISO/IEC 8824: 1990 *Information Technology – Open Systems Interconnection – Specification for Abstract Syntax Notation One (ASN.1)*

ISO/IEC 9595: 1990 *Information Technology – Open Systems Interconnection – Common Management Information Service*

ISO/IEC 9596-1: 1991 *Information Technology – Open Systems Interconnection – Part 1: Common Management Information Protocol*

ISO/IEC 9834-1: 1991 *Information Technology – Open Systems Interconnection – Procedures for the Operation of OSI Registration Authorities – Part 1: General Procedures*

ISO/IEC 10026: *Information Technology – Open Systems Interconnection – Distributed Transaction Processing* (in preparation)

ISO/IEC 10040: 1992 *Information Technology – Open Systems Interconnection – Systems Management Overview*

ISO/IEC 10164: 1992 *Information Technology – Open Systems Interconnection – Systems Management – Part 1: Object Management Function*
Part 2: State Management Function
Part 3: Objects and Attributes for Representing Relationships
Part 4: Alarm Reporting Function
Part 5: Event Report Management Function
Part 6: Log Control Function
Part 7: Security Alarm Reporting Function

ISO/IEC 10165-1: 1992 *Information Technology – Open Systems Interconnection – Structure of Management Information – Part 1: Management Information Model*
Part 2: Definition of Management Information
Part 4: Guidelines for the Definition of Management Information
Part 5: Generic Management Information (in development)
Part 6: Requirements and Guidelines for Implementation Conformance Statements Proformas Associated with Management Information (in development)

ISP 11183-3. *International Standardized Profiles, OSI Management – Management Communication Protocols – Part 3: Basic Management Communications* (expected 1992)

ISP 11183-2. *International Standardized Profiles, OSI Management – Management Communication Protocols – Part 2: Enhanced Management Communications* (expected 1992)

POSIX. *IEEE 1003.7 System Administration Interface for Computer Operating Systems Environments*

Jeffree T., Langsford A., Sluman C., Tucker J. and Westgate J. (1992). (Westgate, 1992) *Technical Guide for OSI Management*. NCC-Blackwell

Waters G. (ed.) (1991). *Computer Communication Networks*. Maidenhead: McGraw-Hill

10

Current practice and future directions

Objectives

- to review the current state of distributed systems management and network management products
- to comment upon ongoing research
- to identify open issues
- to indicate a possible synthesis for management standards and distributed system management products
- to provide a scenario illustrating many of the topics discussed throughout the book

10.1 Distributed systems management products today

Data communications, computer networking and distributed processing are fast-developing fields. If the authors were to offer a detailed analysis of specific products on the market at the time of writing there would be the risk that the information in this chapter was out of date even before it was published. The reader would then be left with a historic account; a snapshot at a moment in time. For this reason the approach throughout this book has generally been to focus on the fundamental aspects and principles of the management of distributed systems rather than to deal with the specifics of actual systems. However, in this final chapter, the authors feel that the risk of obsolescence must be taken, by commenting upon the current state of distributed systems management, its products and those areas which could benefit from further research and development.

There is no lack of products which offer a 'management' capability, especially for local area networks (LANs) using the accepted standards of Ethernet, token ring, token bus and Fiber Distributed Data Interface (FDDI) specifications. But, with the exception of FDDI, which has benefited from the parallel development of network management standards, management for the other forms of LANs has developed after the products themselves have been widely installed. Typical of these are Novell's Netware and Microsoft's LAN Manager products. In consequence, the management offered is largely proprietary and so inhibits interworking or, where interworking is possible using TCP/IP, it is based upon the Simple Network Management Protocol. It is thus not directly compatible with OSI Management Standards. Because these products have been developed principally for the small LAN market, the architectures do not scale well to large systems with more than a hundred or so components. As an exception, Banyan's 'Vines' product is applicable to larger, multi-segment LANs and can be considered appropriate in systems with hundreds of attachments. Only recently have suppliers begun to offer products which provide management communications supported by either OSI lower layers (CMIP), by TCP/IP (CMOT), or by the IEEE logical link layer communication protocols for LANs (CMOL).

The management capability offered by many LAN suppliers largely consists of monitoring simple parameters such as the status of network attachments, statistics of network traffic (both successful and unsuccessful transmissions) together with a limited number of alarm signals to announce fault conditions. These are supplemented by a minimal control capability to start and stop monitoring and, in some instances, the facilities for down-line loading of communications software. In general all these procedures are operator driven. They are without facilities for closed loop control based upon a programmed response to a change in a monitored value or to a notification. The management facilities provided are targeted almost exclusively at the communications network. This appears to be the case even where the suppliers of the corresponding networking products do provide means for sharing files and distributing output to remote printers and graphical output devices. That is, the management tools are confined to those needed for *network management* rather than those for *distributed systems management*.

The long distance communications carriers have long realized the value of having management capability within their communication networks to provide them with all the benefits of rapid fault location, monitoring for performance bottlenecks and the capability for remote diagnostics and network reconfiguration. More recently, they have begun to respond to customer pressure to provide external interfaces to their internal management systems. And, also responding to the developing market, they have seen a business opportunity in offering network management products. As examples, AT&T are offering a Unified Network Management Architecture within which to place their communications product range, including their more recent Accumaster® products. The management interface is provided through the Accumaster Integrator®, which offers control over a number of network element systems for both voice and data transmission. In the UK British Telecom, as part of their Cooperative Network Architecture, offer a similar product, Concert®, through which to manage networks.

The computer suppliers also provide network management products which can be applied to both local and wide area networking environments. Some address both voice and data networking. Others concentrate primarily on satisfying the data communication requirement. Examples include IBM's System Network Architecture, Digital Equipment Corporation's Enterprise Management Architecture and ICL's Community Management. Where there are powerful computing resources, usually associated with a large mainframe computer attached to the network, these suppliers have taken steps to integrate the management of the communications network with that of the network attachments. This integration is typically restricted to the products of a single manufacturer though, from some product suppliers, they may be extended to accept devices from leading manufacturers. These architectures provide user support functions through software products like IBM's NetView, Digital Equipment Corporation's DECmcc (management control center) and Hewlett-Packard's OpenView.

Possibly because the earlier products focused upon architectures dominated by large, centralized mainframes, the tendency was for the management architecture to be centralized. More recently, for example in Digital Equipment Corporation's Enterprise Management Architecture, this tendency is being overcome. IBM appear to be taking a similar stance in their SystemView product range. The change towards a distributed architecture for management is to be welcomed. It responds well to the recognized need in many organizations for the management of the organization to be distributed, with extensive delegation of authority and responsibility. Even where the management of an organization is not distributed, the distributed management architecture of the information technology system is not a disadvantage. It is always possible to implement a centralized management system upon a distributed architecture. However, the converse (mounting a distributed management system upon a centralized architecture) is not possible.

Matching the spirit of the trend to using object oriented paradigms, the Enterprise Management Architecture provides an object-based framework for management of large distributed systems (Fehskens, 1989). The interface between managers and managed objects is provided by a system component called a Director, and domains are used in order to group objects, such as network components, into spheres of influence. ICL uses the domains concept to group resources and activities which support a specific class of information processing service (the **service domain**).

These more integrated products offer a greater capability than the LAN management products. As well as providing monitoring functions and configuration specifications to assist in network start-up, they offer improved user interfaces and programmer interfaces, and they are backed up with data repositories. All these enhance the operator's ability to deal with network complexity. The user interface provides higher level language facilities to interface to the basic monitoring and control functions provided by the management software. Because the interface can also offer facilities to tailor the format of information, this information can be displayed to the operator in ways which make it easier to assimilate. Programmer interfaces allow specific analysis routines and even allow a measure of closed loop control to be incorporated with network management, though the onus of providing such facilities tends to fall upon the system programmer. Using a database or repository which holds system-generated management data, operators have the capability to generate data logs and audit trails. In fault situations, these systems enable them to browse through the system history looking for analogous events, which may help diagnosis by indicating the likely cause of failure. Once established, the same repository can supply a record of the steps taken to cure or to circumvent a fault. This minimizes the mean time to repair the system and return it to operation, thus increasing the availability of the distributed system and its resources.

The concept of a repository of management information appears in many forms in these products. Typically, a repository contains not only references to the actual managed resources, but also, especially for object based implementations, references to the classes of objects with which the management systems will have to interact. These references supply the system with the basic data from which to construct standard management operations. The repository also contains the values of parameters needed to set attribute values and the values of attributes read from remote managed systems. Management tools may access the data in the repository as though it were a knowledge base. The 'help' facility in ICL's Community Management products provides a degree of computer assistance in fault finding by identifying analogues to observed fault situations and advising the operator on possible courses of action to be taken to fix the fault.

10.2 The need for tool integration

In the world of small stand-alone computers, the main management tasks involved in keeping the system running are maintenance of system and applications software, and occasionally changing the system configuration. These are fairly simple tasks requiring, at most, a few hours a year of a person's time and access to a manual. In the world of large mainframes, the situation is different. The management task is significant. It may require a large staff to cope with the various aspects of management and the many different management environments, each supplied with its own set of management tools. The staff could include system programmers, application programmers, user support staff (help desk), an operations manager (to look after the day-to-day operation of the system), and a system manager (who is in charge of the system, the staff and maintenance contracts, and makes policy decisions). The current trend in distributed systems is to interconnect small computers which, once a number have been joined in a network, form a more complex distributed system. The effect of this is to force the problems of managing a large system onto those people who have hitherto had to deal only with the management of small systems. It is neither practical nor cost-effective to replace the small systems managers with the staff necessary to run a large system, as there are many systems involved, often geographically separated, with different management policies reflecting local management requirements. The only way in which the small system manager can adapt to the practices of maintaining a large system is with the help of specialized management tools. These tools should have common system interfaces so that they can share information and work in harmony with one another; and they must have common user interfaces so that the manager can use the tools without having to learn the details of a profusion of different interfaces.

As well as providing tools for monitoring and control, some of these management systems (for example, NetView) contain tools for the planning and organizing aspect of systems management. However, the resulting large suite of software, often developed over a period of time and subsequently adapted to the systems management product, has not always been integrated in a coherent manner. Different components of the total package can have the idiosyncratic 'look and feel' of their origins. The consequence can be that although the same function is performed by the differently packaged components, the presentation or the means of providing the function differs from component to component. This highlights the need for integrated tools.

The ratification of standards for network management and the development of conforming products will increase the possibility for inter-working between the network management capabilities of systems. Through the activities of the Network Management Forum (NMF) the market leaders have declared that their (distributed) network management products will use the Common Management Information Protocol of OSI. Already, demonstrations have been provided of the inter-operation of OSI-based management systems. At the Telecom '91 exhibition in Geneva, Digital Equipment Corporation and British Telecom were able to show the former's DECmcc product managing the latter's components. In the same demonstration British Telecom's Concert product was demonstrated managing Digital Equipment Corporation's networking products, both using CMIP over an OSI network.

Another note-worthy milestone, also reached during 1991, has been the specification of a Distributed Management Environment (DME) by the Open Software Foundation (OSF). OSF, like the NMF, is an association of product and system suppliers. Their remit is broader than that of the Forum because OSF is seeking to apply information technology standards across the range of computing activities, of which network management is just a subset. In DME, they are specifically seeking to provide a broadly based tool set which can be used to manage distributed applications. Its communication base is OSI with CMIS. Because OSF has adopted UNIX™ as its operating system platform, it has also recognized TCP/IP as an alternative data transport protocol. As a consequence, SNMP and CMOT are also supported management communication platforms.

OSF has, in general, avoided the development of totally new products. Where it can, it has preferred to take existing products which meet its requirements. If existing products do not quite meet the need then it looks to build additional functionality on that product. For DME, OSF looked seriously at Digital Equipment Corporation's Enterprise Management Architecture, seeing in it a product which nearly met its requirement. However, in the end it selected components from a number of suppliers which taken together seemed to provide all of the required functionality without the need to develop new components, and a better base for future enhancements. Although this strategy is not without its attendant risks (and DME has already been subject to some revision), it has the benefit of leading to a more broadly based product; one in which more suppliers are well placed to offer product support.

Without seeking to provide an exhaustive catalogue either of components or suppliers, Table 10.1 lists a number of key DME components, initially seen as satisfying the operational needs for distributed systems management identified within this book. The result is a management system

Table 10.1 DME components.

Components	Supplier	Description
Communication support		
CM-API	Groupe Bull	CMIS and SNMP application programming interface
objcall	Tivoli Systems	ANSI C applications programming interface
Postmaster	Hewlett-Packard	Authentication,
Object Dispatcher	Tivoli Systems	address resolution and routing
Data Engine	IBM	Object server
NeL	Wang	Event management
Environment services		
HUGS	Tivoli Systems	Host management
Software Distribution Utilities	Hewlett-Packard	Software distribution
NetLS	Hewlett-Packard and Gradient Technologies	Licence services

which supports both object oriented and procedural based management applications. The target is to have it available late in 1993. However, DME still leaves many higher level management functions to be coded by an organization's in-house system software support team. It is inevitable, in a product with such diverse origins, that the early version will lack some of the desirable coherence and commonality of architecture which would be available in a product from a single design team. Indeed, the initial agreement on DME's constituents was subject to considerable debate and could yet be modified still further.

But, beneficial as these developments are, there is still the lack of equivalent protocols for managing the distributed processing environment. Although the work of IEEE's POSIX group is advancing the definition of managed objects required in the information processing environment (POSIX), definition of procedures is largely limited to software distribution and associated management control. The onus of capturing management policy and realizing it within the intelligence of the distributed processing environment is still the responsibility of the business analyst and systems programmer. For these reasons the coherent management of multi-vendor systems with a unified set of tools for distributed systems management is still in the future.

10.3 Future directions

The management of objects which have to be implemented in a variety of programming languages and run on different computers, supported in a consistent manner by different operating systems, but employing a common architecture, is still an important area for research. For the present, different manufacturers will use their own proprietary and often *ad hoc* techniques to integrate the facilities required to manage a system into a single coherent entity. Although there are many suppliers offering architectures for their systems and network management products and notwithstanding the recent initiatives of OSF, they have relatively few features in common. Generally the architecture identified by the supplier refer to the design and implementation architecture for the product. It is not intended to embrace an architectural view of the management activity itself from which a product architecture can follow.

Yet without this high level view of architecture, it is difficult, even impossible, to establish a thoroughly generic approach to management of distributed processing. One consequence of this is only too clearly seen in the shortcomings of management standards. Standards have been generated from the 'bottom up', starting with simple, two-party management relationships and a matching 'architecture'. Even then, concepts and techniques are being evaluated, often by standardization committee, and standardized before they have first been implemented in realistic systems and thoroughly tested. The recent initiatives by the Network Management Forum and by the Open Software Foundation are helping to counter this tendency but there is still only limited large scale experience of distribution of information technology's management functions.

Research programmes, which adopt a systematic and coherent approach to management, are currently taking place. The authors of this book are engaged in two of them, the UK Domino project (Sloman *et al.*, 1992) and ESPRIT DOMAINS project (Fink, 1991). Both are investigating the concepts of management domains as means of handling system complexity and ability to scale, heterogeneity and standards. Current research, which should lead to advances in the medium term (4 to 5 years) affects complexity, heterogeneity and policy specification. In addition there could be matching advances in the 'look and feel' of user interfaces to management systems and in techniques for automating management.

Chapter 6 highlighted the importance of appropriate languages and language bindings in making distributed systems easier to manage. The DOMAINS project is researching and developing an object oriented language for specifying both the syntax and behaviour of objects of significance to management. In doing this, it is exploring ways in which to overcome the limitations imposed by GDMO, which uses natural language to express behaviour (see Chapter 9). The DOMAINS management language builds upon the template structure specified by GDMO. The language can be compiled to generate executable objects. In research to investigate languages to express management intent within the hierarchical organization of management, Yemini and colleagues (1991) discuss a manager–agent delegation model. Sets of management statements are submitted to agents to specify required operations. The approach overcomes some of the weaknesses of OSI management, which cannot readily specify filtering or discrimination constraints on groups of objects. The description adopts the OSI terminology of **agents**, thereby extending the management support activities of OSI agents. There seem to be close analogies between the agent defined by Yemini and colleagues and a **target**, as defined by DOMAINS, in which a target acts as a domain to which authority has been delegated.

Ability to scale and complexity will become important issues for future distributed systems. Already there are systems within a single organization with thousands of attached computing components, thousands of users and tens of thousands of objects to be managed. With the prospect of inter-organizational communications to handle inter-company business transactions and to buy and sell information processing capabilities just like any other commodity, the numbers of users and managed objects will grow to millions. Although the concept of domains offers a promising solution to some of the problems of structuring large scale systems, neither the research nor early products have yet generated significant implementation experience to establish the performance and demonstrate the reliability implications of systems built using domain architectures.

The problems of heterogeneity should ultimately be solved by standards, though they must be the appropriate standards. If managed objects are specified and implemented according to the standards then they can be expected to interwork. Yet standards are, inevitably, compromises and have to accept many different influences. Therefore standards cannot always guarantee to adopt the best technical solution for every eventuality. Because the resources of standards-making bodies are finite, standards can only be cost-effectively generated for those objects in common use. The next section discusses an approach to specifying managed objects in a standard way without the need to have a standard specification for an object.

The research community is only now beginning to address the issue of how to specify management policy. There are obviously many levels of policy from the high-level objectives of a business enterprise to low-level access rules which specify which users can have access to particular sets of resources. As well as establishing the scope of the topic, work is needed to establish notations by which to capture policy statements. One of the more significant issues for the future of distributed systems concerns the application of policies where systems cross organizational and even national boundaries. In these situations there is no single source of authority to control management policy. Protocols are needed to enable managers to negotiate (and so reach agreement on) policies which affect resources and activities falling within different domains of organizational or political responsibility.

For example, the Pythagoras project (Bedford-Roberts, 1991) is concerned with modelling policies in order to create a database of the policies of an organization. Initially its purpose is for users to query the database, matching textual patterns in the policy statements, in order to enable them to ascertain what policies may exist in a specified subject area. The system does not interpret or constrain the contents of policies, although this might be considered as a future development. A **policy** in Pythagoras is a right or responsibility declared so as to prompt action which conforms with an intention. There are two types of occasion when it is normal to apply policy: firstly, when intention and consequent action are separated in time; and secondly, when intention and consequent action are associated with different people. This is consistent with the view, expressed in Chapter 8, of policies being persistent, because the action cannot be an immediate consequence of an intention. Pythagoras makes an interesting distinction between **satiable** and **insatiable** goals, which could respectively be viewed (i) as goals which are achieved by carrying out actions and (ii) as goals to maintain state, that is goals of the form 'keep the department running'.

Deontic logics, the logics of normative systems, are attractive candidates for expressing policies. These logics have operators which denote **obligation** and **permission**, either of states or actions. The natural approach is to equate 'obligation policies' to the motivation policies discussed in Chapter 8, and 'permission policies' to authorization policies. There are, however, differences of emphasis which require the retention of different terminology. At a philosophical level, some people follow Kant's belief that 'ought' implies 'can' more or less strongly. Most flavours of deontic logic actually have the axiom that obligation implies permission, or even define them interchangeably; permission for an action means being not obliged to refrain from the action. By contrast, motivation and authorization policies must be coupled rather loosely, as discussed in Chapter 8. It is clearly of interest when there is a motivation policy for an unauthorized goal, but it is a common situation in human organizations for the goals to be set up before the resources to achieve them have been marshalled, as is the case when a company prospectus is issued. Alchourron (1991) comes closest to these requirements. He defines obligation and permission independently. The possibility of obligation without permission is explicitly discussed and characterized as 'inconsistent norming'. The equivalent situation in management could be described as 'inconsistent policy making'. One unresolved issue is the logical status of policies. Alchourron makes the distinction between the logic of normative propositions and the logic of the norms themselves. As observed by Wieringa and colleagues (1989) there are two ways of interpreting 'It is forbidden to park here'. It may be the observation that a rule exists or the promulgation of the rule itself. One is a proposition with a truth value, while the other is a norm with the effect of a command. Similarly the statement that 'Payroll clerks have authority to read payroll files' may be a correct observation that a policy exists, but it is not necessarily the promulgation of a rule. There may for example be another policy in existence, with higher priority, which denies that authority. If there is to be an attempt to formulate a logic of policies should it be a logic of propositions, of norms, or of both? The path of deontic logic appears to be the correct one to follow in order to set up a theory of policies on a sound basis, but little progress has been made so far.

The value of and need for integrated sets of tools to support all aspects of distributed systems management in a coherent fashion has been one of the main themes of this book. These include the basic operational functions of monitoring, controlling and configuring systems: topics discussed in Chapter 4. Additionally, tools are needed for analysis of the system, to check for behavioural inconsistencies with respect to management policy and to aid human managers in their planning and decision making. Management systems will have to support many manufacturers' products but, to minimize operator training for a given installation, they will demand a common, installation-specific, human interface as a vital part of the tool set. Thus, user interfaces need to be configurable to handle the range and style of distributed systems and products. Although the current trend is towards a graphical user interface which can be tailored and uses windows, icons, menus and pointers, there is not yet any dominant approach and, because it may establish a leading market position, the Motif interface supported by OSF may become the *de facto* standard. Current research needs to be extended to realistically sized networks in order to establish appropriate display techniques and styles.

Management of distributed systems is a particularly complex endeavour where it is both difficult to train and to retain operators. The speed with which it may be necessary to respond to network events may exceed that of which a operator is capable. The outcome of research to investigate techniques for automating the operator function will be of great value to the design of the distributed systems management product. This automation can be trivial where the situation is well understood and the control response is clear. But for complex situations designers may have to fall back on heuristics. Artificial intelligence approaches are being applied in business to assist the process of decision making. Given a 'top down' approach to management and a corresponding architecture for the management process, effective automation of many of the more complex aspects of distributed systems management will become possible. There is therefore every reason to investigate the non-procedural approaches of artificial intelligence to the control of the distributed processing environment, particularly in those applications where it assists operators in decision making.

10.4 Applying open standards to management products

What have current products, research and development, and standardization activities to say about the way in which the open, distributed system of the future may be managed? Management is about the establishment of policies to meet enterprise goals, turning those policies into plans and supervising the activities of resources to ensure that their operations meet the policy requirements of the enterprise. Policies are characterized by motivation or authority. Managers need to have both the motivation and the authority to perform the tasks required of them. A distributed processing environment can lead to the management task being distributed to a number of individuals or processing subsystems which are given responsibility for different parts of the total system. The partitioning of management may be on regional or functional grounds. It is vital that the areas of responsibility are properly delineated. Partition by region is the easiest to visualize and to implement. Where partition is by function, it will cover operational, security and data management aspects. Because security and data management are less overt aspects of systems, the requirement for coherent management policies can be overlooked when the systems in which they occur are distributed. The importance of security is already recognized by organizations and, for that reason, many of them appoint security administrators to play a coordinating role across all systems to which security is applicable. Because distribution of corporate data within computer systems is a relatively novel concept, attention needs to be given to analogous procedures for managing data.

An approach which goes some way to satisfying these observations can be built on the managed object specification technique developed by ISO. It provides a synthesis of many of the features of distributed systems management identified in this and earlier chapters. The crucial step is to recognize that, whereas it is not practical to specify every object to be managed as a standard, it is practical to standardize the method by which any object can be specified and how that specification may be interpreted. The GDMO standard (see Chapter 9) shows how managed object classes can be specified using templates to formalize both syntax and, in principle, semantics. Similarly, the **repertoire** and **discovery** objects enable the manager to discover what object classes a remote system supports and what objects have been instantiated. At present, this capability extends only as far as discovering information about standard classes. However, if the formal specification of the object were also available for inspection, it could be interpreted in a standard manner, irrespective of whether the object's class had been standardized or not.

Some features germane to this concept are already being discussed as OSI management **definition objects**. These give access to the syntactic structure of an objects's GDMO specification. But three advances are needed before the approach can be universally applied. First: a language (or languages) is needed so that the semantics of object behaviour can be specified. Once this has been accomplished, it becomes possible to submit formal specifications to automated validation and, for automated or self-managed systems, to proceed to code generation. Second: formal specification of objects must be extended to include the specification of **manager object** classes in addition to **managed object** classes. Manager specification would indicate not only the types of operation which managers could emit and the types of notification to which they could respond, but their behaviour specifications would also identify the rationale for emitting operations and responding to notifications. Analysis shows that management behaviour is categorized by sets of rules, determined by and derived from policy. Supplying these sets of rules to a manager (loading them when the manager is a computer process) determines the manager's actions and enables sequences of management operations to be specified. This facility for providing managers with the rules by which distributed systems are to be managed pin-points the third of the required advances. It must be possible to capture policies as a **policy object** in such a way as to derive from them the implied sets of rules and domain structures. These can then be communicated to automated manager processes, identifying the sets of managed objects for which the process has responsibility.

Once these things have been accomplished, it will become possible to automate at least a part of the organizational aspect of management (the deriving of plans, their representation as rules, the organization of domains according to policy and the structuring of discovery and repertoire objects) and all of the operational aspects of distributed systems management, in a standard manner.

These desirable developments can support future systems whose architectures and implementations are built along these lines. But an approach which can only handle new things would be only a partial solution to managing distributed processing environments whose peculiar characteristic is to develop by evolution and accretion. The final link in the chain therefore comes from interfacing these unified aspects of management to existing resources and management products. In the DOMAINS project, this link is provided by the **shield** which encapsulates a resource. The shield offers an open interface exhibiting the above desirable characteristics while at the same time providing a 'gateway' through which the resource can be accessed in its resource-specific way.

10.5 The application of distributed systems management

The following example scenario brings together some of the many topics that have been identified within this book. It illustrates how managers could utilize the checklist which is provided in Appendix A. The example recognizes that open products are not universally available and asks, 'What is the user to do today when presented with a distributed system requirement?'

Imagine that company ABC Ltd. (identified in earlier examples throughout this book) has successfully merged with DEF Ltd. (The two companies were described in Chapter 8 as being engaged in a joint research activity.) In terms of the interactions between the three categories of managers introduced in Chapter 3, the merger arose because senior managers in the two component organizations adopted a particular business strategy (the merger) to meet the objectives of the business managers. Thus, the rationale for this management change was not driven by information technology considerations. However, there are distributed processing consequences and the following discussion shows how the appropriate IT departments deal with the new situation.

Before the merger, the two companies had used a 64 kbit/sec digital communication link to access the research files at each other's sites. Senior managers expect that following the merger it will be desirable to integrate the various information processing activities of the merged company. These will ultimately extend to the finance, production, sales and personnel departments as well as to the research department. However, because the two companies are separated geographically at the ABC and DEF sites, each component of the merged company will retain a measure of devolved autonomy and responsibility at those sites.

Guided by the checklist of Appendix A, the business managers identify their various requirements for integrating the application of ABC and DEF's components in the merged business. They assess the costs, the benefits and the risks; they consult with the users of the information processing systems and note that, in this merger, each site already has extensive networking of its information technology resources. Departments on one site can therefore readily gain access to departments on the other site though the same communication facilities that were used by the research departments. As a consequence of their investigations, the business managers decide that the first step is to integrate the financial management systems at the two sites. One benefit of this integration is that it gives the finance department access to some excellent financial planning software used by DEF Ltd. and a powerful financial reporting system originally installed by ABC Ltd. At the same time, the research director decides that it is now possible to relax the security restrictions previously imposed upon the interactions of ABC's and DEF's research users' domains (see Chapter 8). This allows a full exchange of information between the research departments.

At this point in planning, the requirements for the integration of the finance departments are handed to the IT departments. Their initial task is to propose a costed, technical solution which meets the requirements. Whereas not all the questions raised by the checklist are relevant to this scenario, the IT managers will note that the purchasing policies of ABC Ltd. and DEF Ltd. before their merger have led to a situation in which there is now a multi-vendor system to be managed. They also identify that the primary requirements are for information availability and for security in the form of protection from external access (mainly attempts to dial into the company's network). Whereas the requirements will impose a number of operational constraints upon the financial department, the distributed systems management implications are:

- that the security manager at the ABC site is to be responsible for managing communication security;
- that each site will provide back-up and disaster recovery for the other;
- that the operational management task is largely one of availability monitoring, fault diagnosis and failure recovery.

Measurement of the inter-research department traffic and a simulation of the expected data traffic between the distributed parts of the finance department show that the existing 64 kbit/sec data link is adequate for the immediate needs of data communication. However, an independent assessment of voice traffic between the two sites shows that this could benefit from the introduction of a high bandwidth (2 Mbit/sec in Europe, T1 in North America) direct link between the sites. By structuring the link into voice and data streams, both types of communication traffic can be accommodated at significantly lower cost. The technical managers note that this strategy gives them:

- a method of directly monitoring the use of the link;
- a reconfiguration capability for reallocating bandwidth between voice and data if performance indicators show that growing data traffic makes a reconfiguration advisable.

Their case is reinforced by showing that communication resilience can be achieved by using the conventional public switched telephone network as a back-up or at times of overload.

Organizationally, the two parts of the finance department constitute a single financial management domain. This embraces all the terminal, workstation and computational resources of the finance department and their use is determined by that department's policies. However, the communication services on the two sites and the inter-site communication link, though used by the finance department, are also used by other departments. They are not managed by the finance department and so are not a part of its management domain. The information technology managers at the two sites have also been given the responsibility for equipment maintenance policy at their respective sites and each of these constitutes a separate maintenance domain. This domain analysis (illustrated in Figure 10.1) shows the managers that there is potential for policy conflict between the information technology departments and the finance department. To avoid already identified con-

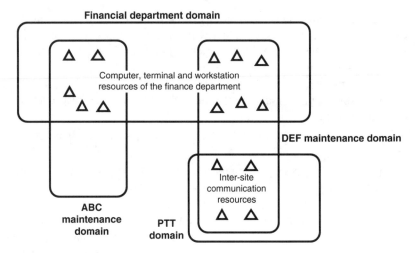

Figure 10.1   Domain overlaps in the merged company.

flicts, senior management sets up a working party to agree operations and maintenance policies. The working party produces its recommendations and adds two important policy guidelines. One states that the potential for policy conflict will continue to be monitored in the operational system. (Clearly, the working party sensibly recognizes that it may not have anticipated every possible conflict.) The second guideline establishes procedures which must be invoked to resolve any conflict that monitoring might reveal.

The ultimate responsibility for the 2 Mbit/sec link is retained by the telecommunication supplier which is supplying the basic communication service. Liaison with the supplier is carried out by the IT department at location DEF on the pragmatic grounds that it is geographically closer to one of the telecommunication supplier's operations and maintenance centres.

The scene is now set for the technical managers to make their costed recommendations. However, senior managers only allow the proposals to go ahead when the finance department has demonstrated the plan for assisting staff in the new working environment. These staff, who are distributed across the two sites, need access to help services. The finance department also proposes a user training plan to explain the changed environment.

These arrangements make little initial change to the local operations of the distributed financial processing system. The finance department extends its licensing arrangements so that the financial planning and financial reporting software can be accessed from either site. The IT departments at each site monitor and maintain the terminals, workstations and computers as in the past. Reports on system performance are passed to the manager located at the ABC site each week, using a conventional file transfer protocol, so that all performance indicators may be printed at one location.

As time passes, inter-site interaction increases. Monitoring reveals that bottlenecks are beginning to develop in the flow of data. A study shows that there could be improvements in application performance if the facilities at the DEF site which are needed by the finance department could be directly monitored from the ABC site. Because the two sites use different computer systems, it is decided (after further analysis) to use the Common Management Information Service (CMIS) as the service to pass management data. Staff in the IT and finance departments are appraised of these changes and of the benefits they are expected to bring. Consultants, brought in by the company, specify appropriate managed objects for the resources at the DEF site from which fault and performance reports can be obtained. The consultants observe that the resources at site DEF are supported by the considerable intelligence of their computers. Therefore, the managed objects are specified as active objects which generate notifications. This is a more efficient use of processing resources than specifying that the objects are to be polled on a regular basis from site ABC. Also, because faults are rare, there are valuable savings in the demands on the communication bandwidth between the two sites. In order to minimize the mean time to recovery in the event of faults, the company is encouraged to purchase a software package providing test management functionality and diagnostic tests to determine resource operation and state. In this way, the enlarged company takes its first steps to evolve its distributed systems towards the use of open distributed systems management standards.

Like any short, hypothetical case study, the analysis has been limited to only a few of the simple issues that are encountered in real situations. The authors could have continued to develop the scenario and the reader may wish to do so, identifying what steps would have to be taken in particular circumstances. Such an analysis, on the part of the reader, would help to reinforce the principles that this scenario has sought to illustrate. These are:

- the management implications of change must be analysed before committing to technical change;
- changes in one area can influence, and result in changes in, another area;
- staff need to be consulted and advised about proposed changes and their consequences;
- management of a distributed system will continue to evolve with the system even after the initial changes and management decisions have been taken.

Study of the scenario shows that it is not possible to separate the management of large distributed systems from the task of software engineering to design and operate those systems. This is because evolution of the distributed system demands a continuing process of analysis, design and performance monitoring. Management is thus an intrinsic aspect of any system engineering method. The key features of the method which this book has identified are:

- the importance of planning;
- the continual assessment of performance through both simulation and actual measurement;
- the need for maintenance, testing and diagnostic capabilities

throughout the (open-ended) lifetime of the distributed system.

10.6 Conclusions

Successful management requires that attention be given to three areas; technology, organization and staffing. Many of this book's chapters have focused upon the technology and its tool support. It is sufficient here to summarize the requirement. The technology influences the nature of the way in which management is performed and, for information technology systems, the speed at which data (and faults) can be propagated. Tools are required for planning to carry out 'what if' analyses, for monitoring and for control. These all require adequate means of interaction with the management system of the distributed processing environment. In addition, management staff need several kinds of documentation. These list the resources and activities being managed; the procedures for their management; and the rationale for decisions taken. In particular, without good documentation, the management of the system will not survive the departure of key staff.

In the final analysis the main issues of managing distributed systems are non-technical. Management quality comes through good organization and good people. This requires that the distributed processing environment and its management tasks are appropriately structured. 'Management domains' are proposed as a technical structuring concept. Two organizational principles underlie the use of domains. The first is to formulate policy and operations in terms of groups of resources. The second principle is that, wherever possible, the groupings shall be independent of the computing application and determined by management need. It may be appropriate to define the domain of, say, terminals in a building which have access to a specific network technology. This domain can be the basis for performing a reconfiguration operation, expressing a security policy and as a unit for performance analysis. The task of structuring is eased by allowing a domain to be defined in terms of subsidiary domains (subdomains) to create hierarchies. Objects may be members of more than one domain; for example, the terminals for the network could also be in the domain of products from a given manufacturer. Potential conflicts, where there are undesirable overlaps in management policies, may be identified through objects with multiple domain membership.

The danger of relying upon the detailed personal knowledge of a few information technology staff and communications specialists is particularly acute. Both classes of staff are in high demand and there is a high rate of staff turnover. The pressure on them to solve urgent day-to-day problems often takes precedence over the need to commit their knowledge to a form where it can be used by others. This pressure should be resisted. Although their knowledge could be consigned to paper, it is better that the knowledge be consolidated into an on-line knowledge base so that it can be accessed through an expert system. In this way, the expertise of the specialist is made readily accessible to operational staff at all times.

This emphasizes the importance of training. Whenever a new product is introduced, its users need to spend time on learning its characteristics and how to use it most efficiently. For some simple products and talented users, learning by use is effective. For many products, time and money spent on formal training sessions is more cost-effective. The hidden costs of learning slowly and making mistakes on the job usually outweigh the visible costs of training sessions. A training programme is required for each staff member, identifying the skills required and planning how they will be acquired.

The need for technical training is obvious, but the need for management training is as great. This should ensure three things. One is that staff are fully aware of the requirements for and disciplines of resource management. The second is that the corporate objectives of their employing organization are explained to them. The third is that operators and managers recognize the relationship of their technology skills to the objectives of their parent organization and so relate the system management need to the corporate need.

But taking account of all these factors is futile unless management attention is also given to the following:

- proper evaluation of task delegation, recognizing the partnership between the administrator (and operator) and the distributed processing environment;

- planning, accompanied by robust strategies for coping with the pace of technical evolution;

- assessment of the extent to which management systems meet the goals of the enterprise.

Regrettably, there is still a lack of sufficient exemplars from which to generalize with confidence. Many organizations are grappling with the problem but solutions, where they exist, are specific. Whereas the potential of managed distributed systems is recognized, few are yet installed. Managers are therefore still on the lower slopes of the learning curve and there is much unknown territory to be explored. One of the merits of distribution, as a strategy, is that it allows a distributed system to be developed through evolution and accretion. Therefore, the system can be installed over time as experience is gained. However, if the growth is unplanned and uncontrolled, this 'step at a time' approach can be the 'Achilles heel' of distributed processing. Programmers have learned the dangers of 'hacking' computer programs by making unplanned additions to code. Likewise, managers need to take a long-term, strategic view of their enterprises' distributed processing requirements and the way in which they will be managed. Unless they do this, they are in danger of 'hacking' their distributed systems, thereby rendering them unmanaged and unmanageable. Managers should draw up:

- a development programme;
- a list of management issues which need to be addressed to achieve that programme;
- a set of criteria to judge the success of the programme.

In performing these activities, managers must be prepared to be guided by analogies from the management of other areas of human endeavour where these are seen to be appropriate. A case could be made for the appropriate professional bodies (for example, in the UK this would be the British Institute of Management or the Institute of Chartered Accountants) to consider establishing a consensus of good management practice. It is the authors' belief that the principles advocated in this book would provide a useful contribution to such an activity.

There is no doubt about the value of the distributed system paradigm. Three things are needed to accelerate its take-up so that more organizations may gain the benefits of distributed processing and networked operations. They require concerted action by the users and managers of distributed systems, the equipment suppliers and the standards makers. First: users must be prepared to identify, with a more coherent voice than hitherto, their requirements and to share whatever experience they have in order to avoid too many false starts. Second: manufacturer groups, such as the Network Management Forum and the Open Software Foundation, must continue to publicize their plans for the development of distributed systems and their management capabilities. The *Roadmap* for networking management (see Chapter 9) is such a publication. Third: standards bodies must also recognize the value of, and develop a programme for, prospective standardization for open distributed systems management to match that coming from the suppliers. Already, one ISO standards subcommittee has recognized that 'the implementation of a release management program would significantly aid in the process' of promoting standardization activities (SC21 N7214, 1992). With published objectives from suppliers, an indication of when standards will be available, and with conforming products, businesses will be able to plan their strategies for the managed evolution of their distributed systems.

References

Alchourron C.E. (1991). Philosophical foundations of deontic logic and its practical applications in computational contexts. In *Workshop on Deontic Logic in Computer Science*, Amsterdam, December 1991

Bedford-Roberts J. (1991). *Concepts from Pythagoras*, Report HPL-91-22, Hewlett-Packard Laboratories, Bristol, UK, February

Fehskens L. (1989). An architectural strategy for enterprise management. In *Proc. IFIP Sym. on Integrated Network Management*, Boston, MA, May 1989. (Meandzija B. and Westcott J. eds), pp. 41-60. North-Holland

Fink B. (1991). DOMAINS – Basic concepts for management of distributed systems. III.2/5. In *Proc. 5th RACE TMN Conf.*, 1991

SC21 N7214 (1992). *ISO/IEC JTC1/SC21 N7214 Rapporteur's Report on SC21 Strategic Planning*, June

POSIX. *IEEE 1003.7 System Administration Interface for Computer Operating Systems Environments*

Sloman M.S., Moffett J.D. and Twidle K.P. (1992). *Domino Domains and Policies: An Introduction to the Project Results*, Domino Report Arch/IC/4, Department of Computing, Imperial College, University of London, UK, February

Wieringa R., Meyer J.-J. and Weigand H. (1989). Specifying dynamic and deontic integrity constraints. In *Data and Knowledge Engineering*, vol. 4, pp. 157-89 Amsterdam: North-Holland

Yemini Y., Goldszmidt G. and Yemini S. (1991). Network management by delegation. In *Proc IFIP Sym. on Integrated Network Management*, Washington, DC, 1991, pp. 95-107. Amsterdam: Elsevier

A

Checklist for the distributed systems manager

A.1 Introduction

This appendix is divided into two parts. The first part provides a checklist of factors which the manager of a distributed system should take into account when requiring, developing, ordering, installing and operating a distributed system. The second part complements the checklist by providing a typical risk assessment proforma to assist managers in their task.

A.2 The checklist

The checklist is divided into a number of sections with topics to be considered in each section. The list aims to be complete. However, it may be that some of the items identified within the checklist do not apply to the reader's particular distributed system. Even so, the manager is advised to consider each point carefully before deciding that the topic is not applicable. Having a rationale for not including a feature or adopting an approach is as important to good management as having a rationale for including a topic.

The sections are:

- Applications
- Requirements

- Security
- Purchase
- Operations
- Maintenance
- User support
- Training

Applications

[ ] What are the applications to be run on this system?
For each application:
  [ ] Have the costs and benefits been identified?
  [ ] Has a business risk analysis been carried out?
  [ ] Has a security risk analysis been carried out?
  [ ] What arrangements are there for user participation in the project?

Requirements

[ ] Is this to be a green field site or will this be a consolidation of existing systems?
[ ] Are there specific requirements for:
  [ ] Security (see next section)
  [ ] Performance
  [ ] Availability
  [ ] Accountability?
[ ] How much of the management will be automated?
[ ] Is this a strategic investment?
Identify the business risks with regard to the following:
  [ ] Is this a multi-vendor system?
  [ ] What standards will be used to support the system?
  [ ] Is the system novel in its use of technology?
  [ ] Will the system be expected to perform new functions?
  [ ] What is the commitment of the project team?
[ ] Will the project team have delegated authority for decision making?
[ ] If future growth is likely, what is the upsizing strategy?

Security

Security administration policies:
  [ ] Who administers the system security?
  [ ] Who coordinates security administrators?

[ ] Who can authorize the registration of new users?

[ ] Have data owners been defined?

[ ] Who can authorize access to data?

Security levels:

[ ] Will the system be partitioned according to different security levels?

[ ] Have the security level(s) to be adopted been identified?

[ ] Will available products support the security level(s)?

Communication security:

[ ] What are the security requirements for message confidentiality/integrity?

[ ] Will available products support these requirements?

System access control:

What are the authentication procedures for:

[ ] In-house users

[ ] Dial-in users?

Data access control:

[ ] What access control system will be used?

Disaster planning:

[ ] Has a maximum down-time, in the event of a disaster, been agreed?

[ ] What plans have been made for data back-up off-site?

[ ] What arrangements have been made for standby equipment?

[ ] Have the procedures for back-up and recovery been defined?

System auditability:

What activities are to be logged;

[ ] Always

[ ] On request?

[ ] Is it defined how the integrity of logs and audit trails shall be ensured?

Legal and regulatory policies relating to security:

[ ] What legal and regulatory security requirements apply?

[ ] Are they being obeyed?

Identification of the cost of the security system:

[ ] What is the cost in terms of system overhead?

[ ] What is the cost in terms of financial terms?

[ ] What is the cost in terms of manpower?

Purchase

[ ]   Have the company purchasing policies been identified for this purchase?

[ ]   Has the contracts department been advised of the implications of distribution/multi-vendor systems?

[ ]   Have the criteria for product and contractor selection been identified?

[ ]   Have the system acceptance criteria been identified?

Operations

[ ]   What is the system monitoring policy?

[ ]   What is the policy for operations review?

[ ]   Have performance goals been set to meet:

    [ ]   User requirements

    [ ]   Management requirements?

[ ]   Have the resources to be managed been identified?

[ ]   What sub-goals (if any) are needed to meet primary goals?

[ ]   What methods will be used to set performance criteria?

[ ]   What methods will be used to determine performance?

[ ]   What is the estimate of the cost of obtaining performance statistics?

[ ]   What benefits will be derived from determining performance?

[ ]   Has it been shown that determining system performance is cost-effective?

[ ]   What method(s) will be used to account for usage?

[ ]   What is the estimate of the cost of obtaining accounting statistics?

[ ]   What benefits will be derived from determining accounting statistics?

[ ]   Has accounting been shown to be cost-effective?

    When establishing system standards for documentation:

    [ ]   Will documents be held on-line?

    [ ]   How will updates be handled?

[ ]   How will operator duties be assigned?

[ ]   How will operations at remote locations be handled?

[ ]   How will remote operations staff be kept in touch?

[ ]   Has the cost of operations been included in financial estimates?

[ ]   How has the tangible benefit of operations been quantified?

Maintenance

[ ]   Is there an enterprise maintenance policy?

[ ]   Will the operations team be responsible for maintenance?

[ ] Will maintenance be subcontracted in whole or in part?

[ ] Have procedures for maintaining a system information base been established?

[ ] How consistent does the (distributed) system information base have to be?

[ ] How frequently must the system information base be checked and updated?

[ ] Has the cost of the update been identified?

[ ] Has the benefit to be derived from the system information base been quantified?

[ ] Is the maintenance of the system information base cost-effective?

[ ] What policy has been set for rectifying faults?

[ ] What is the effective level for spares holding?

[ ] What are the procedures for maintaining system back-up and recovery?

[ ] What special features have been identified for handing remote failure in the distributed system?

User support

How will user information be disseminated:

   [ ] By circular

   [ ] By bulletin board (electronic?)

   [ ] By electronic mail?

[ ] Will there be a help-desk?

[ ] Will there be on-line help?

[ ] Is it certain that help services do not compromise security requirements?

[ ] Will the help services provide special features to operators?

[ ] Has the cost of user support been included in financial estimates?

[ ] How has the tangible benefit of user support been quantified?

Training

[ ] What training policy is to be adopted for operators?

[ ] What special features of the distributed system are important for the operators?

[ ] What training policy is to be adopted for users?

[ ] What special features of the distributed system are important for the users?

[ ] How will users be advised of the special characteristics of the distributed system?

[ ] Has the cost of training been included in financial estimates?

[ ] How has the tangible benefit of training been quantified?

A.3 Business risk assessment questionnaire

A.3.1 Risk assessment: Size
Weight

1. Total systems and programming man-hours for
   the system (5)
   [ ] 100 to 3000   low   −1
   [ ] 3000 to 15 000   med   −2
   [ ] 15 000 to 30 000   med   −3
   [ ] Over 30 000   high   −4

2. What is the system estimate in calendar time? (4)
   [ ] 12 months or less   low   −1
   [ ] 13 months to 24 months   med   −2
   [ ] Over 24 months   high   −3

3. Number of sub-projects within the system. (1)
   [ ] One   low   −1
   [ ] Two   med   −2
   [ ] Three or more   high   −3

4. Length of economic payback (2)
   [ ] Less than 12 months   low   −1
   [ ] 12 to 24 months   med   −2
   [ ] Over 24 months   high   −3

5. Who will perform the work? (2)
   [ ] Mostly by on-site personnel   low   −1
   [ ] Significant portions by on-site personnel   med   −2
   [ ] Mostly by off-site personnel   high   −3

6. Number of departments (other than IT) involved
   with the system. (4)
   [ ] One   low   −1
   [ ] Two   med   −2
   [ ] Three or more   high   −3

7. Approximately how many user department
   people will be necessary to make the system run? (1)
   [ ] Up to 20   low   −1

[ ] 20 to 50	med	−2
[ ] Over 50	high	−3

8. How many different geographic locations will the system encompass? (2)

[ ] One	low	−1
[ ] Two or three	med	−2
[ ] More than three	high	−3

9. How many existing systems must the new system interface with? (3)

[ ] None	low	−1
[ ] One	low	−1
[ ] Two	med	−2
[ ] More than two	high	−3

A.3.2 Risk assessment: Structure   Weight

1. The system may best be described as: (1)

[ ] Totally new system	high	−3
[ ] Replacement of an existing manual system	med	−2
[ ] Replacement of an existing automated system	low	−1

2. If a replacement system is proposed, what percentage of existing functions are replaced on a one to one basis? (5)

[ ] 0 to 25	high	−3
[ ] 25 to 50	med	−2
[ ] 50 to 100	low	−1

3. What is the severity of procedural changes by the proposed system on user departments?[1] (5)

[ ] Low	low	−1
[ ] Medium	med	−2
[ ] High	high	−3

4. Proposed methods and/or procedures:[2] (2)

[ ] First of kind for IT department	high	−3
[ ] First of kind for user	high	−3
[ ] Breakthrough required for user acceptance	high	−3
[ ] Breakthrough required for IT department implementation	high	−3
[ ] None of the above		−0

5. Does the user organization have to change to
    meet requirements of the new system?[1]   (5)

    [ ]   No   −0
    [ ]   Minimal   low   −1
    [ ]   Somewhat   med   −2
    [ ]   Major   high   −3

6. What degree of flexibility and judgement can be
    exercised by the systems architect in the area of
    systems outputs?   (1)

    [ ]   0 to 33% (very little)   low   −1
    [ ]   34 to 66% (average)   med   −2
    [ ]   67 to 100% (very high)   high   −3

7. What degree of flexibility and judgement can be
    exercised by the systems architect in the area of
    systems processing?   (1)

    [ ]   0 to 33% (very little)   low   −1
    [ ]   34 to 66% (average)   med   −2
    [ ]   67 to 100% (very high)   high   −3

8. What degree of flexibility and judgement can be
    exercised by the systems architect in the area of
    database content?   (1)

    [ ]   0 to 33% (very little)   low   −1
    [ ]   34 to 66% (average)   med   −2
    [ ]   67 to 100% (very high)   high   −3

9. What is the overall rating of predetermined
    structure for the new system?   (2)

    [ ]   Highly structured environment – requires
          little or no procedural changes at the user
          level   low   −1
    [ ]   Medium structured environment   med   −2
    [ ]   Low structured environment – requires a
          high amount of procedural changes and user
          education   high   −3

10. Is there any one project on which the system is
    likely to be or is totally dependent?   (5)

    [ ]   No   −0
    [ ]   Yes, but project is of low or normal risk low −1
    [ ]   Yes, and project is anticipated to be high
          risk   high   −3

11. How many estimating questions were unanswered
    or answered with a low confidence factor?   (3)

    [ ] None -0

    [ ] 1–10   low -1

    [ ] 11–20   med -2

    [ ] Over 20   high -3

12. What is the general attitude of the user?[1]   (5)

    [ ] Poor: anti IT solutions   high -3

    [ ] Fair: some reluctance   med -2

    [ ] Good: understands value of IT solutions -0

13. How committed is upper level user management
    to the system?[1]   (5)

    [ ] Somewhat reluctant to unknown high -3

    [ ] Adequate   med -2

    [ ] Extremely enthusiastic   low -1

14. Has a joint IT/user team been established[1]   (5)

    [ ] No   high -3

    [ ] Part-time user representative appointed low -1

    [ ] Full-time user representative appointed -0

A.3.3 Risk assessment: Technology   Weight

1. Is hardware required which is new to the
   organization?[2]   (3)

    [ ] None -0

    [ ] Processor   low -1

    [ ] Terminals   med -2

    [ ] Networking hardware   high -3

2. Is special non-standard hardware required?[2]   (5)

    [ ] None -0

    [ ] Processor   low -1

    [ ] Terminals   med -2

    [ ] Networking hardware   high -3

3. How many vendors are involved in the system
   hardware?   (2)

    [ ] One -0

    [ ] Two   low -1

    [ ] Three or more   high -3

4. Are external network services being used?   (1)

    [ ] No external network -0

    [ ] Yes, but not new to the organization   low -1

    [ ] Yes, and new to the organization   med -2

5. Are program packages being used?   (1)

    [ ] No   high -3

    [ ] Yes – to a small degree   med -2

    [ ] Yes – entirely   low -1

6. Is the system software new to the IT project
   team?   (5)

    [ ] No -0

    [ ] Yes   high -3

7. Is the system software new to the vendor?   (5)

    [ ] Yes   med -2

    [ ] No -0

8. What system management products are supplied
   as standard?   (3)

    [ ] None   high -3

    [ ] Vendor specific   med -2

    [ ] Integrated managements tools -0

9. How good is vendor/supplier support?   (1)

    [ ] Unknown   high -3

    [ ] Adequate   low -1

    [ ] Good -0

10. How knowledgeable is the user in the area of IT[1]   (5)

    [ ] First exposure/little knowledge   high -3

    [ ] Previous exposure but limited knowledge med -2

    [ ] High degree of capability   low -1

11. How knowledgeable is the user representative in
    the application area?[1]   (5)

    [ ] Limited   high -3

    [ ] Understands concept but no experience med -2

    [ ] Has been involved in prior implementation
          effort   low -1

12. How knowledgeable is the IT team in the
    application area?[1]   (5)

    [ ] Limited   high -3

[ ] Understands concept but no experience   med   −2
[ ] Has been involved in prior implementation
    efforts   low   −1

Risk factors

For each factor

Formula	$(S - M)/C$ = factor score
where:	S = sum of answers (weighted)
	M = minimum possible sum[3]
	C = constant to convert to 0–100 range[4]

Risk assessment

Factor range   0–40 = low risk
                 40–60 = medium risk
                 60–100 = high risk

Evaluation

If any of Size or Structure or Technology > 90 – HIGHLY SPECULATIVE
If (Size + Structure + Technology) < 180 –
        TO SENIOR MANAGEMENT FOR SIGN-OFF

Notes

[1] The importance of user involvement is underlined by the application of the highest weighting factor for most questions relating to project or systems interfaces with the users. The value of education in reducing risk can thus be seen.

[2] Answers to these questions are cumulatively scored before application of the weighting factor.

[3] Minimum possible sums are:

Size	22
Structure	21
Technology	16

[4] Constants are:

Size	0.55
Structure	1.35
Technology	1.21

B

Terms and abbreviations

B.1 Introduction

This appendix lists many of the terms used in describing distributed systems and their management. Terms are listed in alphabetical order together with a definition of the term and a reference to the source of the definition. For some terms, more than one definition is provided. In that case, the first definition is the one preferred by the authors. In some instances alternative definitions for terms appear to have little in common or may be contradictory. In these instances, readers may find that there are two or more sets of such definitions representing the terminology adopted by different authors and that, within any one author's set of definitions, there is self-consistency. In some instances, the definitions are derived from the chapters of this book. Where that is the case, a reference is provided to the corresponding chapter.

The appendix also summarizes the terms and their corresponding abbreviations used in this book.

B.2 Definitions of terms

References from one term to another are denoted by the referenced term appearing in *italic* face.

abstraction   a specification of an entity by an interface that controls access of other entities to the entity (Wegner, 1987)

abstraction   the process of suppressing irrelevant detail to establish a simplified model or result of that process (ODP, 1991)

accountability   the principle that individuals should be liable to show how they have acted as stewards for assets within their control (Chapter 6)

295

accounting management a management service that collects, collates and logs usage information that is pertinent to the cost of using or providing a service (Chapter 4)

address a data structure which defines the location of an object

administrative function a function which identifies components and assigns services to them (Chapter 4)

administrator a human management agent

architecture (*of a system*) the structure of a system identifying the interrelationships among its components (ODP, 1991; ISO, 1990)

atomicity the property of anything which is considered not to be capable of further subdivision for a particular level of abstraction (ODP, 1991)

authority the power, obtained legitimately, to perform an action

authority, regulatory a body responsible for policies constraining management policy

binding function maintaining the relationship of interfaces to ensure they are properly matched (Chapter 4)

change management control of changes performed on a system ensuring that they are performed in a consistent manner (Chapter 4)

class a template from which objects may be created (Wegner, 1987) (*of objects*): the set of all objects satisfying a type (ODP, 1991)

clear ~ in data transmitted or stored without encryption (Chapter 5)

communication the transfer of data
the transfer of information (ISO, 1990)

complex service a service which is provided through the use of other services (Chapter 4)

component service an underlying service in support of a *complex service* (Chapter 4)

compound service a *complex service* in which users are unaware that one service is making use of another (Chapter 4)

configuration management installing and interconnecting hardware and software components into a system (Chapter 4)

containment the ability to hide (*encapsulate*) one *object* within another

control a trigger of a series of predefined actions to be taken either by an information system or a user (ISO, 1990)

data the representation forms of information dealt with by information systems and users thereof (ODP, 1991)

discretionary access control a form of access control permitting users to control the sharing of information (Chapter 5)

domain a set of related entities which have been grouped for management purposes a set of objects that are directly or indirectly managed by a single management centre (ANSA, 1988)

a collection of resources . . . and people operating within . . . a particular administration (Gomberg, 1987)

a concept which describes the relationship of an agent to its manager (MAP)

the set of privileges that a subject possesses (Sandhu and Share, 1986)

domain

management a set of managed objects, to which a common systems management policy applies (ISO, 1992b)

security a domain to which a common security policy applies (Chapter 5)

domains

disjoint domains with no members in common

overlapping domains which have at least one member in common

enabling service the *component service* which supports a *main service* (Chapter 4)

encapsulation (*of an object*) the hiding, from external view, of the methods by which an *object*'s data and operations are implemented

end-to-end encryption a form of encryption which provides security of information from its source all the way through to its destination

event a happening associated with a change of state

asynchronously generated information passed from agent to manager (MAP) (Authors' note: this definition is more correctly applied to an *event report*)

fault handling the management of abnormalities in system operation (Chapter 4)

gauge an abstraction of the (numerical) value of a dynamic variable

generic name (*of services*) a name referencing a class of service (Chapter 4)

implicit overlap (*of domains*) a situation in which two *domains* contain different *managed objects* which refer to the same real-world entity (Chapter 8)

inheritance the ability of an object class to express the properties of its *superclass*

instance the realization of a *class*

interface a place where interactions can occur which defines a language for interaction and constraints upon the statements that may be made in that language by parties to the interface (ANSA, 1988)

interface

exported an interface specifying the service which is available from an entity

imported a specification of services provided through other interfaces

information any kind of knowledge about things, facts, concepts and so on in a universe of discourse that is exchangeable among users (ODP, 1991)

language a notation and an interpretation which defines the meanings of statements of the notation (ANSA, 1988)

language
> **concurrent** a language with multiply active threads (Wegner, 1987)
> **object-based** a language which supports objects as a language feature (Wegner, 1987)
> **object-oriented** a language whose objects belong to classes and with class hierarchies which may be incrementally defined by an inheritance mechanism (Wegner, 1987)

link encryption a form of encryption which provides security of information transferred over data links

main service the *complex service* with which users interact when they are aware that the service uses other, *enabling service(s)* (Chapter 4)

managed object an *object* which supports a management interface (Chapter 8)

management (*of networks*) monitoring and controlling the resources of the network and their corresponding characteristics, status and relationships (MAP)

management action policy a *policy* which motivates or authorizes management action (Chapter 8)

management role object an *object* which defines the range and nature of management authority (Chapter 8)

mandatory access control a form of access control based upon fixed access rules (Chapter 5)

modality (*of a management action policy*) a qualifier of a *policy* defining whether it is concerned with authorization or with motivation

model a representation of a system, simplified for the purpose of description or calculation (ANSA, 1988)
> a structured set of definitions which is closed and unbound to the real world (ISO, 1988)

name a symbol – usually a human readable string – identifying some resource or set of resources (Shoch, 1978)

name space a naming regime applying to a set of names

network a series of nodes connected by communication channels (MAP)

notification information emitted by a (managed) object relating to an event that has occurred within the (managed) object (ISO, 1992b)

object a set of operations and a state that remembers the effect of operations (Wegner, 1987)

open system the representation within a generalized abstract model of those aspects of a real open system that are pertinent to its communication with other real open systems (ISO, 1992a)
(Note: this definition is limited in scope by the consideration of Open Systems Interconnection)

open systems interconnection (OSI) the interconnection of open systems in accordance with ISO standards and CCITT recommendations for the exchange of data (ISO, 1992a)

OSI management facilities to control, coordinate and monitor the resources that allow communication to take place in the OSI environment (ISO, 1992a)

outsourcing (*of operations management*) the provision, to an organization, of an integrated operations and maintenance service by a third party

planning definition of expected system behaviour in an open distributed environment including specification of monitoring and control action in order to meet policy objectives (ODP, 1991)

policy the plans of an organization to meet its goals (Chapter 8)

policy constraint a predicate which must be satisfied for the *policy* to have effect (Chapter 8)

policy set the set of members of a *domain* to which its policies apply (Chapter 8)

policy subjects the *users* to which a *policy* applies (Chapter 8)

policy target (objects) the *objects* to which a *policy* is directed (Chapter 8)

port an abstract interface to a communications object (ODP, 1991)

process an entity presenting an interface of executable operations or entry points and one or more threads of control that may be active or suspended (Wegner, 1987)

process
    concurrent a process that may have multiply active threads of control (Wegner, 1987)

processing
    distributed the class of information processing activities in which discrete components of the overall processing activities may be located in more than one system, at more than one location, or where there is any reason which necessitates explicit communication among the components (ODP, 1991)

protocol a set of semantic and syntactic rules that determine the behaviour of entities . . . performing communication functions (ISO, 1990)

real open system a real system that complies with the requirements of open systems interconnection standards in its communication with other real systems (ISO, 1992a)
(Note: this definition is limited in scope to Open Systems Interconnection)

real system a set of one or more computers, associated software, peripheral equipment, terminals, human operators, physical processes and means of communication that form an autonomous whole capable of performing information processing or information transformation or both (ISO, 1992a)

relationship that which exists between objects which are not independent (ANSA, 1988)

route the specific information required to forward data to its specified address (Shoch, 1978)

security interaction policy a policy, for the security mechanisms and parameters to be used in an interaction, negotiated between the parties in the interaction (Chapter 5)

server a named instance created from a service type on which operations can be invoked

service an abstraction of a particular set of operations provided to users to allow them to perform a particular function

shadowing a form of help service in which an operator monitors and guides user operation (Chapter 6)

smart card a security device, similar in appearance to a credit card, and containing a processor and storage (one of its uses is for authentication)

state the condition of an object that determines its behaviour (ODP, 1991)

subscriber a service user which consumes accountable resources provided across a contracted service interface (ISO, 1992c)

symbolic name an ordinary name through which a user identifies an entity (Chapter 4)

system something of interest both as a whole and as composed of parts (ODP, 1991)

> a set of connected things, parts, elements working together in a regular relation (ISO, 1990)
> (see **real system**)

system, distributed a system whose components are explicitly not collocated

systems management policy a coherent set of rules which, when applying to a managed object, constrain behaviour (ISO, 1992d)

thread a chain of actions where at least one object participates in the chain (ODP, 1991)

> a locus of control and a stack (Wegner, 1987)

trader an object which performs *trading* (ODP, 1991)

trading the interaction between objects in which information about new or potential contracts is exchanged via a third party object (ODP, 1991)

type a predicate (an object or data element is of a type if the predicate holds (true) for the object or data element) (ODP, 1991) the set of all items with a particular common characteristic (ANSA, 1988)

a behavioural specification that may be used to generate instances having behaviour (Wegner, 1987)

unique identifier   an immutable identifier for a system entity (Chapter 4)

user   (of a system) anyone or anything which uses a system (ISO, 1990)

version control   the management of software in the course of its service life cycle and/or for different versions of hardware and software computation platforms (Chapter 4)

B.3 Abbreviations

ACE	Access Control Entry
ACL	Access Control List
ANSA	Advanced Systems Network Architecture
APDU	Application Protocol Data Unit
ARPANET	Advanced Research Projects Agency Network
ASN.1	Abstract Syntax Notation One
CCITT	International Telegraph and Telephone Consultative Committee
CMIP	Common Management Information Protocol
CMIS	Common Management Information Service
CMOL	Common Management information protocol Over Logical link layer
CMOT	Common Management information protocol Over TCP/IP
DES	Data Encryption Standard
DME	Distributed Management Environment
DoD	US Department of Defense
DOMAINS	Distributed Open Management Architecture In Networked Systems
Domino	Domain Management IN Open systems
DTI	UK Department of Trade and Industry
EDI	Electronic Data Interchange
FDDI	Fiber Distributed Data Interface
GDMO	Guidelines for the Definition of Managed Objects
ICS	Implementation Conformance Statement
ID	Identifier

IEC	International Electrotechnical Commission
IEEE	Institute of Electrical and Electronics Engineers
IP	Internet Protocol
ISDN	Integrated Services Digital Network
ISL	Interface Specification Language
ISO	International Organization for Standardization
IT	Information Technology
ITSEC	Information Technology Security Evaluation Criteria
LAN	Local Area Network
MICS	Management Information Conformance Statement
MOCS	Managed Object Conformance Statement
MRO	Management Role Object
NMF	Network Management Forum
ODP	Open Distributed Processing
OID	Object Identifier
OSF	Open Software Foundation
OSI	Open Systems Interconnection
PICS	Protocol Implementation Conformance Statement
PIN	Personal Identification Number
POS	Point Of Sale
PTT	Post, Telecommunications and Telephony
QoS	Quality of Service
SNMP	Simple Network Management Protocol
RF	Radio Frequency
ROS	Remote Operations Service
RSA	The Rivest, Shamir and Adleman public key encryption algorithm
TCSEC	Trusted Computer System Evaluation Criteria
TCP	Transmission Control Protocol
TMN	Telecommunications Management Network
WORM	Write Once, Read Many times

References

ANSA (1988). *ANSA Reference Model*

Gomberg D.A. (1987). *A Model of Inter-Administration Network User Authentication and Access Control*, Mitre Corporation

ISO (1988). *ISO/IEC JTC1/SC21 N2551 ODP Definitions and Glossary*, March

ISO (1990). *ISO/IEC JTC1/TSG1 N285, Description list of concepts & named terms – Version 4*, February

ISO (1992a). *ISO/IEC DIS 2382-26 Information Processing Systems – Vocabulary – Part 26: OSI Architecture*

ISO (1992b). *ISO/IEC 10040 Information Technology – Open Systems Interconnection – Systems Management Overview*

ISO (1992c). *ISO/IEC 10164-10: Information technology – Open Systems Interconnection – Systems Management – Part 10: Accounting Meter Function*

ISO (1992d). *ISO/IEC JTC1/SC21 N 7118 Third Working Draft for Management Domain Architecture*

MAP. *MAP/TOP Specification 3.0*

ODP (1991). *ISO/IEC 10746-2: Basic Reference Model of Open Distributed Processing – Part 2: Descriptive Model*

Sandhu R.S. and Share M.E. (1986). Some owner based schemes with dynamic groups in the schematic protection model. In Symposium on Security and Privacy, Oakland, CA: IEEE Computer Society, pp. 61–70

Shoch J.F. (1978). Inter-Network Naming, Addressing and Routing, In *Compcon Fall '78*, pp. 72–9

Wegner P. (1987). Dimensions of Object-Based Language Design. *IEEE Computer* **25**(10), 12–20

Index

academic systems   37
acceptance tests   170, 173, 185
access control   117,132, 247
access control list   122, 205
access rules   200, 205, 217
accountability   117, 145
accounting management   98
ACL   132
address   103, 105
addressing schemes   178
administrative functions   94
administrative systems   29
administrator   223
agent   269
agent role   238
aliases   104, 106
ancestors   204
ANSA project   20
ANSI   121, 124
atomic actions   96, 214, 217
attribute   192, 240
audit trail   117, 134
authentication   117,120
authority   207, 215
availability   116

back office   33
behaviour   243
binding functions   94
bridges   174
business   30
business manager   54
business risk   59, 144

call-out schedules   184
capability   122
CCITT   232
change management   93
class   196
clear   123
CMIP   246
CMIS   246

CMOT   251, 262, 266
communications security   136
complex service   98
component service   98
compound service   98
conditional (package)   242
confidentiality   116
configuration management   93
containment   191
control functions   92
corporation   30
cube model   21
culture   32, 38

Data Encryption Standard   123
data transmission   136
denial of service   112
deontic logic   270
dependent (conformance)   248
DES   123
diagnostics   79, 177
discretionary access control   122
discriminator   238
disjoint domains   201
Distributed Management Environment
   (DME)   266
distributed processing   5
distributed processing environment   5
distributed system   5
'do it yourself'   169
domain   15, 195
DOMAINS   24, 268
Domino   24, 268

eavesdropping   120
electronic data interchange (EDI)   34
electronic funds transfer (EFT)   121
electronic security   119
enabling service   98
encapsulation   190
encryption   123
end-to-end encryption   123

enterprise 30
event log record 245
event forwarding discriminator 245
extended management
 architecture 239, 264

fault detection 75
fault diagnosis 79
fault handling 74
fault recovery 78
fault resolution 83
Fiber Distributed Data Interface
 (FDDI) 262
filter 235, 247
financial information services 32
front office 33

general (conformance) 248
generic name 106
goal 206, 211

help – context-sensitive 150
help – user-sensitive 150
help desk 148, 150
help shadowing 152
human-computer interface 41, 43

identification 122
IEEE 233, 262
incremental testing 176
Information Technology Security
 Evaluation Criteria (ITSEC) 136
inheritance 242
insatiable (goal) 270
instance 191
integrity 116
international standard
 profile (ISP) 250
Internet Protocol (IP) 250
ISO Security Architecture 115, 137
ITSEC 136

kernel 160
key management 124

layer management 236
licence management 157
life cycle costing 60
link encryption 123
local area network (LAN) 262
log 235
logical access control 121
logical security 117, 121

maintaining 168
maintenance agreement 183
managed object 191
management information base 236
management role object 223
management style 58
manager 193, 223
manager object 191, 235
manager role 238
mandatory (package) 242
mandatory access control 122, 216
marginal costing 60
mediation device 253
message authentication 121
metric 86
metric object 246
modality 211
monitoring 70
motivation 206
multiplexors 174

name allocation 106
name binding 243
name registration 106
name space 106
name structuring 106
NETMAN project 21
network element 253
Network Management Forum
 (NMF) 233, 266
non-repudiation 117, 182
notification 192, 238

object class 241, 243
object identifier 104, 241
office automation systems 39
Open Distributed Processing
 (ODP) 232
Open Software Foundation
 (OSF) 233, 266
Open Systems Interconnection
 (OSI) 232
openness 2
operational manuals 181
operations 238
operations system 253
organization 30
overlapping domains 201
owner 221, 223
ownership 221

package 242
parametric modelling 89

parent set   204
path name   104
performance measurement   85
performance optimization   91
petrochemical industry   34
physical security   119, 131
planning   168
point-of-sale systems (POS)   34
policy   206, 270
policy set   195
POSIX   233, 267
post-project review   62
potential event report   245
power   206
pre-tender actions   168
procuring   168
'programming in the large'   93
proof of delivery   117
proof of origin   117
prospective (standardization)   232
protocol   236
protocol implementation conformance
   statement (PICS)   248
public key encryption   123
Pythagoras project   269

quality assurance   170, 179
Quality of Service (QoS)   18, 68

RACE programme   21
real-time   161
reference monitor   121, 218
registration authority   242
relay   175
repertoire object   272
responsibility   222
retrospective (standardization)   232
risk – business-related   144
risk – cost-related   144
risk assessment   133
risk management   133
Roadmap   256
routers   174, 191
RSA   124

satiable (goal)   270
scheduler   235
secret key encryption   123
security   112
security alarm   118
security framework   115

security interaction policy   125
security management   134
security mechanisms   118
security objectives   116
security policy   124, 129, 216
security risk   59, 133
security standards   115, 121, 124,
   135, 138
senior manager   54
service   236, 246
service domain   264
shield   273
short-list   169
simulation   159
Simple Network Management Protocol
   (SNMP)   250, 266
smart cards   121
software down-load   157
stable storage   83
standard operating procedures   183
subdomain   197, 202
subject   207, 211
superdomain   202
support manager   54
symbolic name   103
systems management   236

target   205, 210, 211, 269
TCP   250
Telecommunications Management
   Network (TMN)   252
test libraries   177
test plans   171, 173
testing   168, 172
third-party networks   174
top   243
trader   154
traffic padding   122
training   40, 45
training manuals   180
transaction processing   255
Trusted Computer System Evaluation
   Criteria (TCSEC) 136, 216

unique identifier   103
user   204, 223

version control   93
viewpoint analysis   19

wayleaves   171